The Grandees

AMERICA'S SEPHARDIC ELITE

by
STEPHEN BIRMINGHAM

A DELL BOOK

Published by
DELL PUBLISHING CO., INC.
750 Third Avenue
New York, New York 10017

Dell ® TM 681510, Dell Publishing Co., Inc.
Reprinted by arrangement with
Harper & Row, Publishers, Inc.
New York, New York
Printed in the United States of America

First Dell printing—April 1972

FOR ROGER H. KLEIN,
IN MEMORY

Sephardim:

". . . Many sufferings, which they
had endured for the sake of their
faith, had made them more than
usually self-conscious; they considered themselves a superior class
—the nobility of Jewry."

The Jewish Encyclopedia

CONTENTS

AUTHOR'S NOTE

THERE are a number of people whom I would like to thank for their gracious and generous help to me in the gathering of information for, and preparation of, this book. I am particularly indebted to Mrs. Lafayette A. Goldstone of New York, who turned over her large—and very comfortable—library to me, as a temporary office, where I was able to study her collection of Sephardic Judaica. I am also indebted to Mrs. Goldstone's son, Mr. Harmon Hendricks Goldstone, who was also helpful with anecdotes, family documents and reminiscences, as well as a vast amount of genealogical detail. Thanks are also due to Mrs. Henry S. Hendricks, and her sister, Miss Emily Nathan, for insights into the Hendricks-Nathan-Seixas-Solis family complex, and for access to the Hendricks Collection of family papers. In this connection, I am also deeply grateful to Dr. James J. Heslin and his staff at the New-York Historical Society for their courteous assistance.

For their help and suggestions, I am also grateful to Mr. Piza Mendes, Mrs. Leonard J. Wolf, Mr. and Mrs. Frederic S. Nathan, Mr. and Mrs. Lloyd P. Phillips, all of New York, and to Dr. Solomon Gaon of London, Mr. Edouard Roditi of Paris, Mr. Ralph A. Franco of Montgomery, Alabama, and the late Mr. Thomas J. Tobias of Charleston, South Carolina. Rabbi Herbert C. Dobrinsky of Yeshiva University deserves a special word of thanks, as do Dr. Jacob Marcus, Director of the American Jewish Archives in Cincinnati, Mr. Victor Tarry of New York's Shearith Israel Congregation, and Mrs. Peter Bolhouse of the Newport Historical Society.

I would also like to add a personal note of thanks to my fellow writers and friends, Geoffrey T. Hellman and James Yaffe, who both took time to offer useful suggestions and to point me in rewarding directions.

It was Mr. John L. Loeb, Jr., of New York who first called my attention to Dr. Malcolm Stern's extraordinary book, which became in a sense the cornerstone of my book. I am also particularly grateful to Mrs. Godfrey S. Rockefeller for reminiscences and documents pertaining to the Gratz family, and to Dr. Frank A. Seixas for information about the Seixas family. I would also, at this point, like to thank once again my friend and agent, Carol Brandt, who guided the project from the start, and Miss Genevieve Young of Harper & Row, whose editorial taste is as faultless as her eye is finicky. I would also like to thank the librarian and staff of the Rye Free Reading Room, for letting me keep books long after their due dates, thus adding gentle encouragement to the project; and I want to thank Dr. Rachel Dalven for scholarly assistance, Sra. Elena Zayas of Rye, who translated a number of letters from the old Spanish, and Mrs. Mildred Dicker of New York, who typed the manuscript in record time.

While all these people were an enormous help to me, and while the book could not have been written without them, I alone must stand accountable for any of the book's errors or shortcomings.

S. B.

1.

THE BOOK

IN 1960, there appeared what must have been one of the least heralded books in the history of American publishing. It was called *Americans of Jewish Descent*, and was put together—not "written" exactly—by a scholarly New Yorker named Malcolm H. Stern. The book consisted almost entirely of genealogical charts, and represented a labor of mindboggling proportions.

Americans of Jewish Descent weighs close to ten pounds and is beautifully bound and printed on heavy, expensive stock. It is just over three hundred pages long, including an elaborate index, and traces the ancestry of some 25,000 American Jewish individuals back into the eighteenth, seventeenth, and even the sixteenth centuries, under family headings that list everyone from the Aarons to the Zuntzes. It was never intended to be a best seller; a limited first edition of just 550 numbered copies was printed. Nonetheless, though unheralded, unacclaimed by the critics, and unnoticed by the vast majority of the American reading public, the book created an immediate and profound stir among a small group of American Jews who had long considered themselves an elite, the nobility of Jewry, with the longest, richest, most romantic history: the Sephardim. They were the *oldest* American Jewish families, and they traced themselves back to the arrival of what has been called the "Jewish Mayflower," in 1654, and even farther back to medieval Spain and Portugal, where they lived as princes of the land. Despite its price—forty dollars—and its size, the book was soon gracing the coffee tables and bookshelves of some of the most elegant and prestigious houses in the country and a second printing was ordered. The book was suddenly The Book, and was being studied for the tiny errors that appeared, almost inevitably, in a volume of this one's size and scope—three centuries of interconnected family trees.

The Book created no stir at all among Sephardic Jews who lived not at elegant or prestigious addresses but in Sephardic communities in such places as Cedarhurst, Long Island, and The Bronx. These Sephardim had no Jewish Mayflower to trace back to, no ancestors who had fought in the American Revolution. They had arrived in the United States, under quite different circumstances and after a quite different history, during the first three decades of the twentieth century and as refugees from the fires of revolutions in Turkey, the Balkans, and Asia Minor. They had spent the first generation of their emigration struggling to emerge from the ghetto of New York's Lower East Side. Had they had access to Malcolm Stern's book, it would merely have confirmed the impression among these Sephardim that the *old* Sephardim were the ultimate snobs, who treated all Jews of lesser vintage with condescension, aloofness, and utter disdain. *Americans of Jewish Descent* includes only those Americans descended from Jews who arrived in the United States before 1840. All who arrived since are thereby automatically excluded from the vellum pages and, as it were, the club.

What Dr. Stern had done, intentionally or not, was to compose a curious combination of a Jewish *Who's Who* and *Social Register*—fatter than the former, much harder to get into than the latter. The Book immediately emphasized a distinction which everyone knew existed but which most people preferred not to talk about, between the old, established Jewish families and the Johnny-come-lately arrivals, the distinguished upper crust and the brash parvenus. With its 1840 cutoff date, Dr. Stern's book eliminates, as he explains in a preface, "the large migration of German Jews in the 1840's, which achieved its greatest impetus following the European revolutions of 1848." Dr. Stern says that this date is "arbitrary," but it isn't really, because it eliminates those Jews to whom the Sephardim consider themselves specifically and emphatically superior. These are the "upstarts"—Kuhns, Loebs, Schiffs, Warburgs, Lehmans, Guggenheims, and their like

—who achieved such importance in banking and commerce in the latter part of the nineteenth century; who, by the sheer force of their money, grew to dominate the American Jewish community; and whom the older-established Sephardim therefore looked down upon and actively resented. The Germans have been not only upstarts but usurpers.

Though he does not make a point of this, the 1840 cutoff also makes it possible for Dr. Stern himself to slip under the wire and into the privileged pages. He descends from one Jacob Stern, who emigrated to Newark in 1837 —from Germany, of all places.

With the publication of Dr. Stern's book, small nuances of Jewish social position were reversed overnight. In New York, for example, there had always been a difference in social weight between the two unrelated Loeb families who headed two rival banking houses—Kuhn, Loeb & Company and Loeb, Rhoades & Company. The former were considered "old Loebs," and the latter "new Loebs" (they were sometimes labeled "real Loebs" and "*not* real Loebs"), since one family had arrived perhaps thirty years earlier than the other. Dr. Stern's book, however, sensationally revealed that the new Loebs were actually older than the old ones, by virtue of a grandmother who was descended from an old, genteel, if slightly impoverished, southern family named Moses. This didn't make the Loebs Sephardim exactly, but it got them in The Book, and the old "old" Loebs were not admitted. The banker John L. Loeb, of the new "old" Loebs, promptly bought a number of copies of The Book and sent them to friends—including quite a few Christians whom, in his researches, Dr. Stern had discovered to be of Jewish descent. To a few of the latter Dr. Stern's book must have come as something of a shock.

Who would expect, for example, to find the Rockefellers in The Book? They are there, along with such old-family members of American society as the DeLanceys, the Livingstons, the Goodwins, the Stevensons, the Ingersolls, the Lodges, the Ten Eycks, the Tiffanys, the Van Rensselaers, the Hopkins, and the Baltimore McBlairs.

The Book made it clear that there were also two kinds of Lazaruses—the old and the new. The old, who include the poet Emma Lazarus, and who for many years were among the very few Jews who summered splendidly in

Newport, are prominently in The Book. The new, who include the wealthy owners of Federated Department Stores, are not. Similarly, though the name Levy is now a common Jewish name in America, there are certain Sephardic Levys who stem from an extremely old family. One of the first Jews to set foot on American soil was one of these Levys; they went into fur trading, banking, and government service, and had nothing to do with making rye bread.

Barnaby Conrad, the author, was startled to find his name in The Book. His family, socially prominent in San Francisco, had always boasted of its descent from Martha Custis, whose second marriage was to George Washington. Yet one of Conrad's many-times-great grandfathers was one of those early Levys. Discovering this, Mr. Conrad had his genealogy Xeroxed and mailed to several of his family-proud relatives. His mother's comment was: "At least we were *good* Jews."

In New York society, a rumor had long existed that the Vanderbilts were Jewish. Dr. Stern's book was no sooner out than it was confirmed that some of them indeed were. Mrs. William A. M. Burden, whose husband had recently been appointed U.S. ambassador to Belgium by President Eisenhower, was in The Book. Mr. Burden's mother was the former Florence Vanderbilt Twombly, and of course the Burdens were members of a long list of New York clubs that traditionally have been closed to Jews, including the Brook, the Links, the Racquet and Tennis, and the River. Once again, it was those Levys at work high up in Mrs. Burden's family tree. In 1779, it seemed, Abigail Levy married a Dr. Lyde Goodwin. Was Dr. Goodwin also Jewish? Perhaps, because for some reason one of his sons, Charles Ridgely Goodwin, changed his name to Charles Goodwin Ridgely. He married a Livingston; their daughter married a Schott; their daughter married another Schott; and *their* daughter married a Partridge, Mrs. Burden's father. When this was pointed out to her, and that Jewishness is said, by tradition, to descend from the distaff side of a union—as it would appear to do in her case—Mrs. Burden said politely, "Thank you very much for telling me."

Americans of Jewish Descent is, in a sense, a cross-reference to *The Social Register,* since whenever names listed in *Americans* are also listed in the *Register,* this fact is noted. But *Americans* contains information that is a good deal more personal and gossipy, and states its facts with much more bluntness, than its non-Jewish counterpart. For example, spinsters are pointedly labeled "Unmarried," and as deaths have occurred not only the fact but the manner of death is indicated. Next to the name of the deceased one can find such notations as "Drowned," "Suicide," or "Murdered." As listees in The Book have become baptized, this has been noted, but sometimes the information provided is quite arbitrary. Next to the name of Rebecca Franks, for instance, in addition to her dates —"B. 1760, Philadelphia, D. Mar. 1823, Bath, England" —and her marriage to Sir Henry Johnson is the cryptic comment "Meschianza," which turns out merely to refer to a large party that Miss Franks attended during the American Revolution. Some of Dr. Stern's remarks seem to verge on the libelous. The word "Insane" appears after a number of names. Again in the Franks family, he notes that Calman Solomons was "in bad repute with Jacob Franks," who was his uncle but obviously some family father figure. Referring to Calman's brother Moses (a bad strain in the Franks family here, quite obviously), *Americans of Jewish Descent* advises that he died "in Charleston, S.C. Debtor's Prison, 1745." Dr. Stern also makes, or appears to make, social value judgments such as when, in the case of DeWitt Clinton Judah, he notes that Mr. Judah was married, but omits the wife's name with this comment: "An Irish cook."

The Book shows that the earliest generations of Sephardim in America were astonishingly prolific, with twelve, fifteen, and even twenty children to a marriage. When Ziporah Levy Hendricks died in 1832, she had fifteen children and no less than seventy grandchildren. Remembering family birthdays was no problem because one occurred nearly every week. Frances Nathan Wolff had, in the Hart-Seixas-Nathan-Hendricks family complex, ninety-nine first cousins. Gershom Mendes Seixas, born in New York in 1746, one of a modest brood of eight children, eventually fathered sixteen of his own. His younger brother, Benjamin, not to be outdone, had twenty-one. As a result, today there are thousands who can claim some degree of kinship to one or more Seixases.

From the very beginning, a tight pattern of intramural marriages was formed. Today the intermarriages between

members of the Jewish first families present a dizzyingly
labyrinthine design. Amelia Lazarus, for example, née
Tobias, had six brothers and sisters, no less than four of
whom married Hendrickses. One brother married a Hendricks first then, for his second wife, he chose another Tobias. The Hendrickses, meanwhile, were every bit as loyal.
Uriah Hendricks, whose first wife was a Gomez, and whose
second was a Lopez, had ten children, two of whom married Gomezes. In the next generation, the thirteen children
of Harmon Hendricks married, among others, two Tobias
sisters, two Tobias brothers, a Gomez first cousin, and
two Nathans. And consider the descendants of Abraham
de Lucena, one of the earliest arrivals. In the first American generation of the distaff side—his daughter married a
Gomez—there were three Gomez-Hendricks marriages; in
the next, there were four Hendricks-Tobias unions, two
Hendricks-Nathan marriages, two Gomez-Dreyfous marriages, and one Gomez-Nathan marriage. Meanwhile, Gomezes were marrying other Gomezes, and a disturbing pattern of insanity—clear from Dr. Stern's book—that began
to appear did not seem to discourage these close unions.

A measure of the intricacy of the interrelationships may
be grasped by considering that the 25,000 individuals listed
in Malcolm Stern's book are all grouped under a little
more than two hundred family dynasties. It is no exaggeration to say that, today, all the descendants of the early
Jewish families are, in some way, related to one another.
The late Lafayette Goldstone, a retired New York architect, was so fascinated with his Sephardic wife's elaborate
ancestry that, suspecting that she was indeed related to
everybody else, he attempted to plot all the American Sephardim on one large, all-encompassing chart. Years, and
hundreds of charts, later, he was forced to admit that the
tightly inter-knotted families had presented him with a task
that could not be executed.

Dr. Stern's book also reveals how, through the long cor-
ridor of years, the Sephardic Jewish community in America
—from the tight-knit, proud entity it once was—has steadily lost members as Sephardim have turned from Judaism
to Christianity. The Book shows that prior to 1840 more
than 15 percent of the marriages recorded were between
Jews and Christians, and that of the total number of mixed
marriages only 8 percent involved the conversion of the
non-Jew to Judaism; members of only another 5 percent

showed any indication of wishing to remain identified as Jews, or as members of the Jewish community. At the same time, as the years pass, and the Sephardic family trees stretch their branches downward into the present, one begins to see another phenomenon. The old Sephardic names with their Spanish and Portuguese musicality— Lopez, Mendes, Mendola, de Sola, de Silva, de Fonseca, Peixotto, Solis—begin gradually to be replaced by the somewhat harsher-sounding Ashkenazic, or German, names, as the old Iberian families feel the influx of the Germans throughout the nineteenth century, as the Sephardim and Ashkenazim intermarry and the Germans— as the Sephardim complain—try to "dominate" with their stiff-necked ways.

But the processes of Germanization and Christianization have by no means been complete. The old Sephardic families continue to compose a tight-knit, proud, and aristocratic elite who know who is "one of us" and who is not; who see each other at weddings, coming-out parties, and funerals; and who worship, with their own particular variations in the orthodox Jewish service, at the Spanish and Portuguese synagogues such as New York's Shearith Israel, the oldest in the United States. They lead lives of wealth, exclusivity, privacy, a privacy so deep and so complete that few people remember that they still exist— which is just what the Sephardim prefer, for the Sephardim have by nature been shy, reticent, the opposite of showy.

2.

WHO ARE THEY?

How much each person knows and understands about the past is one of the great preoccupations of the Sephardim everywhere. With some, it is a hobby; with others, an obsession. This is very Jewish. After all, the concept of *zekhut avot,* or ancestral merit, is said to provide the spiritual capital of the Jewish people. In this is embodied the idea that the past must be correctly interpreted in order that it can be passed on to enrich future generations. But there are also strong overtones here of a belief in predestination —that meritorious ancestors offer a kind of guarantee that their descendants will be meritorious also.

When one is dealing with hundreds of years of family history, and when family history relates to political and religious history, confusions and contradictions are bound to arise. And when family histories interconnect and tangle in such a variety of ways as they do within the Sephardic community, and as they have done for centuries, there are bound to be jealousies and rivalries and no small amount of bickering. This makes the Sephardic community a lively place. Where everyone professes to be an expert on the past, and where everyone wants to claim the best ancestors—and where there are many claimants for the same people—everyone must be on his toes.

Take New York's Nathan family. The Nathans are indirectly descended from Abraham de Lucena, one of the first Jews to set foot on American soil in 1655, and, in the process of their long history in this country, the Nathans are now "connected," if not directly related, to all the other old families—the Seixases, the Gomezes, the

Hendrickses, the de Silvas, the Solises, and Philadelphia's distinguished Solis-Cohens. Like Massachusetts Adamses, Nathans have managed to produce men of stature in almost every generation. These have included such figures as the late New York State Justice Edgar J. Nathan, Jr., who was also Manhattan borough president under Mayor La Guardia, and United States Supreme Court Justice Benjamin Nathan Cardozo, and—looking further back—Rabbi Gershom Mendes Seixas, called "the patriot rabbi," who was the spiritual leader of Shearith Israel during the American Revolution. During the war, he closed his synagogue in New York and moved the congregation to Philadelphia rather than ask his flock to pray for George III. Later, he assisted at George Washington's inauguration. His niece, Sarah, married a cousin, Mendes Seixas Nathan, a banker who was one of the little group who gathered one day under a buttonwood tree in lower Manhattan to draw up the constitution of the New York Stock Exchange. Annie Nathan Meyer, the founder of Barnard College, who was a granddaughter of Isaac Mendes Seixas Nathan, once wrote: "Looking back on it, it seems to me that this intense pride, accompanied by a strong sense of *noblesse oblige* among the Sephardim was the nearest approach to royalty in the United States. The Nathan family possessed this distinguishing trait to a high degree." As a child, she recalled, the subject of cheating at school came up. She never forgot her mother's clipped comment: "Nathans don't cheat."

Nathans are also proud to assert that "Nathans have never been poor." The first Nathan arrived in New York with a comfortable amount of money given him by his father, a prosperous merchant in England. So it has been for as far back as Nathans can trace their lineage, which, according to some members of the family, is a long way indeed. Once a Nathan was asked: "Is it true that your family traces itself to King Solomon?" The reply was: "At the time of the Crucifixion, it was said so."

Today, nearly two thousand years later, there still prominent and active Nathans. Emily de Silva Solis Nathan is an attractive, Spanish-looking woman with an oval face and olive skin, and an air of quiet cultivation and scholarly efficiency. She heads a New York public relations firm which represents such distinguished clients as Washington's Smithsonian Institution. Her brother was

Justice Nathan, a cousin was Justice Cardozo (the family
law firm was Cardozo & Nathan), and another cousin was
Emma Lazarus, who wrote, among others, the poem
("Give me your tired, your poor,/Your huddled masses . . .") that is engraved on the base of the Statue of
Liberty. A nephew, Frederic Solis Nathan, also a well-
known New York lawyer, is first assistant corporation
counsel to Mayor Lindsay. Nathan men, quite clearly,
favor the law. Emily Nathan lives in a large, airy apartment filled with antiques and the quiet feel of "old money," overlooking Central Park. A few blocks to the north,
she can see the handsome colonnaded façade of Shearith
Israel, which her ancestors helped found.

Emily Nathan's growing-up years were properly private
schooled, governessed, servant tended. The Nathans were
a large and—rather typically of the Sephardim, who tend
to feel most comfortable when in each other's company—
extremely close family. With the Nathan children and their
parents in the big old brownstone in West Seventy-fifth
Street lived not only a grandmother, Mrs. David Hays
Solis (whose maiden name had also been Nathan), but
also a maiden aunt, Miss Elvira Nathan Solis. Aunt Ellie,
as she was called, was a sweet-faced, blue-eyed, fragile-
looking lady who dressed with spinsterly restraint and always smelled of sachet. The children loved the smell of
Aunt Ellie's closets and played hide-and-seek there among
the neatly hung rows of dresses. Aunt Ellie was of indeter-
minate age, either older or younger than her sister, the
children's mother—they never knew. Age was a taboo
subject in the Nathan household; the children were told
it was bad form to ask people how old they were and, as
Emily Nathan says, "There were no drivers' licenses in
those days." (Not even Dr. Stern was able to uncover
Aunt Ellie's birth date for his book.)

Aunt Ellie was a great favorite of the children. In the
evenings, while the children were being given early supper,
she would often leave the adult company in the drawing
room to join the children in the dining room and tell them
stories. They were tales of Revolutionary heroes and heroines—of brave soldiers who plotted to blow up British
ships in New York Harbor, of a woman who slipped
through enemy lines to carry food to Revolutionary troops,
of a sailor imprisoned at Dartmoor during the War of
1812 who later rose to occupy the highest rank in the

United States Navy, though he started as a cabin boy sleeping on a folded sail. Aunt Ellie's stories were rich with the smell of gunsmoke, the slash of cutlasses, colored red with blood spilled in patriotism's great cause.

In those days, the Nathan family portraits were arrayed in the paneled dining room of the Nathan brownstone, where the children ate, and only gradually did Emily Nathan begin to relate Aunt Ellie's stories—"which at first seemed to me to be nothing more than wonderful eighteenth-and nineteenth-century fairy tales"—to the faces on the dining room walls.

"Was that a relative?" Emily Nathan would ask in the middle of one of the stories.

"Yes, we are connected," Aunt Ellie would reply.

The sense of history, and the sense of a certain long continuity between family past and family present, gradually began to give the little girl a sense of pride and a sense of security. "Later on," Emily Nathan says today, "when certain things happened to me as a Jew that might have upset some people—when I encountered prejudice, for instance, or heard of acts of bias and anti-Semitism—I was able to view them with a certain understanding. Things that would bother other people didn't bother me because I knew, thanks to Aunt Ellie's stories, where I fit into the scheme of things. I was able to rise to occasions."

Gradually, as Emily Nathan grew up, the dining room portraits seemed to grow until they loomed not only over the big room but over the entire Nathan family. Implacable, with, for the most part, stern and unsmiling faces, the old pictures seemed to dominate the Nathans' lives, reminding them daily of what it was to be a Nathan. Some of the ancestors, Aunt Ellie reminded the children, had not always been on the best of terms with one another. One of Aunt Ellie's whimsical little jokes was to say, at breakfast, looking up at the portraits: "I see your great-great-grandfather has a black eye this morning. He's been quarreling again with your cousin Seixas."

For years the Nathan children, and eventually the grandchildren, clamored for more of Aunt Ellie's stories. She seemed to have an endless supply, and could hold them spellbound for hours. Backward and backward she went, back into the Middle Ages, back into Moorish courtyards that dripped with bougainvillea and the splash of stone fountains. For now she was telling of Nathans who had flourished in Spain and Portugal during the centuries of Moorish rule, and of Nathans who had struggled to survive after the Catholic Reconquest. There were Nathans who had seen their synagogues desecrated, who had stood trial for "Judaizing" before Inquisitional courts in the *plazas mayores* of Seville and Toledo during the fifteenth and sixteenth centuries, who had gone to the stake proudly rather than relinquish their faith. There were other Nathans who had pretended to accept Christianity, continuing to worship as Jews in secret places, and there were others who had escaped—some to Holland, some to England, whence the earliest American Nathan emigrated in 1773.

The children liked Aunt Ellie's Spanish stories best, for they were more colorful, peopled as they were with beautiful ladies wearing tall combs and mantillas, royal courts with armored knights in swords, horse-drawn chariots pulled through the night on desperate missions, dukes and princes sighing for maidens' hands. She also told of doubloons being buried by moonlight in a garden, of men thrown into dungeons to be forgotten for years, only to make brilliant escapes; of a man warned by cryptic messages from his king that the Inquisition was at hand; of another whose servants were able to smuggle him to the safety of his ship by hiding him in a sack of laundry. On and on Aunt Ellie's stories went, weaving a vast, rich tapestry of gold and royal purple threads, heroic in size and wonder, spanning more than a thousand years of time, filling the minds of the little Nathans with visions of, quite literally, castles in Spain.

"Yes, we are connected," Aunt Ellie would assure them. "We are connected."

When Emily Nathan's parents died, the family portraits were divided between Emily and her sister, Rosalie. Today half the collection (many of which are very old and precious) hangs in Emily's apartment, and half is in that of Rosalie, who is now Mrs. Henry S. Hendricks. Like her sister's, Mrs. Hendricks' apartment overlooks the park (it is in one of New York's "great" apartment buildings, on Central Park West), and it is similarly filled with antiques and family treasures in porcelain, old books, and heavy antique silver. Mrs. Hendricks is very much a grande dame in New York's Sephardic community. There are even some who would insist that she is *the* grande dame. Rosalie Nathan Hendricks not only has her Nathan heritage working for her, but she is also a Hendricks —by marriage as well as by virtue of the fact that several of her own cousins are Hendrickses—and the Hendrickses are every bit as grand a family, if not even grander, than the Nathans. The Hendricks family—in Spain the name was Henriques—founded the first metal concern in America, a copper-rolling mill in New Jersey which processed copper that was mined around Newark. The Hendrickses sold copper to both Paul Revere and Robert Fulton, and became America's earliest millionaires, in fact, before there was such a word.

Not long ago, Mrs. Hendricks (who has two daughters), realized that the name, with her husband's death, has died out in the male line. In order that the Hendrickses and their works on this earth should not be forgotten entirely, Mrs. Hendricks gathered together a collection of Hendricks family account books, ledgers, business and personal letters, many written in the Spanish cursive script, and other memorabilia that had been collected for over two hundred years, and presented everything to the New-York Historical Society. The Hendricks Collection is an astonishing one, consisting of more than 17,000 manuscripts and dating as far back as 1758, and at the time of her gift there was considerable comment in the press. Who were the Hendrickses? everyone wanted to know. The name didn't seem to ring any sort of bell. Reporters rushed to the New York Public Library. No Hendrickses are listed in the central file, and they are in neither the *Dictionary of American Biography* nor its predecessors, the *National Cyclopaedia of American Biography* and *Appletons' Cyclopaedia of American Biography*.

This, it turns out, is exactly how the Hendrickses have preferred it to be. "The Hendrickses never liked personal publicity," says Mrs. Hendricks, a compact lady in her seventies. "Some people just *say* they don't like publicity. We *meant* it. We considered publicity a preoccupation of commonplace people. We were quiet people who did what had to be done in a quiet way. We left publicity to the lightweights."

When Mrs. Hendricks was gathering together her vast gift—it occupies two dozen file boxes—a number of her relatives, and other members of the Sephardic community, expressed the opinion that the papers should rightly go to the American Jewish Historical Society. But Mrs. Hendricks, a determined woman who, one suspects, does not spend much time on opinions that run counter to her own (when she enters receptions or synagogue functions, the way parts before her like the waters of the Red Sea), was adamant. The recipient should be the New-York Historical Society. "I thought they belonged here, in the general community, since we are an old New York family," Mrs. Hendricks says.

Mr. Piza Mendes, a smooth-faced man past seventy who looks at least twenty years younger (he has not a trace of gray hair), does not think Mrs. Hendricks knows much about Sephardic history, and does not hesitate to say so. Mrs. Hendricks, meanwhile, thinks little of Mr. Piza Mendes' historical theories. Though the two are distantly connected (via the pre-Revolutionary Rabbi Gershom Mendes Seixas), grew up together, and see each other often at the same parties and committee meetings, they are nearly always politely but firmly at loggerheads. Anyone about to discuss the Sephardic past is warned by Mrs. Hendricks to "Watch out for Piza!" Mr. Mendes, meanwhile, says airily, "Rosalie doesn't usually know what she's talking about." It has been this way for years. Mr. Mendes, comfortably off, keeps a midtown office where he manages the affairs of his estate, and spends his spare time studying Sephardica.

People like Mrs. Henry Hendricks feel that Mr. Piza Mendes spends entirely too much time trying to elevate the memory of his father, the late Reverend Henry Pereira Mendes, who for nearly half a century, from 1877 to 1920, was rabbi of the Shearith Israel congregation. Mr. Mendes, the feeling is, is trying to raise his father to a kind of sainthood, a position inappropriate to a religion that does not have saints. Certainly no man reveres his father more and, in this regard, Mr. Mendes offers an elaborately illuminated chart of his father's ancestry. This family tree, less dispassionate than those of Dr. Stern, concentrates mostly on ancestors who achieved positions of merit or heroism. One grandfather, for example, David Aaron de Sola of Amsterdam, is noted to have been a "voluminous scholar." But a closer scrutiny of the Mendes family tree reveals—in a kind of capsule history, as it were—the story of the Sephardim, where they came from, and what they endured. The earliest Mendes ancestor uncovered was Baruch ben Isaac Ibn Daud de Sola, who lived in the ninth century in the Spanish kingdom of Navarre, then a desolate region whose rise to prominence and power was still more than a hundred years away. In the next generation, however, we find Michael Ibn Daud de Sola, who has moved to the southern city of Seville, a great Moorish capital, where he has achieved the title of "physician." From here on, in Mr. Piza Mendes' family tree, we can watch the de Sola ancestors rise to positions of prominence in Moorish Spain. One ancestor was a "scholarly Hebrew author," and another was a "rabbi and Hebrew poet." At last, in the late thirteenth century, we see a de Sola given the ennobling "Don." He was Don Bartolomé de Sola, and was given his title by Alexander IV of Aragon.

For several generations, all goes well with the de Solas. (One was "Rabbi of Spain.") Then, in Granada, in 1492, we see that Isaac de Sola was "banished," and "fled to Portugal." Through the long Inquisitional years, the de Solas vanish from record, and we imagine them wandering across the face of Europe, from city to city, trying to find a place to put down roots. In the sixteenth century, a de Sola turns up in Amsterdam. But, in the meantime, some de Solas must have remained in Portugal, somehow able—helped by pretending to convert to Christianity—to escape the Inquisitors, because, as late as 1749, we see Aaron de Sola, born in Portugal, escaping to London, where he "threw off his Marrano name," the Christian alias he had used to keep his pursuers at bay. That same year his son also fled from Lisbon, but he chose to go to Amsterdam. From here on, in both Amsterdam and London, and eventually New York, we see the de Sola family regathering its strength down to Eliza de Sola, who married Abraham Pereira Mendes II, father of the rabbi whom Mr. Piza Mendes reveres so much.

Meanwhile, on the Mendes side of the family tree, there were equally colorful figures. There was Dona Gracia Mendes, for example, a great beauty who was known in Portugal by her Christian alias, Lady Beatrice de Luna. When her wealthy husband died, she went—still as Lady Beatrice—to Antwerp, where, with her looks and money, she became a great social figure. She lived in a palace and gave great balls to which all the titles of Belgium including the king vied for invitations. She also proved herself to be a shrewd businesswoman and, trading her husband's fortune on the Antwerp bourse, she vastly increased it. At a masked ball a hooded stranger in a black cape whispered to her, "Are you a secret Jewess?"—an unpopular thing to be in Belgium at that time. It was warning enough to Lady Beatrice, who withdrew her money the next morning from her Antwerp banks and went to Amsterdam, where an enclave of well-placed Sephardim was rapidly gathering. Here it was safe to resume her real name of Dona Gracia Mendes, and she did so—and prospered in the Dutch stock market.

Mr. Piza Mendes credits his father with helping to found New York's Montefiore Hospital; he was also influential in the establishment of the New York Guild for the Jewish Blind, whose annual fund-raising ball has become the most fashionable event in the city's upper-crust Jewish life. Perhaps his most significant deed was choosing his successor, the beloved Dr. David de Sola Pool, who was also Shearith Israel's rabbi for almost half a century. Rabbi Mendes spotted the young scholar, who happened also to be a relative, when he was a student at Heidelberg.

Dr. Pool, who is now rabbi emeritus, has himself been deeply interested in the Sephardic past, and he is the author of two massive volumes: *An Old Faith in the New World,* a history of the American Sephardim, and *Portraits Etched in Stone,* a series of biographical sketches of the Sephardic Jews who repose in America's oldest Jewish cemetery, in New York's Chatham Square. Dr. Pool, now in his eighties, has an oval, high-foreheaded, serenely contemplative face and a white beard. It has been said that when he passes through the synagogue he looks like the figure of God Himself.

"Dr. Pool wouldn't like me to say this, but he is a Christ-like figure," says Lloyd Peixotto Phillips, a member of Shearith Israel, with a twinkle in his eye. Mr. Phillips is a bustling, vigorous, outgoing man who is a trader on the New York Stock Exchange. Today he has a few outside customers, but he busies himself primarily with his own portfolio—on the telephone all day, buying and selling stocks in considerable quantity and, one gathers, with considerable success; the Phillipses have an East Side apartment, a country home in New Jersey, and a winter place in Palm Beach. One would not expect a man like Lloyd Phillips—who gives the impression of being all business—of caring much about his Sephardic family past.

But he does. He has shelf after shelf of old books, family papers, and family trees, showing how the Phillips family started out in eighteenth-century Newport, and how his mother's family, the Peixottos, trace themselves back to Portugal, and an escape into Holland and the Dutch West Indies. In the process of their evolution, both the Phillips and Peixotto families became variously connected by marriage to the other old families, and the names Gomez, Hendricks, Seixas, Nathan, Hays, and Hart all turn up in a multitiered Peixotto-Phillips family tree. Mr. Phillips likes nothing better of an evening than, over a glass of Scotch, perusing the old family documents, diaries, newspaper clippings yellowed with age, letters, scraps and bits of family history.

All this leaves his pretty, non-Sephardic wife, Bernice, whom he calls Timmie, somewhat at a loss. "I never realized any of this," she said with a little laugh not long ago. "When we were married, and I was having informal cards printed up, I was at Tiffany's and realized I didn't even know how to spell Peixotto. I couldn't understand how that could get to be a Jewish name." Mrs. Phillips shrugged a little self-effacingly, smiled again, and said, "We were French Jews, you see, and they—well, the French Jews never amounted to all that much."

3.

"NOT JEWELS, BUT JEWS . . ."

THE Spanish-Portuguese part of their collective past is of enduring importance to the Sephardim of America. It is what gives these old families their feeling of relevance, of significance, of knowing where they "fit into the scheme of things," as Emily Nathan puts it. This is because, in both Spain and Portugal in the years before they were forced to flee, the Jews—as a people, a race—had been able to reach heights of achievement unlike anything that had happened elsewhere in their long history. Their position was unique in the world. Who, after all, were the passengers of the *Mayflower?* "Ragtag and bobtail," Aunt Ellie used to say with a sniff. On the other hand, the first Jews who arrived in America, in 1654, were members of ancient noble families, people of consequence, men and women of property and learning who, for reasons over which they had no control, found themselves on the opposite side of the Atlantic from where they had intended to be. It is also true that, had it not been for their Spanish heritage and experience, the Sephardim would never have found themselves in America at all. And it is interesting to speculate why—considering the vast disparities of time, of place, of culture—the Jews can be said to have found their greatest successes and their fullest freedoms within the context of the two civilizations of modern America and medieval Spain.

The word *Sephardim* stems from Sepharad, the land where the Hebrew wanderers are said to have settled after Jerusalem was captured by the Babylonians and their Temple was destroyed. Generally—though the truth is lost in myth and mystery—the Sepharad is thought to have been a region in Asia Minor. The Book of Obadiah is tantalizingly vague: "And the captivity of this host of the children of Israel shall possess that of the Canaanites, even unto Zarephath; and the captivity of Jerusalem, which is in Sepharad, shall possess the cities of the south." Over the centuries, however, Jewish tradition—a relentless and often illogical force of its own—has associated the Sepharad with another peninsula, thousands of miles to the west, the Iberian. It has even been suggested that the Spanish and Portuguese Jews, who have for so long considered themselves the grandest of the grand, simply appropriated the Sepharad for their own. They said it was Spain and Portugal, and therefore it *was*.

Spanish-sounding names do not necessarily indicate Sephardic Jews, though they sometimes do. (The singer Eydie Gorme is a Sephardic Jew, though not of a "first cabin" family.) Spanish and Portuguese Jewish ancestors can often be spied under various disguises of nomenclature. The name Alport, for instance, was in some cases formerly Alporto, meaning "from Portugal," and the same is also true of such names as Alpert, Rappaport (which itself is spelled a variety of ways), and even Portnoy.

The Seixas family, who do have a Spanish-sounding name, offer an example of what can happen to Jewish names. After escaping from Spain during the Inquisition, some of the Seixases made their way to what is now Germany, where the name became Germanized to Sachs, Saks, and even made its royal way into the Saxe-Coburg-Gotha complex. Meanwhile, some Seixases remained in Spain as secret Jews, while others became honest converts—or so we are to suppose, since there is no way now of testing their sincerity—to Catholicism, and actually aided the Inquisitional courts against their own kin and former brethren. Today, Jewish Seixases and Catholic Seixases may be excused, when they come in contact, for eyeing each other a trifle warily. (Vic Seixas, the tennis player, has resisted efforts from New York's Seixas and Nathan families to draw a connection with him; he has not answered their letters. The Seixases slyly point out that Dr. Stern's book lists a certain Victor Montefiore Seixas in the nineteenth century—so the name Victor was in the family even then.) "Not all Seixases are real Seixases," Aunt Ellie used to say. On the other hand, she was not above mentioning certain prominent Catholic families—in both the United States and Europe—and reminding the children, "We are connected with them also."

José Fernández Amador de los Rios, the Spanish historian, would have agreed with Aunt Ellie's appraisal of her family. He has said: "It would be impossible to open the history of the Iberian Peninsula, whether civil, political, scientific or literary, without meeting on every page with some memorable fact or name relating to the Hebraic nation." Even that is an understatement. For six hundred years—from roughly the eighth through the thirteenth centuries—the Jews *were* Spanish history.

There had been Jews on the Iberian Peninsula since pre-Christian times. There is a tradition that Jews founded the city of Toledo, the name of which, scholars say, derives from the Hebrew *toledot,* meaning "generations." During the Dark Ages following the fall of the Roman Empire, Spain consisted of a shifting collection of primitive Visigothic city-states, governed by a multitude of undistinguished kings, each of whom had his tiny region which he tried to control, and was usually battling for power against local nobles and bishops of the Church, sometimes winning bloodily, sometimes being overthrown. The condition of the Jew depended on the whim of the king, who either persecuted the Jew or used him in the tradition of the "court Jew"—as a financial middleman through whom money passed in its endless journey from the pockets of the peasant class into the vaults of the royal exchequer. Taxes on Jews were quaint, arbitrary, and capricious rather than confiscatory. In Portugal under Sancho II, for example, Jews were required for a while to pay a "fleet tax," and had by law to "furnish an anchor and a new cable for every ship fitted out by the Crown." In one of the many Spanish kingdoms, the Jews were taxed on such basic foods as meat, bread, and water. In another, there was a Jewish "hearth tax," and in another there was a "coronation tax" plus a regular yearly tax "to pay for the king's dinner."

This was nothing like the heavy pressure of taxation Jews faced elsewhere in Europe, where the Jew had, it must have seemed, to pay for every act of his life from the first to the last. Jews were taxed for passing through certain gates, for crossing certain bridges, for using certain roads, for entering certain public buildings. They were taxed for crossing the borders of the tiny Rhineland states, for buying or selling goods, for marrying. Jewish babies were taxed at birth, and no Jew could be buried until his burial tax was paid. Jewish houses were taxed according to the number and size of their rooms, which encouraged families to crowd together in as small a space as possible. In peacetime, soldiers were billeted in Jewish quarters, and houses of prostitution were placed there, in an attempt to break down Jewish family life. To rape or kill a Jewish child was considered no crime.

By contrast, the Jewish quarters of such Spanish cities as Seville, Córdoba, and Granada were the best neighborhoods of their cities, occupied by the most beautiful houses —gracefully built around airy courtyards—and Christians vied with each other to buy houses there. It was a far cry from the ghettos of the Rhineland, where streets were too narrow for a wagon to turn around, where open sewers ran, where the Jew paid a tax to leave his quarter and another to return, and in which he was locked at night. Jews in the rest of Europe, who had heard of the life their brothers lived in Spain and Portugal, looked longingly and enviously at what lay across the Pyrenees.

Then, at the beginning of the eighth century, came the Moors.

It is popular in Spain today to speak of "the years of Arab occupation," leaving the implication that these Arabs were no different from the nomadic illiterates who wander the African desert on camels and wear burnooses. It is hard, even today, for a Spaniard to accept the fact that the Moorish conquest of the Iberian Peninsula was the first conquest since Roman times of an inferior land by a superior people. Other invaders of Europe—the Huns, the Turks, the Normans—were barbarians. But the men who, in 711, overcame the scattered city-states of Spain were the bearers of the great Islamic culture which had flourished in such sophisticated cities as Damascus and Alexandria. They brought with them the flow of knowledge from northern Africa to southern Europe—sciences Spain had never been exposed to before, including algebra, chemistry (or alchemy), architecture—and even introduced such unheard of amenities as indoor plumbing.

The Moors, during their half millennium of rule, turned the city of Córdoba—one of several Spanish cities that responded strongly to the Moorish impact—into one of the most glittering and exciting in the world, with its great mosque, its libraries, gardens, palaces, university buildings, and what were then the most opulent private houses in Europe. Muslim historians claim that at one point under Moorish rule the city had a population of over a million; now it has shrunk to 190,000. There are said to have been more than 3,000 palaces, public baths, and mosques, plus over 80,000 shops. The main library had a collection of over 400,000 volumes. In Granada, the Moors created the incomparable Alhambra, that shimmering complex of towers, pavilions, courtyards, pools, fountains, and gardens, each arched window of each great hall designed to frame a particular picture of exquisite beauty. The Alhambra is a triumph of Moorish aesthetics, and its fountains, an engineering miracle—their graduated upward thrust dependent on gravity, with a water source located high on a mountainside above—operate with the same precision today as they did seven hundred years ago. In a room off the Courtyard of the Lions, a mosaic Star of David is prominently displayed on one wall, a reminder that the Jews and the Moors were both Semitic peoples, with ancient shared pasts.

Until recent times, in fact, when opposing nationalistic aims turned the two peoples apart, the followers of Judaism and Islam had deep interrelationships. Never in their history did Jews have a longer and more meaningful encounter with another religion than in Spain. As the Moors surged forward and upward in Spain, achieving power and grandeur, they bore the Jews upward with them. As the Moorish occupation moved northward—at its height, in 719, the Moors held nearly the entire peninsula—the Jews helped the invaders by opening towns and fortresses to them, enabling them to go on to further victories, and for this the Jews were rewarded with high positions. The role of the Jews in the Arab conquest would be remembered, of course, later on when the tide began to turn the other way.

Immediately, the Jewish and the Moorish respect for education and culture recognized each other and went hand in hand. The Jewish and the Moorish skills in politics and the arts were kindred, and instantly in sympathy. Under Moorish rule, the Jews of Spain were no longer restricted to the narrow roles of moneylenders or tax collectors. In the list of popular Jewish occupations we see "bullion merchant" drop to twelfth place, well behind such humdrum trades as "lion tamer," "juggler," and "mule seller." Leading the list, by contrast, is "physician," followed by "public official," and "clerk of the treasury." Moorish sophistication and breadth of mind encouraged Jews to become inventors, artisans, soldiers, lovers, mystics, scholars—out of the darkness and solitude and "outsider" always feels, into the shining circles of magic and poetry.

By the eleventh century, the Jewish stamp was firmly on the land, and the twelfth, thirteenth, and fourteenth centuries in Spain and Portugal represent a kind of golden age for Jews. From 1200 on, Jews virtually monopolized the medical profession, a fact that was to cause serious trouble for both Jews and Christians later on, and in the kingdom of Aragon it was said: "There was not a noble or prelate in the land who did not keep a Jewish physician." Jews adorned the other professions, and Jewish advocates, judges, architects, scientists, and writers were heavily relied upon by the courts of both Aragon and Castile. Jews were equally important in their financial service to the kings of Spain, where, in one report, we find them "in key positions as ministers, royal counsellors, farmers of state revenue, financiers of military enterprises and as major domos of the estates of the Crown and of the higher nobility." In addition, Jews provided the country's apothecaries, astronomers, map makers, navigators, and designers of navigational and other scientific instruments. Jews were also prominent as merchants dealing in silver, spices, wine, fur, timber, and slaves.

There were isolated outbreaks of anti-Semitism from time to time. The Crusades of the eleventh and twelfth centuries frequently provided excuses for local pogroms, the rationale being: "Let us purify our own home as well as the land of the infidel," and the number of these occurrences increased as Christian Spain began its long push southward again, dividing the land more equally between Christianity and Islam, and as the Moorish influence began to wane. But in general, through these centuries—1100 to 1390—fresh breezes of tolerance and intersectarian understanding seemed to blow across Iberia.

This was partly because Christian kings tended to follow the enlightened examples of their Moorish predecessors. Having seen what the Jews had done for the Moors, the Christian kings were eager for Jewish favor. A number of kings considered themselves the protectors of the Jews, and in many places the Jews literally belonged to the Crown. Two of the greatest kings, James I of Aragon and Ferdinand III of Castile, were decidedly pro-Semitic. Ferdinand III was fiercely possessive of what he called "my Jews," and was quick to put down any attempt to persecute them. He often described himself as a "king of three religions" and, in proud reply, a Castilian rabbi declared to his congregation: "The kings and lords of Castile have had this advantage, that their Jewish subjects, reflecting the magnificence of their lords, have been the most learned, the most distinguished Jews that there have been in all the realms of the dispersion; they are distinguished in four ways: in lineage, in wealth, in virtues, in science." When Ferdinand III died, his son, Alfonso X, erected a monumental mausoleum for his father, and ordered the dead king's eulogy inscribed upon it in Castilian, Latin, Arabic, and Hebrew. After death, Ferdinand became known as Ferdinand the Saintly.

His son, known as Alfonso the Wise and Alfonso the Learned, was in many ways more remarkable than his father. He patterned his rule after that of the Moorish king Abdulrahman III, whose reign had been majestic, broadminded, and tolerant, and Alfonso's may have surpassed Abdulrahman's in its magnanimity and influence. In his researches, Alfonso always turned to Jewish scholars, "the best," and he founded the celebrated center of astronomic learning at Toledo. Part of the scientific output of this institution, the Alphonsine Tables, were to figure importantly in the navigational thinking of the young Christopher Columbus.

Up to Alfonso's time, the official language of the royal court, of diplomacy, and of the universities had been Latin. Since it was the language of the Church, of their persecutors, it was a tongue that the Jews instinctively regarded with aversion. The upper-class Jews preferred Castilian, and the lower classes spoke Ladino, or Judeo-Spanish, written in Hebrew characters, among themselves. Alfonso and his Jewish scholars codified Castilian, abolished Latin, and declared Castilian the official language of Christian Spain, to the great rejoicing of the Jewish community.*

* Prayer books in Spanish synagogues were promptly reprinted in Castilian, an interesting contrast to the attitudes of American Ortho-

These were years when, according to the historian Americo Castro: "In the commercial sphere no visible barriers separated Jewish, Christian, and Saracen merchants. . . . Christian contractors built Jewish houses, and Jewish craftsmen worked for Christian employers. Jewish advocates represented gentile clients in the secular courts. Jewish brokers acted as intermediaries between Christian and Moorish principals. As a by-product, such continuous daily contacts inevitably fostered tolerance and friendly relationships, despite the irritations kept alive in the name of religion." In the south, in Andalusia, still under Moorish control, it was the same: a civilized society that made no distinction as to creed, where Jew, Moor, and Hidalgo lived in accord and mutuality, though it is interesting to note that the term "blue blood" originated here. In those with light skin, the blue veins of hands and wrists showed through the skin. The Moors were not Negroes but they were dark and tanned from the sun. Their "blue" blood did not show.

During these years, Spanish Jews enjoyed the privilege, almost universally denied to Jews elsewhere, of wearing arms. Contemporary accounts describe dashing Jewish knights, elegantly fitted out, riding through cities on horseback, swords glittering in the sun. Many bore elaborate multiple names, and had been given the title of "Don." From Portugal, a report to King John II remarks: "We notice Jewish cavaliers, mounted on richly caparisoned horses and mules, in fine cloaks, cassocks, silk doublets, closed hoods, and with gilt swords." Jews organized their own sports and amusements, participated in jousts and tournaments of their own, and these often had a particularly Jewish flavor. In one popular pastime, Jewish knights, to the blare of horns and bugles, tilted with wooden staves at an effigy representing Haman, the Biblical enemy of the Jews in the Book of Esther, and, at the termination of the game, burned Haman on a mock funeral pyre while everybody sang and danced.

Then why did it end? What caused three tranquil centuries to turn suddenly into something so different, so violent and bloody, and so prolonged that it has continued

---

dox Jews of the twentieth century, who thoroughly disapprove of Reform congregations, where English, the language of the country, is spoken.

into modern times? What sent Spain hurtling in a new and terrible direction? Actually, it was a combination of many forces, some obvious, some subtle, some planned, some accidental that changed life totally for the Jews of Spain. True, Moorish power, which had helped bring the Jews to power, was on the wane. By 1480, Granada was the last Moorish stronghold on the peninsula. But long before that, factors had begun to accumulate and align themselves against the Jews.

Though Spain and Portugal were isolated and cut off, emotionally as well as geographically, from the rest of Europe, they cannot have been unaware of what was going on elsewhere, where conditions for Jews were steadily worsening. There was the problem of dress, of identification. When Pope Innocent III introduced the Jewish badge in 1215, he particularly stressed that his reason was that Jews had been dressing and looking far too much like other people, that intermarriages with Christians had occurred as a result. The prevailing feeling was that Jews were "different," and that their difference must be made unmistakable. The yellow badge became the Jews' greatest insult, "the mark of the beaten, reviled, scorned, abused by everyone," according to one medieval writer. The position of the Jew in various lands could be gauged by the size of the badge each country prescribed. In France and Italy, the circular badge was relatively small. Germany required the largest badges and in the most reactionary city-states of Bavaria the badge was soon deemed not degrading enough, and laws were passed enjoining Jews to wear only the colors yellow and black, and to walk barefoot.

At the Spanish Jews' heated insistence, the papal bull decreeing the badge was not enforced in thirteenth-century Spain. (In some cities, Jews were allowed to buy exemptions from the badge; in others, the edict was simply ignored.) For many years, Jewish scholars and rabbis had worn the cope—a long embroidered cloak, open at the front and clasped at the throat with a brooch—when they walked the streets. They considered the cope an appropriate ecclesiastical vestment, even though it belonged specifically to the costume of the Christian Church.

Still, the Jews must have been aware that the tide was beginning to run against them. Many Spanish moneylenders were still Jews, as were tax collectors—two professions that have never rated high in popularity among the general populace. The old dark myths began to be unearthed again of the abominations that supposedly took place in synagogues, that on Good Friday the Jews crucified young Christian boys and drank their blood. By unhappy coincidence, while these rumblings and mutterings were being heard, the Black Plague marched across the European continent, and Jewish doctors, helpless in its path, were accused of poisoning their Christian patients. Bigotry, fed by fear, flourished.

The Seventh, and last, Crusade ended unsuccessfully in 1270. The spirit of the Crusades had always been as much commercial as religious—with the profitable sacking and looting of the land of the infidel just as important (if not a good deal more so) than the claiming of his immortal soul. The Seventh was a failure in terms of loss of both life and money and, all over Europe, the prevailing mood toward the infidel grew harsh and bitter. Purification of the blood and homogeneity of faith became twin preoccupations. If the infidel of the East was now too costly to reach, then where could he be found? Eyes turned homeward, and there he was. The century following 1270, then, can well be labeled a Home Crusade, with ridding the homeland of "outsiders" a major theme.

Meanwhile, Moorish power in Spain was declining. The Islamic hand that had pulled the Jews upward was no longer outstretched. Both Jews and Moors who saw the writing on the wall began converting to Catholicism, and now the *Conversos*, or New Christians, created a problem all their own. It was often the *Converso* who became the greatest enemy of his former religion, the most virulent anti-Semite, who took it upon himself to lead the attack against the "reprobate Jews." Such a *Converso* was Don Pablo de Santa María, who, before his conversion in the early 1400's, was named Selemoh ha-Levi.* The former chief rabbi of Burgos, he now became the bishop of Burgos. It is a monstrous irony that this ex-rabbi, famous throughout Spain for his scholarship, should have become the scourge of the Jews.

Don Pablo's specialty was accusing the *Conversos,* of which he was one, of secretly betraying their faith, of

* This *Converso* name change is fairly typical. The *Converso* felt a need to advertise his new faith with special enthusiasm, and often selected the name of a Catholic saint.

"Judaizing." He was the first to draw the distinction between "faithful" *Conversos* and the "faithless" ones, between true Christians and false. The more Christian zeal a *Converso* displayed, Don Pablo pointed out, the greater was the likelihood that this *Converso* was a secret Jew or *Marrano*—literally "pig" in Spanish. (It has also been said that these Jews were called Marranos because they "ate pork in the streets," so badly did they want—and need—to be taken for true Christians.) Don Pablo obviously did not intend his own extreme zeal to be considered in this light.

He rose rapidly and became tutor to Prince John, the future John II of Castile, father of Isabella. He also placed in high positions in the Church and government many members of his large family, many of whom shared his anti-Semitic obsession. (His wife and sons, on the other hand, renounced him.) Don Pablo repeatedly urged the reenactment of old Visigothic laws under which a new Christian relapsing into Judaism could be punished with the death penalty, and he wrote these grimly prophetic words: "I believe that if in this our time a true *inquisition* were made, numberless would be those who would be given over to the fire amongst those who would really be found *judaizing; who*, if they are not down here more cruelly punished than public Jews, will be burnt forever in eternal fire."

And, of course, the fact is that he may have been right. "Numberless" Jews may indeed have made the gesture of converting only because they considered it prudent, and had simply taken their old religion underground. Others who may have been sincere converts at the outset may have suffered second thoughts. The *Converso* immediately found himself an object of extreme suspicion since, thanks to the efforts of Don Pablo, "New Christian" had become synonymous with "false Christian." The *Converso's* former co-religionists had little use for him and so the *Converso* became a sort of social outcast. Whereas he had had status as a Jew, he must have begun to think little of a religion that treated its converts with so little charity. Who could blame him for returning, in private, to his old faith?

Don Pablo used the pulpit, the most effective medium of communication of his day, to spread his views. When one of his coagitators declared, in a sermon, that he possessed positive proof that one hundred circumcisions had been performed on sons of Judaizing Christians, the prelate was rebuked and called a liar by the king, but the episode demonstrates another force that was working against the Jews. Medieval Spain was a ceaseless battleground for power, not only Christian versus Moorish but a three-way struggle between the kings, the bishops of the Church, and the feudal nobles. The Moors and, in turn, the kings, had been the Jews' protectors. Now, as Spanish cities grew and became more important, the dukedoms of the fourteenth and fifteenth centuries were coalescing. The kings had used the Jews and the bourgeoisie in their struggle against the lesser nobles; the nobles, meanwhile, were aligned with the Church. Now the nobles sided with Don Pablo de Santa María and other bishops to wrest the Jews away from the kings.

At the heart of the billowing anti-Semitism was, of course, envy—a human trait and a trait predominant in what has been called the Spanish temper. The Jews had simply become too rich, too powerful, too important in too many walks of life. Just as the Crusades had been of a mixed religious and commercial motivation—conversion of the infidel no more important than pillaging his fields and emptying his vaults—so did the episodes of prejudice and the scattered anti-Jewish pogroms that broke out in the fourteenth century have only partly to do with matters of faith. They were undertaken in jealousy, with intent to get back, by force, what less fortunate non-Jews believed to have been unrightfully taken away from them. As Chancellor Pedro López de Ayala wrote in his diary after a particularly savage pogrom in Seville, in which the rich Jewish quarter of the city was looted and many were murdered: "And it was all cupidity to rob, rather than devotion."

The pogroms spread like brush fire, and it was clear that a terrible twilight was at hand. In 1390, the Jews of Majorca were forbidden to carry arms. The question of the Jewish badge—"yellow, in circumference four fingers, to be worn over the heart"—became specific. Riots took place in several cities, and suddenly in 1391 in Seville— in direct defiance of orders from his king—a priest named Don Ferrán Martínez led an armed mob into the judería. After scattering the king's soldiers, Martínez and his men massacred more than four thousand Jews, looted and burned their houses. Pogroms were now an institution

across the face of Spain, and they erupted in Toledo,
Valencia, Barcelona. After each pogrom, forcible mass
baptisms and conversions were inflicted on the Jewish sur-
vivors. These Jews, presented with a faith that wielded a
cross in one hand and a knife in the other, were also called
Conversos, and, needless to say, went into a category all
their own.

Through the next twenty years conditions grew steadily
more severe, and thousands of Jews emigrated from Spain,
scattering across the face of Europe. In 1421, Saint Vincent Ferrer and the Chancellor of Castile dictated a long
series of anti-Semitic and anti-Moorish laws. Jews and
Moors alike were required to wear identifying badges;
they were forbidden to hold office or to possess titles; they
were excluded from such trades as those of grocer, carpenter, tailor, and butcher. They could not change their resi-
dences. They could not hire Christians to work for them.
They could not eat, drink, talk, or bathe with Christians
under the new laws. They were forbidden to wear anything but "coarse clothing." One Jew complained:

> They forced strange clothing upon us. They kept us
> from trade, farming, and the crafts. They compelled
> us to grow our beards and our hair long. Instead of
> silken apparel, we were obliged to wear wretched
> clothes which drew contempt upon us. Unshaved, we
> appeared like mourners. Starvation stared everyone in
> the face. . . .

However, the legislation did have the effect that it
claimed it desired. Conversions stepped up markedly, while
the line between "faithful" and "faithless" *Converso* became very dim. In the years following Don Pablo de
Santa María, it was easier to suppose that everyone was
faithless, and bloody battles continued—in Toledo in 1467,
in Córdoba in 1473, and, in 1474, an incredible uprising
where a young *Converso* led a bloodthirsty crowd in Segovia in a raid against other *Conversos*. In the middle of
this maelstrom, this tumult of cross- and countercurrents,
of warring factors and faiths and ideologies, of opposing
ambitions and thrusts for power and money, there stepped
a youngish pair of royal newlyweds, Queen Isabella of
Castile, and King Ferdinand of Aragon.

It was a dynastic union, and had been planned that way

by—the ironies do not cease—a small group of Jews from
the very highest court and banking circles of Spain. The
two principal matchmakers were Don Abraham Senior of
Castile, and Don Selemoh of Aragon, men of such prominence that they had never taken the trouble to be baptized.
("Yes," Aunt Ellie would assure the children when she
spoke of these great men. "We are connected, we are connected.") It was their grand notion to bring the two great
kingdoms—which had been gradually coalescing from the
multitude of minor ones—into a single, even greater whole.
Their idea represented an early form of nationalism not
unlike de Gaulle's in modern France; both men were in-
tensely chauvinistic, dedicated to making Spain the mightiest nation in the world. It was Don Abraham of Castile
who invited Ferdinand to his house and put him up there
while Ferdinand paid formal court to Isabella, and who
brought Ferdinand on his first secret visit to inspect his
bride-to-be. It was Don Selemoh who served as the in-
termediary in the presentation of a magnificent golden
necklace to Isabella, Ferdinand's engagement gift, purchased, of course, with Jewish money. It was Don Abraham who, in conversations with his royal house guest, was
the first to suggest that one of Ferdinand and Isabella's
future offspring might be wed to a Portuguese prince or
princess, thus placing the entire Iberian peninsula under
one rule. The two men negotiated on all details involving
Isabella's dowry to her husband.

In Granada a splendid catafalque rises above the place
where, in simple leaden caskets, the Catholic monarchs
rest. The king, or at least his marble effigy, lies with his
hands folded on his chest, looking very regal, his head not
even denting the stone pillow beneath it—an indication, it
has been said, of his cranial capacity in life. His queen
lies at his left, hands folded, and for some reason that has
never been explained, her head is turned away from her
husband, her eyes seemingly fixed contemplatively on the
middle distance, giving her a look that is both thoughtful
and estranged, and the disturbing mood created by the
pair is one of disunion and disaffection. Certainly this must
have been the queen's attitude toward her husband while
she lived. He was a perpetual adulterer, and his many mistresses, and the ensuing bastard children with which he
scattered the Spanish landscape, must have been a heavy
cross for the queen to bear. It was a notably unhappy mar-

riage, with Isabella emerging as the more interesting partner in it.

This stern, practical, pious, thorough woman, who treasured her rents and her "power to be feared," had—through the efforts of Don Abraham Senior and Don Selemoh of Aragon—married a man almost totally her opposite. Where Isabella was direct and forthright, Ferdinand was devious and sly. Where Isabella was plain, Ferdinand was dashing and handsome. A contemporary describes his "merry" eyes, and "his hair dark and straight, and of good complexion." For all her jealousy, it was said that Ferdinand "loved the Queen his wife dearly, yet he gave himself to other women." Also, "He enjoyed all kinds of games such as ball, chess or royal tables, and he devoted to this pleasure more time than he ought to have done." At the same time, "He was also given to following advice, especially that of the Queen, for he knew her great competence." Also, she was some two years older than he.

Although history has labeled Ferdinand and Isabella as archenemies of the Jews, it is hard to believe that they themselves were anti-Semitic. The royal household had a very Jewish complexion, and the king and queen were literally surrounded by Jews. Some, like Don Abraham Senior, had not converted, while others were *Conversos*. These included Hernando de Pulgar, the queen's confidential secretary, and the queen's confessor, Fray Hernando de Talavera. The king and queen depended enormously on these men, and on the guidance and support of other *Converso* advisers, and before Ferdinand assumed his father's throne he had officially increased the power of the *Conversos* at court. The general bailiff of Aragon, the grand treasurer, and the rational master, were all members of the Sánchez family, baptized Jews. *Conversos* also held the three top military posts in Ferdinand's command—heads of the fortresses of Perpignan and Pamplona, and commander of the fleet off Majorca. The king's private chamberlain, Cabrero, was an ex-Jew.

Isabella's household was no different, and *Conversos* about her included her closest woman friend, the Marquesa de Moya, who closed Isabella's eyes at her death. It was the same everywhere in Spain. In Aragon, the vice-chancellor of the kingdom, the comptroller general of the royal household, the treasurer of the kingdom of Navarre, an admiral, a vice-principal of the University of Saragossa, were all members of the large and powerful La Caballería family, as were several pivotal members of Ferdinand's council. Don Juan Pacheco, Marquis of Villena and Grand Master of the Order of Santiago, was descended on both sides from an ex-Jew named Ruy Capón, and Don Juan's brother, Don Pedro Girón, was the equally exalted Grand Master of the Order of Calatrava. Their uncle was archbishop of Toledo, and an ex-Jew—everyone knew. At least seven of the principal prelates of the kingdom were of Jewish descent, including at least two bishops. Why, then, with Jews and ex-Jews serving them in so many important areas, did Ferdinand and Isabella permit a policy to develop that was so patently destructive and disruptive of their mightiest ambition—a great and unified Spanish nation? How could a policy of ferreting out, and separating, the true Christians from the false, the faithful converts from the secretly "Judaizing" ones, have possibly been considered practical, much less wise? The crucial, and virtually unanswerable, question became: who was Jewish and who was not? In the three generations that had passed since the massacre of 1391, thousands of Jews had been baptized. Throughout the fifteenth century, many of the wealthier New Christians had married into families of the old Catholic nobility.

Did Ferdinand and Isabella merely surrender to popular sentiment—which was not at all like them—or did they actually believe that the Jew had infested Spain and had to be removed? That anti-Semitism had become popular there is no doubt. It is also possible that when the Jewish court physician failed to save the life of one of her sons, the Infante Don Juan, Isabella may have become embittered against the Jews and been reminded of old myths of Jews as poisoners of wells and children. And anti-Semites among the *Conversos* had begun to tell the monarchs that most of the conversions were only feigned, and recalled an ancient Castilian legend that developed under the reign of Peter I. Peter, it was said, used to wear a waistband given him by his wife, Doña Blanca, who wanted to expel the Jews. His mistress, Doña María de Padilla, obtained the waistband with the help of an old Jew who was powerful at court, and the Jew placed a curse on it so that the next time Peter wore it—at a court ceremony, when he was in his full regalia—the waistband suddenly turned into a serpent and, before the eyes of the horrified onlookers, coiled itself around the king's neck and strangled him.

The Inquisition was first suggested to the king and queen by the Dominican prior of Saint Paul in Seville, backed by the papal nuncio, Nicolao Franco. The king and queen agreed, it is said, "reluctantly" that an "inquisition," or inquiry, be undertaken, but placed the leadership of it in the hands of the great Cardinal of Spain, the Archbishop of Seville, Pedro González de Mendoza, who assured their majesties that the approach to Judaizing *Conversos* would be evangelical—through education, argument, and preaching, rather than force. But the lower clergy, the lesser nobles, and the general public quickly became impatient with the cardinal's gentle ways and called for sterner measures. Of the cardinal's methods, the historian Andrés Bernáldez wrote: "In all this, two years were wasted and it was of no avail, for each did what he used to do, and to change one's habits is a wrench as bad as death." In 1479, the king and queen—still reluctant—gave in to the popular pressures surrounding them and founded the Inquisition.

Anti-Semitism became official, and the rulers embarked upon a policy of systematic expulsion. In 1481, Jews were ordered confined to their *juderías*. Next, a partial expulsion was ordered of all the Jews in Andalusia. In 1483, Jews were decreed expelled from Seville and Córdoba and, in 1486, from Saragossa, Abarán, and Teruel.

On January 2, 1492, Isabella and Ferdinand arrived in Granada, the last state in Moorish power, to accept its final surrender and receive its keys. Slowly the banner bearing the Cross was raised over the Alhambra while, just as slowly, the crescent of Islam was lowered. It must have been a moment of unparalleled emotion, of momentous impact, as the Moorish King Boabdil the Young moved, on foot, toward the mounted Ferdinand, to offer the symbol of capitulation after over seven hundred years of Moorish sway. His head was high and proud. The Christian *Reconquista* was complete. Spain's medieval era had come to an end. As the Cross and royal banner rose above the tower of Comares, the royal knights at arms chanted, "Granada, Granada for King Ferdinand and Queen Isabella." Around her, the queen's chapel of singers began to sing the solemn hymn of thanks, *"Te Deum Laudamus."* Granada's fall must indeed have seemed decreed by divine will. The queen, overcome, fell to her knees and wept. She was not quite forty-one years old.

At this stirring moment when the youthful king in his turban walked slowly toward her, carrying the keys, when she flung herself to her knees convinced she must be witnessing an act of God's holy will, did she remember the old accusations of how, seven centuries before, it was the Jews who "opened the gates" to ungodly Moors? Did she give weight to the powerful and long alliance of the two cultures, and did she now see the Jews and the Moors as inseparable enemy forces? Did she finally convince herself that what the churchmen and the nobles had been telling her was true, that Spain could triumph only if permanently cleansed of all unconverted Moors and Jews? It is more than likely, because three months after Granada's fall the famous Expulsion Edict of 1492 was issued, with the solemn words:

> It seems that much harm is done to Christians by the community or conversation they have held and hold with Jews, who pride themselves on always attempting, by whatever means, to subvert our Holy Catholic faith . . . instructing our faithful in the beliefs and ceremonies of their law . . . attempting to circumcise them and their sons . . . giving or taking to them unleavened bread and dead meats. . . .
>
> We order all Jews and Jewesses of whatever age that before the end of this month of July they depart with their sons and daughters and manservants and maidservants and relatives, big and small . . . and not dare to return.

Figures are unreliable, but it is estimated that somewhere between 165,000 and 400,000 people emigrated from the peninsula in the months that followed. Obviously, the figure for those who chose the alternative, and remained to accept baptism, is even shakier, but it is generally placed at about 50,000. As Jews poured out of the country, the Sultan of Turkey, Bajazet II, is said to have commented that he "marvelled greatly at expelling the Jews from Spain, since this was to expel its wealth." He said, "The King of Spain must have lost his mind. He is expelling his best subjects," and he issued an invitation to Jews who so wished to come and settle in Turkey.

It is no coincidence that Columbus' expedition was

launched that same calamitous year. It too was an extension, with the same mixed religious and commercial motives, of the Crusades; after the fall of Granada, the Home Crusade might be said to have been completed. The next logical step was westward, across the Atlantic.

One of the charming legends that have been perpetuated about Queen Isabella is that she impulsively, one might even say girlishly, offered to pawn (or sell—the stories vary) her jewels to finance Columbus on his voyage. Like so many charming legends, this one turns out to be nothing more than that. True, Isabella's treasury was nearly empty. But her coffers were rapidly filling up with property confiscated from departing Jews. Jews filled other roles in the expedition.

When he first plotted his course, Columbus used charts prepared by Judah Cresques, known as "the map Jew," head of the Portuguese School of Navigation in Lisbon. The almanacs and astronomical tables that Columbus gathered for the trip were compiled by Abraham ben Zacuto, a Jewish professor at the University of Salamanca. It was Señor Zacuto who introduced Columbus and the officers of his expedition to the prominent Jewish banker Don Isaac Abravanel, who was one of the first to offer Columbus financial backing. When still more money was needed, and when Isabella was at the point of abandoning the project for lack of funds, Abravanel turned to other Jewish bankers, including Luis de Santangel, Gabriel Sánchez, and Abraham Senior, who had played such an important role in bringing Isabella and Ferdinand to the altar. It is because of these bankers that the expedition was able to leave Spain under the Spanish flag and, as a result of their part in the undertaking, Columbus' first word back to Spain about his discovery was addressed not to the queen—which would have been courteous—but to Señores Santangel, Sánchez, and Senior, his bankers, which was practical. As a result of these activities, Professor H. P. Adams of Johns Hopkins has commented: "Not jewels, but Jews, were the real financial basis of the first expedition of Columbus."

There is also a distinct possibility that Columbus himself was a Marrano, the son of parents named Colón, who had escaped from Spain to Genoa during one of the pogroms. He was certainly a very odd sort of Genoese. Why, for example, did he write and speak such poor Italian—

and yet speak Castilian Spanish so fluently that he could move with ease in the highest circles of the Spanish court? Nothing but puzzles and blind alleys surround the actual place and circumstances of Columbus' birth. For centuries, Portugal has refused to honor Columbus, claiming that he was a "foreigner," and yet it is known that for several years before his expedition he lived in Portugal and was married to a Portuguese girl. (In 1968, Portugal remedied the situation by erecting a statue of him on the Portuguese island of Madeira.) Was Columbus a secret Jew? A large school of thought believes so. He certainly surrounded himself with Marranos and *Conversos* when he was making up his crew. Aboard the *Santa Maria,* both Mestre Bernal, the physician, and Marco, the ship's surgeon, were Jews. The first man ashore in the New World was probably also a Jew: Luis de Torres, the official interpreter for the expedition. He had been brought along on the voyage because the expedition expected to reach the Orient.

Though the monarchs' Expulsion Edict was quite specific, there was a certain leeway in its interpretation. Bribery was not unknown in the fifteenth century, and Portuguese officials were even easier to bribe than those of Spain, which was saying very little. The first Jews affected by the edict were the poorest, who could afford no bribes; richer and more prominent people could make arrangements. The royal matchmaker Abraham Senior, for example, who had served the king so well—he had helped the king pay off many of his mistresses, and came to his assistance whenever his amorous adventures threatened to be dangerous—was among the Jews who were given permission to take whatever personal possessions they wished out of the country, after a few routine donations were made to certain ministers and public causes. The government's debt to Senior—in the stunning amount of 1,500,000 *maravedis* —was also ordered paid. Senior, however, after thinking it over, reported to his old friend and former house guest King Ferdinand that he would prefer to remain in Madrid, and that he would accept baptism as the price. The king was delighted, and the Senior family was baptized in the palace and changed its name to Coronel. Don Abraham, after all, was an old man, and perhaps he had grown weary of the struggle. His friend and former colleague Don Isaac Abravanel, offered the same terms, chose to leave Spain rather than convert, and thus the great Abravanel name was carried out into Europe and, eventually, the United States.

The Jews who could not muster the price of a bribe were herded out of Spain like cattle. They were allowed to take nothing with them. To sell their houses or goods, they were forced to take whatever a buyer might deign to give them, and whatever they received was ordered turned over to the king. According to one chronicler: "They went around asking for buyers and found none to buy; some sold a house for an ass, and a vineyard for a little cloth and linen, since they could not take away gold."

While Columbus was assembling his fleet in Cádiz, he watched the harbor, which was filled with tiny boats waiting to carry away the Jews. If indeed he was the son of parents who were clandestine Jews, he must have viewed the hectic scene with queerly mixed emotions. The ships assigned to take the refugees were overcrowded, badly managed, and faced late-winter storms at sea. Those who boarded Turkish ships—sent by the sultan himself—found the Turkish sailors less hospitable than their leader. Some Jews had hit upon the idea of swallowing gold and silver pieces in order to take their money with them. Of these a rabbi whose father was one of the early exiles wrote: "Some of them the Turks killed to take out the gold which they had swallowed to hide it; some of them hunger and the plague consumed, and some of them were cast naked by the captains on the isles of the sea; and some of them were sold for man-servants and maid-servants in Genoa and its villages, and some of them were cast into the sea."

When Aunt Ellie reached this point in her stories, the children's eyes would be as wide as saucers.

4.

THE TWENTY-THREE

ON the first day of September, 1654, a tiny privateer, the *Saint Charles,* sailing under the French flag, appeared in what is now New York Harbor. It was something of a surprise to the fortress colony of New Amsterdam, which had been established on the tip of Manhattan island barely thirty years earlier, to learn that twenty-three of the *Saint Charles* passengers were Jews.

More than 150 years had passed since the Expulsion Edict, and the Catholic monarchs had long ago been placed in their uncomfortable-looking repose. And yet the twenty-three were victims of the monarchs' edict also, part of a continuing stream of escapees from Inquisitional Spain, Portugal, and all Spanish and Portuguese possessions on both sides of the Atlantic, where the Inquisition had been quickly established.

The dispersion following the Expulsion Edict was chaotic, following no set paths. Jews who refused to convert scattered in all directions—southward into Africa, eastward into Greece and Turkey, northward into Europe. Only one rule applied: the richer the Jew, the more liberal he could be with his bribes and, therefore, the freer he was in his choice of destination. The poorest Jews fled across the Gibraltar straits into the mountains of Morocco. The richest went to Holland—and for good reason. This tiny, doughty country had, from as early as the fourteenth and fifteenth centuries—just as it has today—a record and reputation of tolerance, of treating "outsiders" with respect and kindness. And so the Jews who escaped to Holland from Spain and Portugal found not only a friendly atmosphere where they could reestablish their congregations, but also a place where they could practice their businesses and professions. The city of Amsterdam was already an important money capital. In Holland the Sephardim were soon prospering again and occupying positions very much like those they formerly had held in Iberia. By the early seventeenth century, the Sephardim were an important part of the Dutch economy.

And the Netherlanders of the sixteenth and seventeenth centuries were the most cultivated people in Europe. This was the great era of Dutch painting, of Frans Hals and Rembrandt and Vermeer. It was an age of opulence and luxury, and in Holland ordinary burghers enjoyed comforts in their homes that were found only in the palaces of princes elsewhere. Across the North Sea, in England, members of the royal courts were still eating with their fingers, throwing their bones to mongrel dogs who roamed, snarling, under dinner tables. They were using their sleeves for napkins, strewing the royal halls with rushes instead of rugs, and had barely begun to discover the use of window glass. The rich of Amsterdam, meanwhile, were living in houses with thick carpets from the Orient and beautiful furniture, eating off porcelain plates with all the table silver of modern times. The affinity between the elegant Dutch and the aristocratic Sephardim was easy to understand.

Because the oldest Sephardic families in America can usually point to a Netherlands interlude in their collective past, they have an added point of pride. As one of the New York Nathans says today: "We were ladies and gentlemen in Spain, and we became ladies and gentlemen in Holland." Cream rises to the top, regardless of its location.

In the years following Columbus' discovery, Dutch explorers, along with explorers from other European countries, fanned out across the Atlantic, establishing colonies in North and South America, the Caribbean islands, Africa, and the Orient. As the Dutch established colonies, Sephardim from Holland followed them, helping the Dutch put their colonies in business. As a result of the Dutch colonial thrust, Sephardic communities can be found today virtually wherever the Dutch had outposts—Guiana, Polynesia, the West Indies. The oldest Jewish cemetery in the New World is the Sephardic burying ground on the Dutch West Indian island of Curaçao.

A particularly important Jewish settlement had been

made in Brazil. Discovered by a Spaniard, Brazil was claimed for Portugal in 1500 by the Portuguese explorer Pedro Álvarez Cabral. Soon other nations were eyeing this vast and fertile land and its rapidly growing sugar industry. In 1624, the Dutch West India Company—backed by the Dutch government—launched a full-scale military campaign against Brazil and captured Recife, which brought Brazil into Dutch hands.

Jews, many of them Marranos, had settled in Brazil during the century of Portuguese rule. With the Dutch victory and the abolition of the Inquisition—along with new arrivals from Holland of Sephardim who followed the Dutch conquest in a now familiar pattern—there was a great rush of reconversion to Judaism. Ex-Catholics were welcomed back into the synagogue, and before long Recife had a thriving and openly Jewish community.

The position of Jews in Brazil was now equal to that of the Protestant Dutch, with the same rights and privileges, and was considerably superior to that of the conquered Portuguese Catholics, whom the Dutch naturally endeavored to keep powerless. Unfortunately for the Jews, this state of affairs lasted only thirty years. In 1654, after a long and bloody siege by the Portuguese, the Dutch surrendered Recife, and Brazil became once more a colony of Portugal. The Jews' situation had changed utterly. The grim hand of the Inquisition reached out again.

But the leader of the Portuguese invaders, General Barreto, was a reasonably lenient man. He ordered the Jews out of Brazil, but he didn't hurry them unduly. In his diary, David Franco Mendes, one of the leaders of the Brazilian Jewish colony, and another early member of the ubiquitous Mendes clan, describes the situation:

> . . . And it came to pass that in the year 1654, the Portuguese came back, and from the Hollanders took their lands by force. And God had compassion on His people, and gave it favor and grace in the eyes of the mighty ruler, Barreto, who should be favorably remembered, and he caused it to be proclaimed throughout his Army that every one of his soldiers should be careful not to wrong or persecute any of the children of Israel, and that if any should wilfully transgress his command his life would be forfeited. . . .

General Barreto's proclamation pardoned "All nations, of whatever quality or religion they may be . . . for having been in rebellion against the Crown of Portugal. . . . The same shall apply to all the Jews who are in Recife and Murits-Stadt." To find a conqueror in such a forgiving mood is rare indeed. The Jews (and the other Dutch colonists) were given three months to conclude their affairs in Brazil, and were told, according to Mendes' diary, that they

> could sell their houses and goods at an adequate price and in the most advantageous manner. And he gave permission to our brethren initiated into the covenant of Abraham (who now number more than six hundred souls) to return to our country here. And he commanded that if there were not enough Dutch ships in the harbor, as many Portuguese ships within his dominion should be given them until a sufficient number should be obtained. And all our people went down to the sea in sixteen ships, spread sail, and God led them to their destination to this land.

"This land," in the case of David Franco Mendes, was familiar and sophisticated Holland. Of the sixteen ships that set sail that May, fifteen arrived at their Netherlands destination. The passengers of the sixteenth had a different fate. Blown off course and separated from its sister ships, it was set upon by Spanish pirates. Its passengers were taken prisoner, its cargo was confiscated, and the ship was set afire and sunk. The prisoners were told that as Jews they would be taken to a Mediterranean port, where they would be sold as slaves. But soon—it is not clear how many days or weeks later—the pirate vessel was sighted by the *Saint Charles,* which was captained by a Frenchman named Jacques de la Motthe. In a skirmish at sea, the pirates were defeated and the prisoners rescued and taken aboard the *Saint Charles,* which, it turned out, was bound for a place David Franco Mendes describes in his journal as "the end of the inhabited earth," a hamlet that consisted mostly of warehouses, called New Amsterdam.

Captain de la Motthe was not exactly a cordial host, and the Jews may well have wondered if they might have been better off in the hands of Spanish pirates. His boat was small and already overloaded, and de la Motthe insisted that they abandon much of their personal belongings. When his ship dropped anchor in what is now New York Harbor, and when the twenty-three Jews prepared to go ashore, de la Motthe refused to let any of their remaining goods off his ship until every stiver of their passage money had been paid. It is clear that, collectively, the twenty-three Jews had not enough cash to pay for a second set of transatlantic tickets, having already paid for passage from Recife to Amsterdam and wound up in the opposite direction.

The Jews tried to reason with de la Motthe, arguing that they would soon be receiving help from friends and relatives in Holland, but the captain was adamant. Poor, without food, houses, or friends in the new land, but, thanks to their considerable Dutch connections, at least able to speak the language of the Dutch colony, the twenty-three went ashore with only the clothes they wore on their backs. They set up a camp of sorts on the banks of the Hudson, just outside the settlement, and began a long struggle to come to terms with de la Motthe.

On Monday, September 7, 1654, about a week after their arrival, the Jews were ordered to appear before the Worshipful Court of Burgomasters and Scepens of the City of New Amsterdam. According to the court records, translated from the Dutch:

> Jacques de la Motthe, master of the bark St. Cararina [*sic*], by a petition written in French, requests payment of the freight and board of the Jews whom he brought here . . . according to agreement and contract, in which each is bound *in solidum*, and that therefore, whatever furniture and other property they may have on board his bark may be publicly sold by order of the Court, in payment of their debt. He verbally declares that the Netherlanders who came over with him, are not included in the contract and have satisfied him. Solomon Pietersen, a Jew, appears in Court and says that the nine hundred and odd guilders of the 2,500 are paid, and that there are twenty-three souls, big and little, who must pay equally.

Who was "Solomon Pietersen, a Jew"? He is not included in the pages of Dr. Stern's book, nor does he appear to have been one of the twenty-three *Saint Charles* passengers. Had he preceded the twenty-three in some way? Perhaps so. His willingness to go before the court in their behalf indicates that he had a certain familiarity with the burgomasters of New Amsterdam, and he obviously spoke fluent Dutch. There is also evidence (his name, for one thing) that Pietersen was an Ashkenazic,* or German, Jew, and—for all his helpfulness—there are indications that Pietersen's efforts were not universally appreciated by the twenty-three Sephardim, who considered Pietersen's origins decidedly lower class—a Sephardic-Ashkenazic conflict that would billow in America for centuries to come. In any case, Pietersen's plea got the Jews an extension of time, but not much, for the record continues:

> That the Jews shall, within twice twenty-four hours after date, pay according to contract what they lawfully owe, and in the meantime the furniture and whatever the petitioner has in his possession shall remain as security, without alienating the same.

During the two-day moratorium, the Jews' only hope was that help might somehow appear in the harbor from friends in Holland, even though the friends had no idea they were in America, and probably by this time assumed they had been lost at sea. When twice twenty-four hours had elapsed, the court was reconvened and de la Motthe appeared to demand the specific sum of 1,567 florins. He also placed in evidence a list of the Jews' property held on shipboard. The list was pathetically scant, consisting mostly of articles the Spanish pirates had not wanted. Through all this the woebegone little group remained silent.

What were their names, these unwelcomed and unwilling pioneers? The court records mention only one or two specific names, and spellings are offered capriciously. The court preferred to treat the "twenty-three souls, big and little" as a group, and in phraseology ominously reminiscent of the Expulsion Edict. Many records of America's first Jewish community are lost or incomplete and are

---

* From Ashkenaz, a people mentioned in Genesis, who in medieval rabbinical literature became identified with the Germans.

complicated by Marrano aliases. But from what can be pieced together about them, it seems probable that the twenty-three consisted of six family heads—four men (with their wives) and two other women who in all likelihood were widows, since they were counted separately—and thirteen young people. The heads of these families were Asser Levy, Abraham Israel De Piza (or Dias), David Israel Faro, Mose Lumbroso, and—the two women—Judith (or Judica) Mercado (or De Mercado, or de Mereda) and Ricke (or Rachel) Nunes.

The court was clearly of two minds about their situation. The colony needed able-bodied men, and had made it a policy to welcome immigrants, indigent or wealthy. But the court could not ignore de la Motthe's fiercely worded petitions, and de la Motthe was eager to be on his way. The solution was a compromise. The court offered the Jews a further delay, of four days this time, and then directed that if their debt was not settled the captain could "Cause to be sold, by public vendue, in the presence of the officer, the goods of Abraham Israel [De Piza] and Judica de Mereda, being the great debtor, and these not sufficing, he shall proceed in like manner with the others to the full acquittal of the debt and no further."

By now the Jews and their predicament had become the talk of New Amsterdam, and the pros and cons of the case were being argued all over the colony. As a result, when the four days had passed, with no salvation in the form of a ship appearing, and when the Jews' property was brought ashore and arrayed on the pier to be sold at auction, a group of New Netherlanders who had been defending the Jews arrived early, began buying up items at nominal prices, and then handed them over to their original owners. It was one of the earliest recorded examples of what might be called Christian charity in America. This was not, however, a development calculated to please M. de la Motthe, who, as soon as he learned what was happening, ordered the sale stopped. He then turned matters over to a young Dutch lawyer named Jan Martya.

Under normal procedure, petitioners before the Worshipful Court of Burgomasters had to bring their cases to the court on days when it was scheduled to be in session, and each case had to wait its turn. But a ruling did exist which stated that in return for "each member of the Council, five guilders; and for the Court Messenger two guil-

ders," the Worshipful Court would hold a special hurry-up
session and forget about what other cases might be pending. It was a provision that obviously favored the rich, and
Martya, acting in de la Motthe's behalf, paid the necessary
guilders and an "Extraordinary meeting" was promptly
announced at the *Stadt Huys* (State House), which was
actually a chamber over a taproom where "beer was sold
by the whole can, but not in smaller quantities." One gathers that beer had its place in the normal proceedings of the
court.

All over again, the case against "David Israel and the
other Jews" was recited, and Martya added in sterner
tones:

> Whereas their goods sold thus far by venue do not
> amount to the payment of their obligations, it is
> therefore requested that one or two of the said Jews
> be taken as principal which, according to the afore-
> said contract or obligation, cannot be refused. There-
> fore he hath taken David Israel and Moses Am-
> brosius* as principal debtors for the remaining bal-
> ance, with request that the same be placed in con-
> finement until the account be paid.

This, revealing that legal language has grown no less
convoluted over the years, was the first time prison had
been mentioned. And the Jews, who had no guilders with
which to pay for their share of the court's attention, could
do nothing but ask for the mercy of the court. But the
court decreed:

> . . . having weighed the petition of the plaintiff and
> seen the obligation wherein each is bound IN SOLI-
> DUM for the full payment [we] have consented to
> the plaintiff's request to place the aforesaid persons
> under civil arrest (namely with the Provost Marshall)
> until they have made satisfaction.

It was not, however, a total victory for de la Motthe,
because the decree contained a proviso that may have come
as a surprise to him. The order sent the two men to debt-
or's prison only provided that "He, de la Motthe, shall

---

* Probably Mose Lumbroso.

previously answer for the board, which is fixed at 16 stivers per diem for each prisoner, and is ordered that for this purpose 40–50 guilders proceeding from the goods sold shall remain in the hands of the Secretary, together with the expenses of this special court." Collecting his money was becoming an increasingly expensive chore for de la Motthe.

With two men jailed and the sale resumed, the prospects for the twenty-three were discouraging. September passed, and October nights were growing chilly. Though there was scattered help from sympathetic residents of the little colony, the encampment by the river faced slow starvation. Then Solomon Pietersen—who had made himself the chief defender of the twenty-three—stepped to center stage again.

In the small print of the agreement the Jews had signed when taken aboard, Pietersen uncovered a helpful fact. The passage money was not owed to de la Motthe alone. The other officers, and even the crew, of the *Saint Charles* were entitled to a share. Armed with this, Pietersen went to each officer and sailor and, in individual pleas, asked each to wait for his money until the ship's next call the following year. Each would be paid then, he promised, and with full interest. To de la Motthe he pointed out that the proceeds of the sale nearly equalled his personal share, and this he could keep. On October 26, 1654, the Worshipful Court declared:

> Solomon Pietersen appeared in Court and exhibited a declaration from the attorney of the sailors, relative to the balance of the freight of the Jews, promising to wait until the arrival of the ship from Patria. Wherefore he requests to receive the monies still in the Secretary's hands for Rycke Nunes, whose goods were sold, over and above her own freight debt, in order to obtain with that money support for her. Whereupon was endorsed: Petitioner Solomon Pietersen as attorney was permitted to take, under security, the monies in Secretary's hands.

And so, after an ordeal of nearly two months, the settlers who had inadvertently become America's first "minority group" were free—or at least somewhat free—to make a living.

And they could practice their religion. With the boys over thirteen, there were probably enough males to form a minyan to celebrate the first Rosh Hashanah in America on September 12, 1654 (5415 according to the Hebrew calendar). Within a year, the congregation of Shearith Israel—"Remnant of Israel"—was founded. The settlers were not allowed a house of worship, but they could hold services in their own houses; a few years later, they were permitted to rent quarters for services. At first they were refused land for a cemetery but, by 1656, they had acquired "a little hook of land" for a burial ground. Its exact location is unknown. By 1682, the congregation was permitted to purchase the Chatham Square Cemetery, which exists today. It was not until 1730 that the congregation succeeded in erecting the first synagogue building in America, a tiny structure in Manhattan's Mill Street.

The parnas, or president, of the synagogue that year was Emily Nathan's great-great-great grandfather, as Aunt Ellie would remind the children. A Nathan—Emily's brother, Justice Edgar J. Nathan, Jr.—was parnas until his death in 1965. His son Edgar Nathan III now serves.

Today, New York families such as the Nathans, the Seixases, the Cardozos, and the Hendrickses—who are all able to locate the names of the earliest settlers far back in the tangled branches of their family trees—can view the settlers' accomplishments with a certain quiet pride. In the years around the turn of the last century, when Mrs. William Astor was throwing her celebrated balls for the people Ward McAllister had labeled "the Four Hundred"—and when a later-arriving German-Jewish elite had begun high-hatting Mrs. Astor and calling itself "the One Hundred"—one of the little Nathans, no stranger to the family's intense sense of hubris, asked his mother, "Who are *we?*" "We," said Mrs. Nathan with a little smile, "are the Twenty-Three."

5.

"THESE GODLESS RASCALS"

AT the heart of the Jews' early difficulties, and a factor that would continue to cause them grief for a number of years, was the openly hostile and anti-Semitic attitude of Governor Peter Stuyvesant. In the land where the Pilgrims, just a few years earlier, had come to find religious freedom, bigotry was no rarer, nor were its expressions much different, than today. At the height of the de la Motthe affair—on September 22, 1654—Stuyvesant had written to the headquarters of the Dutch West India Company in Amsterdam to say:

> The Jews who have arrived would nearly all like to remain here, but learning that they (with their customary usury and deceitful trading with the Christians) were very repugnant to the inferior magistrates [members of the Worshipful Court] as also to the people having the most affection for you; the Deaconry also fearing that owing to their present indigence they might become a charge in the coming winter, we have, for the benefit of this weak and newly developing place and the land in general, deemed it useful to require them in a friendly way to depart; praying also most seriously in this connection, for ourselves as also for the general community of your worships, that the deceitful race—such hateful enemies and blasphemers of the name of Christ—be not allowed further to infect and trouble this new colony, to the detraction of your worships and the dissatisfaction of your worships' most affectionate subjects.

Peter Stuyvesant, a harsh and despotic man, was a bigot in the classic sense. He had already been reprimanded by the company for his persecutions of Lutherans and Quakers in the colony, and he had made himself generally unpopular with everyone by his efforts to increase taxes and prevent the sale of liquor and firearms to the Indians. What was the basis of his distrust, even fear, of a handful of impoverished Jews? The charge of "usury" was a common one, and Jews had learned, in a grim way, to be amused by it. The ironic fact was that usury was invented by a seventeenth-century Dutch Christian, Salmasius, who published three books on the subject between 1638 and 1640 urging the adoption of usury as an economic tool. His views had been quickly adopted by most Christian, as well as Jewish, moneylenders. Among the Jews, meanwhile, were men who, in Brazil, had been respected businessmen, as they had been in Holland before that. There could have been no real reason to suppose they had come to New Amsterdam to indulge in anything dishonest.

There were, however, certain characteristics of the Spanish and Portuguese Jews that Christians found off-putting. The Sephardim were characterized by a certain dignity of manner, an implacable and unbroachable reserve. They possessed not a little of the Spanish temper. From early portraits we see their high-cheekboned, often haughty, faces. There was a sense of aloofness, of distance, about them that passed for arrogance or extreme self-pride. The records of the de la Motthe hearings all describe the Jews as sitting rigidly in their seats, saying nothing, retreated into the grandeur of silence. But Peter Stuyvesant's attitude shows, more than anything else, that the spirit of the Inquisition had crept, in little ways, all over the world, and that the ancient superstitions and accusations against the Jews had followed it—that the Jews were sorcerers, ritual murderers of children, poisoners of wells, killers of Christ.

There were others who shared Stuyvesant's views. The Reverend John Megapolensis, head of the Dutch Church in New Amsterdam, had, the same year as the Jews' arrival, succeeded—with Stuyvesant's full help—in denying the Lutherans permission to build their own church in Manhattan. A few months later, in a state of alarm, Megapolensis wrote to his archbishop in Holland:

Some Jews came from Holland last summer, in order to trade. Later a few Jews came upon the same ship as De Polhemius;* they were healthy but poor. It would have been proper that they should have been supported by their own people, but they have been at our charge, so that we have had to spend several hundred guilders for their support. They came several times to my house, weeping and bemoaning their misery. If I directed them to the Jewish merchants, they said they would not even lend them a few stivers. Some of them have come from Holland this spring. They report that still more of the same lot would follow, and then they would build here a synagogue. This causes among the congregation here a great deal of complaint and murmuring. These people have no other God than the unrighteous Mammon, and no other aim than to get possession of Christian property, and to win all other merchants by drawing all trade towards themselves. Therefore we request your Reverences to obtain from the Lords-Directors [of the West India Company] that these godless rascals, who are of no benefit to the country, but look at everything for their own profit, may be sent away from here. For as we have Papists, Mennonites and Lutherans among the Dutch; also many Puritans or Independents, and various other servants of Baal among the English under this Government, who conceal themselves under the name of Christians; it would create a still greater confusion if the obstinate and immovable Jews came to settle here. Closing I commend your Reverences with your families to the protection of God, who will bless us and all of you in the service of the divine word.

Though the Jews petitioned Megapolensis, it is unlikely that they came "weeping and bemoaning." This seems quite out of character. The Jews, who had plenty to weep about and bemoan, and who were under no misapprehensions about the very limited degree of welcome they were being given, were not emotional but methodical in their

* Dominie Joannes Polhemius was a Dutch religious who had arrived in New Amsterdam aboard the *Saint Charles*. This letter confirms the fact that the twenty-three *Saint Charles* passengers were not technically the first Jews to set foot upon American soil.

approach to the problem. Early in 1655 they drafted and sent off a lengthy petition to the directors of the West India Company in Holland. This document is remarkable not only in its coolheadedness and tact, its diplomacy and relentless logic, but also for the clarity with which it defines the political and economic position of the Jews in western Europe in the middle of the seventeenth century.

The petition begins with a deferential salutation "To the Honorable Lords, Directors of the Chartered West India Company, Chamber of the City of Amsterdam" and proceeds to a detailing of the Jews' specific grievances. Stuyvesant had refused to give them passports or to let them travel outside the settlement, making it impossible for them to trade. This, the petition points out, "if persisted in will result to the great disadvantage of the Jewish Nation. It also can be of no advantage to the Company, but rather damaging." The petition reminded the directors that "The Jewish Nation in Brazil have at all times been faithful and have striven to guard and maintain that place, risking for the purpose their possessions and their blood." Next the Jews pointed out the economic advantages to be gained by allowing settlers to disperse about the country. "Yonder land," they wrote, "is extensive and spacious. The more . . . people that go and live there, the better it is in regard to the payment of taxes which may be imposed there." They reminded the "high illustrious mighty Lords" that in the past they had "always protected and considered the Jewish Nation as upon the same footing as all the inhabitants and burghers. Also it is conditioned in the treaty of perpetual peace with the King of Spain that the Jewish Nation shall also enjoy the same liberty as all other inhabitants of these lands."

The petition then made its most telling point.

> Your Honors should also please consider that many of the Jewish Nation are principal shareholders of the West India Company. They have always striven their best for the Company, and many of their Nation have also lost immense and great capital in its shares and obligations. The Company has consented that those who wish to populate the colony shall enjoy certain districts and land grants. Why should certain subjects of this state not be allowed to travel thither and live there? The French consent that the Por-

tuguese Jews may traffic and live in Martinique,
Christopher, and others of their territories. . . . The
English also consent at the present time that the Portuguese and Jewish Nation may go from London and
settle at Barbados, whither also some have gone.

The reply from Amsterdam was slow in coming, and
the permission it gave was given begrudgingly. Clearly the
directors shared some of Stuyvesant's misgivings. But the
reminder that there were Jewish shareholders of importance in the company was what turned the vote in their
favor. In their letter of instruction to Stuyvesant dated
April 26, 1655, the directors said:

We would like to effectuate and fulfill your wishes
and request that the territories should no more be allowed to be infected by people of the Jewish Nation,
for we see therefrom the same difficulties which you
fear, but after having weighed and considered the
matter, we observe that this would be somewhat un-
reasonable and unfair, especially because of the considerable loss sustained by this nation, with others,
in the taking of Brazil, as also because of the large
amount of capital which they still have invested in
the shares of this company. Therefore, after many
deliberations we have finally decided and resolve to
apostille [i.e., to note] upon a certain petition
presented by said Portuguese Jews that these people
may travel and trade to and in New Netherlands and
live there and remain there, provided the poor among
them shall not become a burden to the company or
to the community, but be supported by their own nation. You will govern yourself accordingly.

One wonders whether, if the loss of Brazil had not driv-
en the price of West India Company stock down, the directors would have been even this sympathetic. In any case,
with this mealymouthed and decidedly reluctant verdict,
the Jews gained their second important victory in the new
land—only one of many more that were to come.

6.

LITTLE VICTORIES

In Holland, where so many of the better off and the intelligentsia had fled, the phoenix was adopted as the symbol of the Sephardic Jews, representing their rise from the ashes of the Inquisition. In the mid-seventeenth-century Dutch colony of New Amsterdam, however, a creature more symbolic of persistence would have had to be chosen —the tortoise, perhaps, because the story of the early years of the first Jewish families in Manhattan is one of endurance.

The chief enemy continued to be Peter Stuyvesant, who had called them "godless rascals." A handful more had arrived by the spring of 1655—"from the West Indies *and now from the Fatherland!*" Stuyvesant wrote with alarm, regarding the trickle of immigrants as something akin to an invasion. Among the newer arrivals joining the original twenty-three was one Abraham de Lucena. Though Mr. de Lucena clearly appears to have been some sort of leader in the little Sephardic community in New Amsterdam, his importance has since become more genealogical than historical, since such old New York families as the Nathans and the Hendrickses find in him a common ancestor. Not much is known about the first de Lucena. It was noted that he came to New Amsterdam from "the Fatherland" —or Holland—it is also recorded that he could "barely speak Dutch." One assumes, then, that he was a recent escapee from the Inquisition, and that he had not tarried in Holland long during his journey from Spain.

Without a democratic government or a clear body of laws, rules in the settlement were subject to wide interpretation, and Stuyvesant made full use of this latitude. In 1655, the "Jewish problem," in Stuyvesant's eyes, loomed so large—there were perhaps twenty families—that he announced that Jews were not wanted as guards or soldiers for the city. This was a devious measure because, in effect, it denied them the right to stand guard over their own homes, which in those days was the most important duty a member of the civil guard had to perform. Stuyvesant based his ruling on what he claimed to be the unwillingness of the colony's regular soldiers "to be fellow-soldiers with the aforesaid nation and to be on guard with them in the same guard house," and he therefore declared "to prevent further discontent" that Jews were to "remain exempt from . . . general training and guard duty." He added the galling statement that, for "the privilege of remaining exempt," each male Jew between the ages of sixteen and sixty would have to pay a tax of 65 stivers—about a dollar in present currency—per month. It was the Jew tax of Europe all over again.

More anti-Semitic legislation followed. In the summer of 1655, Stuyvesant announced that Jews would not be allowed to own their own houses. At a public auction in December a young man named Salvador Dandrada bought a small house, in either defiance or ignorance of this order, at what is now the east end of Wall Street. When it was discovered that Dandrada was Jewish, the purchase was declared annulled and the house placed on the auction block all over again, to be sold to someone else.

Laborious petitions were written to the Dutch West India Company in Holland, itemizing the wrongs and injustices the Jews had suffered, and these were dispatched on their slow journey across the sea. The four principal negotiators were now Salvador Dandrada, Jacob Henriques, Abraham de Lucena, and Joseph d'Acosta and, again, it was the weight of the shares in the company owned by these four men—d'Acosta particularly—that provided them their best leverage. It was enough, at length, to bring about a letter to Stuyvesant from his superiors. The directors told the governor that they had learned "with displeasure" that he had forbidden Jews "to trade at Fort Orange and South River, and also the purchase of real estate, which is allowed here in this country without any difficulty." The directive did not give the Jews complete equality, however.

They were still "not to establish themselves as mechanics
. . . nor allowed to have open retail shops."

The unwillingness to let Jews enter retailing was based
on an interesting economic theory, a holdover from the
old world. In seventeenth-century Holland it was thought
that Jews, because of their supposed "talent" at international and wholesale trade, should be channeled into these
activities, for the good of the country. It is certainly true
that contributions of Dutch Jews to international finance
helped balance Holland's economic position in relation to
her competitors—England, Portugal, and Spain. It was
claimed that retailing "distracted" Jews from their more
important international business, and the same focus of
their attention was deemed necessary in New Amsterdam
as well. Here, after all, trade between the colonies was becoming increasingly important. Why Jews were not wanted
as "mechanics" is, however, not entirely clear.

Jews were also ordered to carry on their religion "in all
quietness . . . within their houses, for which end they must
. . . endeavor to build their houses close together in a con-
venient place"—in other words, in a ghetto of sorts. At
the same time, the directors rather sternly told Stuyvesant
that they expected their orders from now on executed
"punctually and with more respect." It was another victory, and led the way a year later, to Jews being given full
rights as burghers, or citizens, of New Amsterdam.

In 1664, the Dutch ceded their American colony to the
British, New Amsterdam became New York, and the cli-
mate changed again. Instead of Peter Stuyvesant, there
was a reactionary government in England to deal with.
The restrictions continued. Jews were not permitted to indulge in retail trade, nor could they worship in public. It
wasn't long, though, before these rules became impossible
to enforce. The Jews were becoming too important an element in the colony to be kept out of the mainstream of
New York commercial life. They were soon to be a political force to be reckoned with as well. Moses Levy, who
operated a small but profitable general store in Manhattan,
became the first Jew in America to be elected to a public
office when he was chosen "Constable of the South Ward."
Mr. Levy, however, was not impressed by the honor and
announced that he did not wish to serve, preferring to
pay the five-pound penalty for not serving rather than
taking on this time-consuming and low-paying job.

Moses Levy was also one of New York's earliest philanthropists, and in his giving he was laudably ecumenical. In 1711, he was one of seven New York Jews who contributed to a fund for the building of the steeple of the original Trinity Church, the landmark that today stands rebuilt at the head of Wall Street. In 1727, the affluence of Mr. Levy led to a minor misfortune, and to another "first" for Jews that was somewhat less auspicious. Moses Susman, also Jewish, robbed Mr. Levy of "gold, silver, money bags, rings &c," and was caught red-handed. Little is known of Susman, whose name suggests that he was German, except that he spoke no English and possessed "no goods or Chattles Lands or Tenements." The controversy between Susman and Levy may have been an instance of the hostilities that lingered between the older-arrived Sephardim and the newer-arriving Jews from northern Europe. In any case, Mr. Levy decided to deal sternly with the thief, and the court, finding him guilty, demanded the sentence that was in those days customary for men convicted of this crime—that Susman be "hanged by the neck till he be dead, and that he be hanged on Wednesday the twelfth of July between the hours of ten and eleven in the forenoon." Thus Moses Susman achieved the dubious honor of being the first Jew in America to be executed. The record notes that a Mr. Noble was ordered paid "two pounds Current Money of New York" for erecting the gallows.

By the early 1700's, two families, the Levys and the de Lucenas, had become easily the two most prominent Jewish families in New York. Abraham de Lucena, who started out trading with the Indians for pelts, soon became one of New York's most important fur merchants and was among the major contributors when donors were sought for the purchase "in trust for the Jewish Nation" of the first Jewish Cemetery in the New Bowery. His son,[*] Abraham Haim de Lucena, was the second rabbi of the Shearith Israel congregation and was able to afford a large and comfortable house of stone—a sign of advanced status —with a view of the harbor.

Asser Levy, a "connection" of Moses Levy, offered a

_____
[*] Possibly his grandson; the genealogical line is blurred at this point.

similar success story. Six years after reaching Manhattan
on the *Saint Charles*, he had obtained a butcher's license.
By 1678 he had prospered sufficiently to build a slaughterhouse at the water gate at the bottom of Wall Street and,
adjacent to this, he also opened a tavern. Levy's Tavern
was a popular spot because the proprietor was a cordial
fellow who also extended a bit of credit here and there.
Levy's substantial house stood nearby. In 1671, Asser Levy
loaned the Lutherans enough money to build their first
American church. He owned the land on which the first
synagogue was built, and helped support the congregation
by charging them no rent. When Asser Levy died, in 1682,
his estate was valued at the then princely sum of £53 in
cash, plus considerable land and a large inventory of goods
in which he traded as a sideline, including one otter skin
and 504 Jew's harps.

An even more important accomplishment of Asser Levy
was that he had managed to form the first business part-
nership with a non-Jew that has been recorded in America,
taking into the slaughterhouse, tavern and Jew's harp business one Garret Janson Roos. Since there were only six
licensed butchers in the city, each was required to take an
oath of office. Mr. Roos took his oath "on the faith of a
Christian." Mr. Levy, however, took "the oath that Jews
are accustomed to take," and was also granted special permission "to be excused from killing hogs, as his religion
does not allow him to do it." Mr. Roos became head of
the hog-killing department.

It must have seemed as though the golden era Jews had
enjoyed in medieval Spain was about to return in the new
world. Other families were rising to wealth and prominence and, with these, respectability. The Gomez family,
wheat merchants, were rivaling the Levys and de Lucenas
in importance, to the extent that when a Gomez son married Rebecca de Lucena, Abraham Haim de Lucena's
daughter, it was considered a match of two leading American families, of the highest social order. Gomezes also
married Levys and de Leons and Nuneses and Hendrickses.
In 1729, the Gomezes became the first Jews to advertise
their products on any sort of scale, and the tiny weekly
New York *Gazette* carried the following item:

All persons who shall have occasion for good Stone-
Lime next spring or summer, may be supplied with

what Quantity they shall have occasion for by Lewis
Gomez in the city of New-York, at a reasonable
Price.

"You notice," one of the Nathans commented in connection with his advertisement—for Nathans are descended
from Gomezes, too—"what perfect English our family
used, even then."

7.
"GOMEZ, THE ONIONS
BEGIN TO SMELL!"

"THEY walk with heads held high," a contemporary writer said of the members of New York's tiny (perhaps a hundred families in a city of ten thousand) eighteenth-century Jewish community. "These haughtiest of Chosen People must deem themselves the princes of the earth." They may also have walked with a certain feeling of relief. Because, while families like the Gomezes were finding it possible to prosper in the new world, dark and frightening rumors drifted back to them from across the ocean—tales that their rabbis told them in the synagogue of what Jews who had elected to remain in Spain and Portugal were undergoing. Deep in the background of every American Jew's conscience, throughout those Inquisitional years, was an awareness of what was happening to his relatives and coreligionists in the land the Jews called the Sepharad. It was a frustrating awareness, too, because those who had escaped the Inquisition could do absolutely nothing to help those who had not.

And, once the Inquisition had begun, there seemed to be no way to stop it. It grew like a malignant disease for nearly four hundred years, and when at last it died, its death was slow and hard and painful. It was founded in 1479, and the last public burning took place in 1781, but even then the Inquisition was not over. Executions continued under the Holy Office until as recently as 1826. The last man to hang was a young Valencian, who, in public prayer, was said to have uttered—witnesses swore they had heard him—a blasphemous "Praise be to God," instead of the required "Ave Maria." His body swung in the *plaza mayor* for all to see.

It was not, in fact, until July 15, 1834, that the Spanish Inquisition was officially abolished. But the Expulsion Edict remained firmly in effect, and for years after that there were repeated urgings from the press and from the pulpit for "the restoration of our beloved Inquisition." Even by the 1890's, it seems—while Americans were dancing gaily at Sherry's and laughing at the antics of Diamond Jim Brady—Spanish zealots were clamoring to have their Inquisition back, nor had the country seemed to have grasped the fact in its long and arduous process, the Inquisition had destroyed Spain utterly, robbed it of all the bright promise it had once had in the years of the *conquistadores.*

The Inquisition would not die, even though it was based on an unworkable concept. For it set about with fanaticism to perform a labor that could not be done, to erase something that could not be erased, to create something that could not be created, and to solve a problem to which there was no solution, final or even partial. The Inquisition was, by the nature of the visions that bore it, endless, and so, when the end came, Spain lay spent and exhausted and powerless.

Apologists for the Inquisition, and defenders of Isabella, who inaugurated it, point out that the idea was not original with Spain, that Spain's version was based on an earlier Italian effort, and that the punishments it inflicted were no more brutal than those in other countries of the period. The technique of expulsion was not new. In England in 1290 the Jews were ordered out on the grounds that they tried to lure recent converts to Christianity back to "the vomit of Judaism." It has been said that the Inquisition was necessary because Jews had infiltrated Spanish life to such an extent that they had to be removed and that, from the beginning, it had been clear to the Jew that conversion would free him from the possibility of persecution. Also, it has been argued, Jews who were honest about their Judaism were never murdered, tortured, imprisoned, or mistreated in any way. Admission to being a Jew merely resulted in a man's being stripped of his property and bank account, and sent out of the country. But the terrible fact of the Inquisition, regardless of its origins and methods, was that for all its protracted length it was a massive failure. If its aim was to create a homogeneous Spain, its result was the opposite. It tore the country into warring and irreconcilable factions.

The *Conversos,* or New Christians, quickly reoccupied important positions almost identical to those they had held as Jews, those of physicians, lawyers, financial advisers to the nobility, jobs for which training or learning qualified them. Instead of a Jewish conspiracy, it now seemed like a New Christian conspiracy. Meanwhile, the actual strength of their new faith, the fullness of the conversion, was under heavy suspicion—and for good reason. The man baptized at sword point was often less than sincere. When *Converso* doctors lost patients, the old accusations were muttered, and when the government attempted to take untrained men, who happened to be Old Christians, and turn them overnight into brilliant physicians, the results were equally disastrous. In the somewhat lowlier occupation of tax collector, more ironies appeared. When Old Christians took up these tasks they were looked down upon for performing "Jewish" chores, and soon were accused of being Jews in Old Christian clothing. Of this confused situation, a seventeenth-century writer complained:

> Formerly all who applied themselves to the gathering of taxes were Jews and people of low origin; yet now, when they are not so, people look down upon them as Hebrews, even though they be Old Christians and of noble descent.

Between Old Christian and New there grew an unbridgeable gulf of dislike and distrust. A number of ex-Jews, obviously supposing that the move would make them safer from the Inquisition, chose clerical careers and some of them rose to positions of importance in the Church. But even the Church's servants were not spared from suspicion that they were secret Judaizers, and before the Inquisition was over, hundreds of nuns, monks, and friars were marched to the stake. At one remarkable auto-da-fé in Coimbra, which lasted over two days and in which over two hundred suspected Jews were involved, the victims included nuns, friars, curates, priests, canons, professors, vicars, and an unfrocked Franciscan who stubbornly refused to confess that he was not a devout Catholic and was therefore burned alive as punishment.

The doctrine of *limpieza,* or purity of blood, was impossible to enforce from the beginning, with so much of the Spanish nobility already "tainted" with Jewish blood, and so it quickly became nothing more than a tool—a powerful tool, for it was an instrument of blackmail—which any noble could use in dealing with his enemies, or which the Church could use in its endless struggle with the nobility, or which one order within the Church could use against another. In 1560, for example, Cardinal Francisco Mendoza y Bobadilla, annoyed that two relatives were not admitted to a particular military order, pettishly and vengefully turned over to Philip II a document, later called the *Tizón de la Nobleza España* (the Blot on the Nobility of Spain), in which he "proved" that the entire nobility of Spain was of Jewish descent. Apparently the Cardinal's proofs were convincing, for the *Tizón* became a standard Inquisitional reference book, used right up into the nineteenth century, hauled out whenever new victims were needed, republished, and amended at each publisher's whim—many times. For a price, of course, one could have one's name removed from its list.

Meanwhile, *Conversos* who had been converted under duress and who were bitter and resentful of the Church became a faction of their own. Outwardly labeled Marranos, they called themselves, in private, *Anusim,* "the Forced Ones," and continued to practice Judaism.

Soon there was agitated talk of "the *Converso* danger" and "the Marrano peril," and *Conversos,* in terror of their lives, fanned the flames by turning informer on Marranos as well as on each other. In Seville, one of the main centers of *Conversos,* the New Christians, led by Diego de Susan, a wealthy merchant, decided to resist the Inquisition. Diego's beautiful daughter, however, disclosed this secret to her Old Christian lover, who passed it on to the Inquisitors, and many distinguished *Conversos* of Seville were tried, convicted, and sent to the stake.

It was an endless whirlpool of hate and fear. A list was circulated of the thirty-seven signs by which one could recognize a Judaizer. With dismay, it was quickly noted that a number of the thirty-seven signs applied to everybody. There is no way of telling how many Marranos there were at any given point in time, how many had fled, how many remained. Marranos, it was said—and no doubt it was true —worked harder for the Inquisition than most Christians as a way of preserving their disguise. How could you tell the traditional zeal of the fresh convert from what might be smoke screen and deception? There was no way, and the extrazealous *Converso* was as much under suspicion and surveillance as the indifferent one. And thus the Inquisition revealed its essential dilemma: It was suspicious even of itself.

When the Inquisitor of Seville wanted to locate the homes of Marranos, he went up on a hilltop on a Saturday and pointed out homes whose chimneys were not smoking. "You will not see smoke rising from any of them," he said, "in spite of the severe cold. They have no fires because it is the Sabbath."

As the Inquisition's power increased, so did the number of fleeing Marranos, and the number of Judaizers discovered and brought to trial. At the Inquisitional tribunal in Toledo, between the years 1575 and 1610, 175 convicted Judaizers appeared for sentencing. Later, between 1648 and 1794, the number had jumped to 659. Though Judaizing was not the only crime the Inquisitional courts dealt with, it was by far the most popular one. Also punished were those found guilty of being secret Moors (or Moriscos), those guilty of blasphemy, witchcraft, heresy, solicitation in confession, and "those who do not consider fornication sinful." It is interesting to note that while the number of convicted Judaizers rose sharply, the number of persons accused of condoning fornication declined— from 264 in the years 1575 to 1610 to a mere five in 1648 to 1794.

The prisons of Spain filled until there were enough prisoners to hold an auto-da-fé—literally, an "act of the faith" —and these autos quickly became a tremendously popular form of public entertainment. Today, the phrase conjures up scenes of human victims tied to rafters and fed into blazing pyres while a bloodthirsty populace screamed approval. In actuality, the autos-da-fé were reasonably sedate affairs, conducted as public expressions of religiosity and pious justice. Fidel Fita, a fifteenth-century Spaniard, describes the ceremony that was held on Sunday, February 12, 1486, and we see that it was a restrained occasion:

All the reconciled went in procession, to the number of 750 persons, including both men and women . . . from the church of St. Peter Martyr . . . the men were all together in a group, bareheaded and unshod, and since it was extremely cold they were told to wear soles under their feet which were otherwise bare; in their hands were unlit candles. The women were together in a group, their heads uncovered and their faces bare, unshod like the men and with candles. Among these were many prominent men in high office. With the bitter cold and the dishonour and disgrace they suffered from the great number of spectators (since a great many people from outlying districts had come to see them), they went along howling loudly and weeping and tearing their hair, no doubt more for the dishonour they were suffering than from any offence they had committed against God. Thus they went in tribulation through the streets along which the Corpus Christi procession goes, until they came to the cathedral. At the door of the church were two chaplains who made the sign of the cross on each one's forehead saying, "Receive the sign of the Cross, which you denied and lost through being deceived." Then they went into the church until they arrived at a scaffolding erected by the new gate, and on it were the father inquisitors. Nearby was another scaffolding on which stood an altar at which they said mass and delivered a sermon. After this a notary stood up and began to call each one by name, saying, "Is ――― here?" The penitent raised his candle and said "Yes." There in public they read all the things in which he had judaized. The same was done for the women. When this was over they were publicly allotted penance and ordered to go in procession for six Fridays, disciplining their body with scourges of hempcord, barebacked, unshod and bareheaded; and they were to fast for those six Fridays. It was also ordered that all the days of their lives they were to hold no public office such as *alcalde, alguacil, regidor* or *jurado,* or be public scriveners or messengers, and that those who held these offices were to lose them. And that they were not to become money-changers, shopkeepers or grocers or hold any official post whatever. And they were not to wear silk or scarlet or coloured cloths or gold or silver or pearls or coral or any jewels. Nor could they stand as witnesses. And they were ordered if they relapsed, that is if they fell into the same er-

ror again, and resorted to any of the aforementioned
things, they would be condemned to the fire. And
when all this was over they went away at two o'clock
in the afternoon.

Henry Kamen, one of the best historians of the Inquisition, has pointed out that two o'clock is the traditional
Spanish hour for lunch, and that 750 transgressors "reconciled" back into the ways of righteousness was most certainly a good morning's work. As the Inquisition progressed, and the number of penitents grew, the autos-da-fé
became longer, often stretching into the night and sometimes going on for days. Burnings, however, seldom took
place in public in the centers of town, and were performed
in the outskirts of cities, away from the eyes of the morbid
or curious. Also, since so many prisoners died in confinement before being sentenced, a good proportion of the victims were burned in effigy only.

"Scourging" was a more popular form of punishment.
The prisoner was ordered to "discipline his body" with
whips, or often given added discipline by being lashed to
a mule and "whipped through the streets" by the executioner. In these cases, the public was urged to participate
by pelting the victim with stones and garbage. How grateful the prisoner must have been to have returned to the
True Faith. Children and old people were subject to identical punishment—a teen-age youth sentenced to the same
number of lashings as a seventy-year-old woman. The
number of lashings prescribed varied according to the offense, but a hundred was the usual minimum and two hundred the maximum.

An even more bizarre—though effective—device of punishment was the *sanbenito*, a corruption of the words *saco
benito*, or "holy bag." An odd garment, cut rather like a
poncho, the *sanbenito* fitted over the head and hung to
the knees. It was usually of yellow, the color of cowardice,
and decorated with crosses, flames, devils, and other re-
minders of torture. With the *sanbenito* was worn a tall
pointed headpiece, similar to a dunce's cap. A reformed
heretic might be required to wear this strange-looking out-
fit for anywhere from a few months to the rest of his life,
and any relapse to his old Judaizing ways while condemned to the *sanbenito* meant, instantly, the stake. In
addition to the humiliation the *sanbenito* inflicted upon its

wearers, there was the further disgrace that when a penitent was permitted to remove his sack it was displayed, with his name attached to it, in the cathedral "in perpetuity."

Tomás de Torquemada, the first Inquisitor General of the Inquisition, was himself of Jewish descent. He was among those who urged Ferdinand and Isabella to establish the Inquisition in the first place. Both monarchs held him in high regard. The queen consulted Torquemada often and sought his advice on religious matters. He visited her frequently at her palace in Segovia in the years before she took the throne, and he became her personal confessor. Later, he became Ferdinand's as well, and must have listened to some startling accounts if Ferdinand confessed all. Torquemada was known for his thoroughness and singlemindedness. He was called "a scourge of heresy, a light of Spain, the saviour of his country, and an honor to his Order," which was the Dominican. Popes Sixtus IV and Alexander VI praised Torquemada for his dedication to ridding Spain of Jews and Moors, and spoke admiringly of the smooth efficiency of his courts.

A strange, austere, overpowering figure of a man, he comes down through history to us as a compound of myths and contradictions. It was said that he never traveled unless he was accompanied by 250 armed guards and fifty horsemen, that he was pathologically afraid of the dark and could not sleep unless an attendant was at his side to rouse him from his terrible nightmares. It was also said that he never ate unless the horn of a unicorn and the tongue of a scorpion were placed beside his plate. Considering the supply of unicorns' horns in fifteenth-century Spain, he must have dined little. He was praised for his extreme asceticism, yet a portrait of him by a contemporary painter depicts him as a full-faced, dark-complexioned, oddly worldly-looking *bon vivant*. One could describe his face as decidedly Semitic in cast, and this may have had something to do with his attitudes.

It was he, whose own blood was "impure," who first introduced the doctrine of *limpieza* into a Dominican monastery, the one that he built in Ávila and dedicated to Saint Thomas Aquinas. This cold and beautiful building, addressing serene courtyards and gardens, built with money extracted from the victims of his Inquisition, is a major tourist attraction in Ávila today. Torquemada's standards were said to be utterly unimpeachable. In 1484 his pope, Sixtus IV, wrote a letter congratulating him for having "directed your zeal to those matters which contribute to the praise of God and the utility of the orthodox faith." He had a violent temper, and was not even afraid of speaking imperiously to his king and queen. According to one account, Ferdinand and Isabella were offered a ransom of 30,000 ducats by a group of Jews. The king and queen were tempted, and summoned Torquemada for an opinion. When he heard what they suggested, Torquemada is said to have torn his crucifix from his breast, flung it on the table in front of their majesties, and shouted, "Will you, like Judas, betray your Lord for money?"

As the Inquisition progressed over the tortured centuries, it was not always so incorruptible. If the amount of the bribe sufficiently exceeded the amount that could be obtained through simple confiscation, the king was usually willing to listen. In 1602, a group of ex-Jews offered Philip III a present of 1,860,000 ducats, plus handsome cash gifts to each of the royal ministers, if a pardon was issued to "judaizers of their nation for all past offences." And there was more, the king was told, where that came from. The *Conversos* openly admitted to a hoard of wealth amounting to over 80 million ducats held in a secret hiding place. This offer, more than sixty times the amount that enraged Torquemada, resulted in the issuance of a papal decree of pardon, and 410 prisoners were released from the Inquisition.

Torquemada ruled that those who steadfastly refused to renounce their Judaism and to reembrace the Church must die by fire. Only the penitents were given lesser punishments. The results were some extraordinary cases of martyrdom. One of the greatest was that of Don Lope de Vera, who appears to have become actually unhinged by his zeal to be a Jew even though he had not a drop of Jewish blood in him. He had studied Hebrew and become a pro-Jewish fanatic. Denounced and turned over to the Inquisition by his own brother, Don Lope repeatedly declared to the Inquisitors that he wanted to become a Jew. He circumcised himself in his prison cell and stated that he had renamed himself Judah the Believer. While being led to the stake he chanted Hebrew prayers. He was burned alive.

Torquemada's successor as Grand Inquisitor was Diego

Deza. Until he took his post he had been known as a quiet and scholarly man, a friend and patron of Columbus. Like Torquemada, he was of Jewish extraction. He far outdistanced his predecessor when it came to savagery, and under his leadership the Inquisition became more wanton and ferocious than ever before. In 1500 a Marrano woman "of exalted rank" who considered herself a prophetess was arrested at Herrera. Immediately this was seized upon as an excuse for an enormous auto-da-fé. After months of planning, it was held at Toledo and the woman and thirty-eight of her followers—all of them women—were burned. The next day, sixty-seven more—again all women—suffered the same fate. Under Diego Deza, possession of a trace of Jewish blood was enough to call for execution. The archdeacon de Castro, whose mother was from an ancient Old Christian family, was sentenced, made to perform public penance, and had his considerable fortune confiscated, simply because his father had been a *Converso*. At one point, 107 people were burned alive; they were said to have been in a church while a sermon containing pro-Jewish sentiments was being preached.

The excesses of the Inquisition were reaching such heights that the captain of Córdoba complained that the Inquisitors "were able to defame the whole kingdom, to destroy without God or justice, a great part of it, slaying and robbing and violating maids and wives, to the great dishonor of the Christian religion."

Complaints of atrocities began to reach royal ears and, in 1505, Philip and Juana—the daughter of Isabella—ordered Inquisitional activities halted until they should return from Flanders. Then Philip suddenly died, leaving things in Juana's somewhat unsteady hands. Known as Juana la Loca, or Joan the Mad, she stayed, mute and uncommunicative, beside her dead husband's casket during a long macabre journey back across the face of Europe to Madrid. Periodically, Juana would order the casket opened and she would embrace the decaying corpse. While succession was being disputed, the Inquisition was resumed and continued on its dismal course.

Since "reconciled" heretics were being given, they were assured, the gift of eternal life, it was frequently argued that the kindest thing that could be done for a fresh

Christian convert was to speed him, with as little to-do as possible, out of this world and into the next before he had had a chance to change his mind. From the pen of an Inquisitor who witnessed the auto-da-fé of Logroño in 1719 we have this chilling account of an accused Judaizer who "with perfect serenity," said:

"I will convert myself to the faith of Jesus Christ," words which he had not been heard to utter until then. This overjoyed all the religious who began to embrace him with tenderness and gave infinite thanks to God . . . a learned religious of the Franciscan Order asked him, "In what law do you die?" He turned and looked him in the eye and said, "Father, I have already told you that I die in the faith of Jesus Christ." This caused great pleasure and joy among all, and the Franciscan, who was kneeling down, arose and embraced the criminal. All the others did the same with great satisfaction, giving thanks for the infinite goodness of God . . . the criminal saw the executioner, who had put his head out from behind the stake, and asked him, "Why did you call me a dog before?" The executioner replied, "Because you denied the faith of Jesus Christ, but now you have confessed, we are brothers, and if I have offended you by what I said, I beg your pardon on my knees." The criminal forgave him gladly, and the two embraced.

And desirous that the soul which had given so many signs of conversion should not be lost, I went round casually behind the stake to where the executioner was, and gave him the order to strangle him immediately. . . . When it was certain that he was dead, the executioner was ordered to set the four corners of the pyre to the brushwood and charcoal that had been piled up . . . it began to burn . . . the flames rising swiftly . . . when the cords binding the criminal had been burnt off he fell through the open trap-door into the pyre and his whole body was reduced to ashes. . . .

Such demonstrations of "the infinite goodness of God" had, over the years, their desired effect. Even *Converso* families who had been converted with extreme reluctance became, after three or four generations, thoroughly Christianized. An elder might privately consider himself still a Jew, and continue secretly to practice his religion and honor its holy days. But there was a reluctance to pass Judaism on to children for fear of placing them in the Inquisition's relentless path. Often, by the time a child was old enough to be safely told that he was Jewish, he had already been educated to the dogma of another faith and another ritual. Thus the *Conversos* became, gradually, what they were supposed to be: Christian converts.

But the Inquisition was never able to stamp out completely the Jewish faith in Spain and Portugal. Marranos continued to meet in secret places, clearings in woods or cellars of houses, to celebrate the Sabbath and holy days. Their lives involved continuous stealth and deception and fear. How many were there? There is no way of telling. Throughout the provinces of Toledo, Estremadura, Andalusia, and Murcia, it was said in 1488 that of the converts "hardly any are true Christians, as is well known in all Spain," and Hernando de Pulgar, himself a *Converso,* testified that there were "thousands" of secret Jews practicing their religion in Toledo alone. Three hundred years later, in 1787, Joseph Townsend reported after traveling through Spain:

> Even to the present day both Mahometans and Jews are thought to be numerous in Spain, the former among the mountains, the latter in all great cities. Their principal disguise is more than common zeal in external conformity to all the precepts of the Church; and the most apparently bigoted, not only of the clergy, but of the inquisitors themselves, are by some persons suspected to be Jews.

The Marranos gradually altered certain aspects of their ritual. After all, for the appearance of things it was necessary that they attend Catholic masses, and over the years Catholic practices made their inevitable way into Marrano Judaism. For instance, Marranos knelt rather than stood in prayer, and prayers were recited rather than chanted. No prayer books were kept, for they could be used as evidence, and Talmudic doctrine and lore were passed along verbally from one generation to the next. Marranos generally abstained from pork. They had secret Biblical names, which they used only among each other. Catholic wedding ceremonies were required, and a private Jewish wedding would be held afterward. More emphasis was placed on fasting than on feasting, and elaborate measures were resorted to in order to keep a Marrano's Christian servants from discovering that a fast was going on. Servants might be sent out on sudden errands at mealtimes; in their absence, plates were greased and dirtied to make it appear that the meal had taken place. A favorite device was to stage a family quarrel just before mealtime. By prearrangement, one member of the family would run out into the street in a feigned fit of rage, and the others would run after him to try to cajole him. When the quarrel was over, everyone would be too emotionally exhausted to eat anything.

The ancestors of Lewis Gomez, New York merchant and advertiser of "good Stone-Lime," appear to have been somewhat luckier than most Inquisitional Jewish families. Because of their services to a series of Spanish royal houses, Gomezes had been able successfully to remain in Spain long after Ferdinand and Isabella's Expulsion Edict. The Gomezes were connected by marriage to the great Santangel family, Marranos who, before their claimed conversion, had been named Ginillo. The Santangels, with their wealth and power and vast land holdings in Aragon, were natural targets of the Inquisition. Jaime Martin de Santangel was burned in 1488; Doñosa de Santangel six months later. Simon de Santangel and his wife, Clara, betrayed by their own son, were burned in Lérida in 1490. A more understandable betrayal occurred when one of the daughters of Luis de Santangel, along with her lover, was turned over to the Inquisition by her husband. A particularly grisly Inquisitional episode took place in Granada in 1491 when Alfonso Gomez, his wife, the former Violante de Santangel, and her brother, Gabriel de Santangel, were all posthumously condemned of heresy and their families exhumed and burned in public.

Perhaps the Gomez tradition of being men of deeds and few words helped them survive the Inquisition for as many generations as they did. As a family, the Gomezes over the centuries have been both industrious and brainy. It appears to have been Gomez brain power, rather than real estate, that made Gomezes so popular and useful to a series of Spanish kings and queens. In any case, Isaac Gomez, born in Madrid in 1620, had developed such a skill with deeds—particularly money deeds—that he was made financial adviser to the king, following a family tradition. He was one of the king's great favorites.

The king at this time was the melancholy Philip IV, three-time great-grandson of Ferdinand and Isabella, and great-great-grandson (on both his father's and his mother's side) of Juana la Loca, who, through the entanglements of royal intermarriage, turned up three more times in the king's family tree as his great-great-*great* grandmother. A heavy inheritance of her madness had fallen to him. This king was the father of the pathetic incompetent who was to be the last Hapsburg king, Carlos II, called Carlos the Bewitched. Philip himself was once suspected of being the victim of black witchcraft.

This also is the king we see in so many Velázquez portraits—regally astride his horse or standing imperiously in lace and ruffles, clutching his huge plumed hat, with a look of disdain on his far from handsome face with its heavy-lidded eyes, large nose, handlebar moustache, and the inevitable underslung Hapsburg jaw, which his son inherited to such an extreme extent that he could not chew his food. The king was a profligate and relentless womanizer, and his court was haunted by furies, real and imagined, from his frail and mentally retarded son to his belief that devils crept frightfully into the royal bedchamber and had secret intercourse with the queen. Quite obviously, the king was a man who needed a financial adviser, and Don Isaac Gomez (who must have used another Christian name in public) filled the bill perfectly.

It is an indication of the persistence of the Gomez family that they had been able to survive nearly a century and a half of Inquisition since the Expulsion Edict as secret Jews. It is also clear that the king, and probably others of his court, knew the Gomez secret. In any case, it suited Philip to protect Gomez from the Inquisition, and in return Gomez honored his king in faithful fashion. When Philip's sister married Louis XIV of France, Isaac Gomez named his first-born son Louis Moses Gomez, in honor of his monarch's new brother-in-law. Though Philip's own son would one day preside over one of the most ferocious autos-da-fé in history, Philip himself was of a gentler nature, tortured by self-doubt, convinced that his adulteries and promiscuity—over which he felt he had no control—were to blame for the ills that beset Spain. He once wrote: "These evil events have been caused by your sins and mine in particular. I believe that God our Lord is angry and irate with me and my realms on account of many sins, and particularly on account of mine. . . ."

King Philip had promised Isaac that if the officers of the Inquisition ever seemed to have come too close for comfort, and if the king heard of it before Isaac, the king would issue him a coded warning. At dinner he would say to him, "Gomez, the onions begin to smell."

The day came. Unfortunately, by the time the king's message reached him, there was time only to get Isaac's wife and son smuggled out of the country. Remaining behind to wind up his affairs, Isaac was arrested and thrown into prison. It was several years before he was able successfully to bribe his way out, and by then his friend the king was dead. He was forced to take a familiar route, over the Pyrenees into France, where he joined his family.

In 1685 the Edict of Nantes was revoked, there was an outbreak of religious disturbances in France, and a new mood of reaction was spreading across the Continent. Isaac prudently decided to move on to England, where he also had friends and family. In London, thanks to his connections, Isaac Gomez was granted a "letter of denization," which literally made him a denizen, or free man of the country. It was an important document for an alien to have, and one not customarily given to Jews. It indicated that Gomezes were persons of privilege, with full rights of British citizenship, except that of holding public office. Despite these advantages, however, Isaac's son Louis—a young man now—decided that he wanted to seek his fortune in America.

When word reached New York that a member of the exalted Gomez clan was on his way, there was a considerable stir within the little community of Sephardim—particularly among the mothers of unmarried and eligible daughters, who immediately began receiving instructions on how to treat a Gomez. It was said that the Gomezes were so grand that they still used their titles, and had to be addressed as "your grace," and "your ladyship." (This was true; they did.) Young Louis Gomez, however, disappointed the mothers by stopping enroute in Jamaica, where he met, by a prearrangement with her family, the daughter of another high-placed Sephardic family, Esther Marques, and married her. The young couple arrived in New York in 1696.

Louis Gomez (in America he anglicized his first name to Lewis) set himself up in a small store in lower Manhattan selling general merchandise. But soon he saw how important wheat was becoming to the young colony. Wheat, grown in what is now suburban Westchester County, as well as in the West Indies, was being traded back and forth across the Atlantic and was a highly profitable item. Concentrating on the wheat trade, Louis was soon able to write back to his father in London that he was trading wheat "on an enormous scale." He was becoming a rich man.

In 1705, Louis Gomez was numbered among the freemen of the city, and in 1710 a "memorial," which may of course have been in some ways a bribe, from Louis Gomez persuaded the New York City Council to give him permission to ship wheat to Madeira, even though a number of petitions by others had been denied. In 1728, he was elected parnas of the Shearith Israel congregation, an unusual honor since he was, after all, an immigrant and newcomer to the community, among families that had been in New York for two and three generations. It was under his presidency that funds were raised to build New York's first synagogue, in Mill Street. Louis Gomez was as broadminded in his philanthropies as the Levys: his name also appears on the list of those who contributed to the building of the steeple on Trinity Church. When Louis Gomez died, in 1740, he bequeathed "a pair of silver adornments for the five books of Moses, weighing 39 ounces," to his oldest son. The bequest has become a tradition in the family, and the silver ornaments, worn smooth by age, have been passed from eldest son to eldest son through seven generations.

Daniel, the third of Louis Gomez' six sons, was even more enterprising than his father. At the age of fourteen, Daniel joined his father in the wheat business and West Indies trade, and in the course of his wanderings he, like his father, met and married a member of an ancient and redoubtable Jamaican family, Rebecca de Torres. When she died in childbirth five years later, Daniel married another West Indian lady, Esther Levy of Curaçao.

From Daniel's first entry into it, business was good.

Starting with such commodities as wheat and West Indian sugar, he expanded into other goods and commodities. Soon he was trading not only with Madeira but also with Barbados, Curaçao, London, and Dublin. In 1751, an advertisement in the New York *Gazette* offered a new shipment of Daniel's wares from Liverpool, including:

> . . . earthenware in casks and crates, Cheshire cheese, loaf sugar, cutlery ware, pewter, grindstones, coals and sundry other goods too tedious to mention.

The blasé tone of the last phrase is an indication of the advertiser's success.

The list of names of men with whom Daniel Gomez did business reads like a *Who's Who* of Colonial America, and his customers included George Clinton, Walter Franklin, Robert Livingston, Myndert Schuyler, Isaac Sears, John de Peyster and Cornelius Ten Broeck of Albany; the Vallenburghs of Kinderhook; the Kips of Dutchess County; the Abeels, Brinckerhoffs, Beekmans, Barrons, Bogarts, the Rutgerses, the Van Cortlandts, the Van Wycks. His correspondence and bills went to such then-remote towns outside the colony as New Town, New Rochelle, Brunswick, Goshen, Huntington, Bushwick, Albany, the Hamptons, and Oyster Bay. He traded with other colonies as well, and his dealings extended to Boston, New Haven, Norwalk, New London, Allentown, Lancaster, Philadelphia, Princeton, Maryland, and South Carolina.

Though he concentrated on wheat, Daniel bought, sold, and traded nearly every other imaginable commodity, including stockings, suspenders, ginger, buttons, nightshirts, gunpowder, swords, preserved goods, silk, and sailcloth. But through all this diversity of business he still seems to have been searching for some product, some area of trade, that would consume him utterly, to which he could devote himself single-mindedly. Suddenly, in 1710, he found it.

Most people know that the great Astor fortune in America is based upon the fur trade. Only a few people know, however—the few including the old Sephardic families—that the first John Jacob Astor was preceded in the fur trade—and by many years—by a Sephardic Jew, Daniel Gomez. Daniel was, in fact, one of the very first to consider the vast wilderness of the continent that lay on all sides of him, and the numbers of fur-bearing animals that lived there. Daniel was an American pioneer in a business that has consumed adventurers and merchants since the days of the Golden Fleece. He was also the first in America to see how the native Indians could be used in this trade as trappers and skinners.

When, in 1710, Daniel Gomez began buying land in what is now Ulster County, his friends thought he was crazy. He was buying wilderness. Before long, he had acquired nearly 2,500 acres, including most of what is the present-day city of Newburgh, on the west bank of the Hudson River. He was able to buy this land cheaply only because no one else wanted it. It was also said, of all things, that the region was haunted. At the northwestern head of Newburgh Bay there is a rocky point of land which thrusts craggily into the river, and on a misty evening this peninsula, in profile, can indeed acquire an eerie look, as if possessed by spirits. And on this point, for untold hundreds of years before the arrival of the white man, the Algonquin tribes of what are now the New York, New Jersey, and Pennsylvania regions would meet at certain seasons of the year to worship, dance, and commune with their tribal gods and with the Great Spirit. This was a sacred place to the Indians, and before any hunting expedition, or any war, they traveled here in great numbers, often over hundreds of miles, to conduct the ceremonies that, they hoped, would improve the outcome of whatever task was at hand.

It has been said that when Henry Hudson sailed up the great river in 1609 he anchored off this point and watched the Indians performing one of their mystic ceremonies, dancing around a tall fire. In the minds of the Dutch settlers, the point quickly became associated with all sorts of dark deeds and, as Christians horrified at the heathen and mysterious evil rites that were said to be performed on the rocky headland, they renamed it *De Deful's Dans Kammer* (The Devil's Dance Chamber). An old ditty, designed to frighten adventuresome children from visiting the area, went:

For none that visit the Indian's den
Return again to the haunts of men.

The knife is their doom, oh sad is their lot.
Beware! Beware of the blood-stained spot!

All this served to depress local real estate values, and to Daniel Gomez' advantage. He had learned that the "blood-stained spot" also marked the convergence of a number of well-traveled Indian trails, and he selected the Indians' den as a strategic place to establish a trading post.

Attempts had been made since earliest Colonial times to identify the American Indians with the Ten Lost Tribes of Israel, and long lists of similarities between Indian and Judaic ritual had been drawn up, in an effort to prove this thesis. It was pointed out that, like the Jews, the Indians tabooed certain animals as "unclean." Like Jews, they had a sense of personal purity; they worshiped a great spirit called Yohovah; they had high priests; they had puberty rites. The Indians had important holy days in spring and fall, corresponding to Passover and Succoth, and a two-day fasting period corresponding to the Day of Atonement. The Indians had a lunar calendar, a similar counting system, and there are superficial similarities between the Hebrew and Indian tongues (both Hebrew and Indian languages make use of hyperbole and metaphor, and possess no comparative or superlative degree). Anthropologists have since dismissed these likenesses as coincidental, but in Daniel Gomez' day they were the subject of serious study. In the early Sephardic community of New York, these matters were discussed at the synagogue. Just in case they should turn out to be distant brethren, the rabbis had enjoined their congregations against mistreating or exploiting the local Indians. In any case, Daniel and the Indians got along famously right from the beginning. "I am able to understand the Indian thought," Daniel wrote to a friend.

For his post, Daniel Gomez selected a site that was near a spring where the gathering tribes regularly stopped for water, and he began, in 1717, to construct a massive stone blockhouse. Trading with the Indians was not without certain obvious hazards, and his trading post was also a fortress. The walls were two feet thick in the front and in the back, from which direction an attack was considered likelier, they were three feet thick. The house contained two vast cellars which were to serve as vaults to store the goods—knives, hatchets, trinkets, and of course guns and whiskey—that Daniel intended to sell, as well as the furs he intended to acquire.

He was building in the middle of virgin forest, seven miles from the nearest hamlet, Newburgh, which had been settled only eight years earlier. Trees had to be felled for timber, and stones had to be lifted from the ground for walls. The house took six years to build, but when it was finished Daniel Gomez had built an oasis of strength and also of comfort in the wilderness. In the main parlor Daniel had placed a huge fireplace, eight feet wide and six feet deep, designed for business entertaining during the winter months. Twenty to thirty Indians could gather around the fire's warmth to trade and haggle over the prices of lynx, beaver, otter, black fox, mink, and muskrat. In a smaller room, another fireplace, equally large, had the same hospitable and commercial function. Contemporary reports describe Mr. Gomez' house as furnished in "the ultimate luxuries which Gomez brought up from New York." Here he and his two sons—and eventually his second wife—spent the winter fur-trading season. It must have been a lonely life, but Gomezes had always been self-sufficient types, more interested in deeds than in words.

The lonely fort became known as "the Jew's house," and local records refer to Daniel only as "Gomez the Jew." Until recent years the stream that ran by Daniel Gomez' house (and that was once navigable, and doubtless transported some of Daniel's goods for barter) was designated on local maps as "Jew's Creek." For thirty years, Daniel Gomez operated his trading post, at the same time keeping close personal and business ties with New York. Like his father, he was elected parnas of Shearith Israel, pledging the then lordly sum of fifteen pounds a year to the synagogue. As early as 1727, he was listed among the "freemen" of New York, but though the title of freeman, or burgher, permitted its owner certain rights, there were others—including the right to vote—that could be obtained only through naturalization.

In 1737, in a notorious contested election, the right of Jews to vote for the general assembly had been challenged. Daniel Gomez was among the Jewish voters whose rights were in question, and the outcome was later called by William Seward "a stain in the annals of New York which the friends of rational liberty would wish to see effaced." The objection was upheld, and the Jews' rights were denied. Three years later, however, a Naturalization Act was passed. Daniel Gomez was among the first to take advantage of it and become a voter.

At the outbreak of the Revolution, with the arrival of British and Hessian troops in New York, Shearith Israel closed its doors and most members of the congregation moved to parts of the East held by the Revolutionary cause. Only a few Tory-minded Jews remained. These did not include the Daniel Gomezes. Daniel took his family to Philadelphia, the center of the American patriotic movement. He was an old man now, but he nonetheless became one of the founders of a new Sephardic congregation, Mikveh Israel.

He continued to keep track of his affairs in Newburgh, where one of his sons held the fort. It wasn't long before his son was able to write Daniel that he had hired a teenage German immigrant as an apprentice, and was teaching the youth to pound the pelts of beaver, otter, and mink that were making their way down Jew's Creek in Indian canoes. The young man's name was John Jacob Astor—then spelled Ashdor—and the Gomez firm was paying him a dollar a day. Certainly this early association with the Gomezes accounts for the recurring rumor in New York that the Astors are of Jewish descent. There is no proof of this, but there is plenty of evidence of what young Gomez thought of young Astor—a butcher's son with a heavy south German accent, a wildly indecipherable handwriting, and atrocious manners (after meals, Astor would wipe his hands on his shirt). Moses Gomez was, after all, a third-generation American and had no taste for this vulgarian. Soon Moses Gomez could take no more of him and, in dismissing him, explained to his father in a letter: "The fool has no head for this business absolutely"—a remarkably poor appraisal of the man who would found the American Fur Company, and become America's first monopolist.

The Newburgh house still stands. Far from seeming haunted by evil spirits, the house and the lands around it have, over two and a half centuries, had a happy history. There have been a number of owners since the house passed out of the Gomez family, and all have treated it tenderly. One added a second story of brick which contrasts handsomely with the gray stone walls Gomez built —built without mortar, fitted so perfectly that even today the walls stand straight and smooth. Now, though the acreage around it has been reduced to only twenty-seven, the blockhouse is still an elegant country home furnished in "the ultimate luxuries." The present owners, who have lived in it for over twenty years, speak of it with affection. In 1968, Mrs. Jeffrey Starin, wife of the owner, told a reporter from the New York *Times:* "The children talk about the house as having great roots. It gives them a feeling of strength and security. It has stood up in all kinds of weather and, a few years ago, when there was all that talk about bombs and shelters, they used to say, 'Our house will still be standing.' "

But alas, the Gomez name—which withstood so many generations in Spain—has died out in the United States. It decorates, of course, the higher branches of many Sephardic family trees, including the Nathans', but the last male Gomez, we learn from Malcolm Stern's extraordinary book, died in Franklin, New York, in 1926, without issue. He, Joseph Edwin Gomez, Jr., would have been Daniel's great-great-great-nephew. He was one of five children, and Dr. Stern notes above their names: "Children converted with mother, Feb. 3, 1871." If Daniel's ghost was pacing the house in Newburgh when this news was received, there must have been outraged noises in the night.

8

"MAKE YOUR WAY TO THE WINDWARD COAST OF AFRICA"

EVEN after it became a British colony, New York remained very Dutch in feeling. The brick and tile with which the houses were built, the architecture, the machinery, the utensils—everything had been imported from the Netherlands until a replica of a Dutch *dorp* had been created on the tip of Manhattan, a miniaturized Amsterdam. The British had arrived and taken over things, but the Dutch families refused to change their quiet, cultured ways. They continued to live with their mahogany furniture, their Oriental rugs, their delft ornaments, their fine brass and silverware, their paintings by Dutch masters. They continued to worship at the Dutch church, and to speak the Dutch language. So resolutely did they cling to their old-world roots that Dutch was spoken in the Dutch Church of New York right up until the time of the Civil War.

The Dutch were scornful of the British arrivals, and considered them boorish and uncultivated. The people who counted were still the Dutch families—the de Peysters, the Bogarduses, the Lockermans, the Van Cortlandts, the Kierstedes, the Van Rensselaers, the Phillipses, and the Beekmans. The Jews of New York, with their affinity for things Dutch, felt similarly about the British. (England had, after all, had anti-Semitic pogroms, which Holland had never had.) As Revolutionary sentiments were marshaling themselves, there was no question of where most of the New York Sephardim would stand: squarely against the British.

But as the trickle of Sephardic arrivals continued—

along with a much smaller trickle of Jews from central
Europe, who joined the Sephardic congregations when
they got here—Jews were scattering to cities other than
New York, establishing little settlements in Philadelphia,
Charleston, Savannah, and New Orleans to the south, and
in New England to the north, following the pattern of expansion of the American colonies along the eastern seaboard. A particularly important Sephardic community had
been established early in the eighteenth century in Newport, where sons and grandsons of the Twenty-Three,
along with their later-arriving cousins, had settled and were
taking part in Newport's booming trade. By 1750, Newport had outdistanced New York as a commercial seaport,
and Newport's Sephardim were getting even richer than
New York's. There were strong ties between Jewish Newport and Jewish New York. The famous Touro Synagogue
in Newport was built as—and continues to be—a branch
of New York's Shearith Israel, and is owned by the New
York congregation (it pays rent of a dollar a year). But
in terms of eighteenth-century politics, Newport and New
York were somewhat unlike. Newport, after all, was a New
England city. There was more pro-Tory feeling about.
Writing to his young Newport cousin, Aaron Lopez, Daniel Gomez frequently chided him for failing to support the
Revolutionary cause. But young Aaron, though he respected his New York relative, had different ideas. On his
arrival in America he had sworn in his naturalization oath
to "be faithful and bear true allegiance to His Majesty
George the Third." And Aaron had business reasons for
remaining on good terms with the British. He had extensive
dealings with them in Newport's flourishing slave trade.

Aaron Lopez was a very determined young man. He
had arrived in Newport from Portugal—where his family
had been successful Marranos—in 1750 at the age of nineteen, and he had already acquired a wife, another cousin,
five years older than he, named Abigail (Anna had been
her Christian alias in Iberia), and a tiny daughter, Sarah
(alias Catherine). In Newport the little family immediately resumed their Old Testament first names, and Aaron
and his wife were remarried in the Jewish rite.

Men of Aaron's generation had a distinct advantage
over the earliest pioneers such as the Twenty-Three. There
were other Jews, many of them relatives, to welcome them

and help them set themselves up in business. In Aaron's case, there were his Gomez and de Lucena connections in New York, and, in Newport, an older half-brother, Moses Lopez, and still another cousin, Jacob Rodriguez Rivera, who had both become successful merchants. For several years, Aaron Lopez worked for Jacob Rivera while he saved his money so as to get into something on his own. Mr. Rivera was credited with having founded Newport's spermaceti industry, dealing in the whitish, waxy substance that could be separated from the oil of the sperm whale and was the principal ingredient of candlemaking. Between spermaceti and the town's "other" industry—slavery—Newport's harbor was one of the busiest in America, where as many as 150 ships lay at anchor at a time.

Slavery, and their part in it, has understandably become a sore point with the Sephardim, who tend to play down their ancestors' role, or to insist that Jewish merchants who took part in the slave trade did so "only on a very limited scale." Looking at it in historical perspective, however, and bearing in mind the attitudes that prevailed at the time—and remembering man's limitless capacity to overlook his own folly—it is possible to view slavery as it was viewed in the eighteenth century, as just another business. No one questioned the morality of the slave trade. Whether it was right or wrong was something not even considered. It was not in any way a Jewish preoccupation. All the "best people" were involved in it, and a great many of New England's oldest, finest, and most redoubtable fortunes are solidly based on human cargo. (One should not point to the Jews and overlook the Christians.)

In New England, slavery was not only tacitly approved. It was actually touted as an institution of great benefit to the black man, in that it brought him out of the heathen jungle into the civilized land of Christian godliness. A certain elder of the church in Newport would, according to one historian, go to church the Sunday following the arrival of a slaver from the Coast and "thank God that another cargo of benighted beings had been brought to a land where they could have the benefit of a Gospel dispensation." In a volume called *Reminiscences of Newport*, an idyllic picture of slavery is painted, and the attitudes prevalent in Aaron Lopez' day are perfectly defined. "If we look at the relation of master and slave at that time," the author writes, "we must own that the attachment between them was stronger, and the interest manifested in the welfare of each other far greater than anything in our days between employer and employee." He adds, "Few were the complaints of the servitude exacted." True, there were some who regarded slavery with distaste or even horror, but these were regarded as harmless eccentrics. Ministers such as Ezra Stiles and Samuel Hopkins ranted against slavery from their New England pulpits, but to little avail. Every man of substance owned slaves. The Episcopal Church itself owned a plantation in Barbados, and from time to time had to purchase fresh slaves to keep it in operation. And slavery had become such an immensely profitable business that those men engaged in it had no difficulty whatever in turning deaf ears to their scattered critics.

Newport's first human cargo from Africa arrived as early as 1696, and soon afterward began that interesting triangular trade route which the slavers followed for the next hundred years. A ship would set sail from Newport to the west coast of Africa loaded with hogsheads of New England rum. In Africa, the rum would be traded for slaves, who would then be carried to the West Indies, where the third major transaction would take place—slaves traded for sugar, which was then brought back to Newport, where no less than twenty-two stills waited to turn the sugar into rum, which would then make its way back to Africa to be exchanged for more slaves.

The rum, in part, stayed in the African coastal colonies, where it was simply another form of currency, and of course a small portion of it went into the interior of Africa, where tribal chieftains accepted it in payment for their people. But most of the rum eventually went to Europe—to England, France, Holland, Portugal, and Denmark—for all these countries were then engaged in what amounted to an international business. And these were the countries, too, that needed slaves to provide labor in their expanding colonies.

There were opportunities for sizable profits at each corner of the triangular slave trade, and from a great variety of other goods that were bought, sold, and traded along the way. But slaves produced the tidiest yield—between £1,500 and £2,000 profit per shipload being about average, at a time when, to get an idea of comparative prices, a hundred-gallon cask of Madeira wine sold for something like £6. At the height of the slave trade when Aaron Lopez was active, as many as 184 vessels were involved from the state of Rhode Island alone. In the United States, only South Carolina exceeded this figure. This meant that Newport saw the arrival or departure of a slave ship every single day of the year.

Of course it was easier for the men who owned the slaving fleets to justify their curious occupation. Most owners never set foot aboard their ships. They had never seen a slave ship being unloaded or watched the sick and filthy men and women—and children, too—emerge with their black skins gone gray from hunger and confinement below the decks. The same was true of the rest of commercial and social Newport. Slavery was invisible. Slaves were nearly always disposed of in West Indian or southern ports. As Jeremy Belknap, an old Newporter, once recalled: "Very few cargoes ever came to this port. . . . I remember one, between thirty and forty years ago, which consisted almost wholly of children . . . sometimes the Rhode Island vessels, after having sold their prime slaves in the West Indies, brought the remnants of their cargoes hither for sale." Mr. Belknap then wistfully added: "Since this commerce has declined, the town of Newport has gone to decay."

Out of sight was out of mind and, meanwhile, an altogether different sort of character was required for the man who captained a slaving ship, who anchored off the African coast and engaged in the actual barter of human bodies in exchange for hogsheads of rum.

Of a different caliber, too, was the "governor" who operated the coastal "castle" where slaves were herded and corraled until sold. At the height of the eighteenth-century slave trade, as many as forty of these stations were strung along the so-called Slave Coast, the low-lying delta country that stretches for 700 miles between the mouth of the Volta River and Mount Cameroon. Here, those blacks "deemed to make the best slaves" were brought for 350 years. Of the forty castles, fourteen were English, three were French, fifteen were Dutch, four were Portuguese, and four were Danish. But from the figures of a single year of trade—38,000 slaves sold by the British, 20,000 by the French, 4,000 by the Dutch, 10,000 by the Portuguese, and 2,000 by the Danes—it is quite clear that more than half the trade was in British hands.*

Slaves were driven on foot to these castles from their villages in the interior. For this most dreadful stage of their long journey, during which the greatest loss of life occurred, their herdsmen were almost always their own people. The most demoralized positions in the entire slave trade fell to these men. As for the native chieftain who sold off members of his tribe for barrels of rum, he was almost as remote from the death and torture of the business as the powdered and bewigged ladies and gentlemen back in Newport, chatting over teacups, the leaders of business and society who were enjoying the gratifying monetary fruits of the operation at the other end. White or black, slavery was the creation of the nabobs.

On the African coast, price negotiations were in the hands of the slaver captain and the resident governor of the castle. It was all very businesslike, and there were fluctuations in the market just as there were in every other commodity. Sometimes it took months for a satisfactory deal to be completed, but once it was, the slaves were loaded aboard with great dispatch. A captain who "lost" his slaves for any reason was, understandably, not assured a precisely warm welcome back in Newport, and so some care was taken for the slaves' well-being, but no more care than was economically feasible. Slave quarters were in spaces between the decks, three to three and a half feet high. Men were stretched out on their backs, in spaces eighteen inches wide per man, their ankles secured by chains. Women and children lay in a separate compartment, equally crowded but unchained. The journey across the Atlantic took anywhere from six to ten weeks, depending on the weather. Sometimes, if the captain was a lenient one, the prisoners were allowed above decks for short periods to get exercise and a breath of fresh air. Often, during these moments, prisoners tried to fling them-

* Slavery was brought to the colonies by the English. England did get around to abolishing slavery somewhat before the United States did, in 1807. Denmark was the first nation to abolish slavery, in 1792. The northern American states, meanwhile, starting with Vermont in 1777 and ending with New Jersey in 1804, all had adopted state abolition laws before Great Britain did.

selves overboard into the sea. Uncooperative prisoners were punished in such bizarre ways as being tied to ships' anchor chains and dragged in the wake.

There were equally bizarre dangers to be encountered by those employed at various points of the slaving triangle. One of Aaron Lopez' Da Costa cousins, who helped her husband with his end of the business in Kingston, Jamaica, and who happened to be pregnant at the time, one night "went to draw rum to adulterate for the Sunday sale of slaves"* by candlelight. A spark from her candle dropped into the high-proof rum, and the rum, along with the unfortunate woman, went up in flames. Mrs. Da Costa very nearly did for Kingston what Mrs. O'Leary's cow later did for Chicago, for nearby were "rum, brandy and gin shops by the score" which contained thousands of inflammable gallons. Luckily, the "eingine" arrived quickly and the fire was extinguished, though too late to save the lady.

In this, Newport's leading, highly respected, even fashionable industry, young Aaron Lopez—enterprising, handsome, with dark hair, high cheekbones, and large, dark, commanding eyes; small and wiry—was an early success. From the pennies saved while working with his cousin Jacob Rivera, he had been able, within two years, to become a partner in the purchase of the ship *Ann,* described in her bill of sale as "A double deck new brigantine about 113 tons burthen . . . completely finished for the African trade . . . to be sheathed with inch pine boards or ½ inch cedar . . . the awning, a second boat, caboose, colors, small arms, *chains* and *hand cuffs* [these items are underscored in the bill of sale] and every other small utensil to be excluded and provided by the Captain." Not even the implements of imprisonment were dealt in by the owner.*

At 113 tons, the *Ann* was probably about seventy feet in length, a small ship for such long voyages, but few slave ships were larger. Her cost to Aaron Lopez was quoted at "£690 Sterling," not even half the profit that could be made from a single load of slaves. On November 27, 1772, nine months after she had been ordered, the *Ann* lay ready to sail in Newport harbor, her decks loaded with

* Undoubtedly to thin it with water.

such items as Madeira wine, brown sugar, molasses, vinegar, thirty sheep, thirty-nine turkeys, twenty-eight geese, twenty-one ducks. But the largest item, which caused the *Ann* to ride low in the water, was "98 hogsheads and 14 tierces New England Rum," approximately 11,000 gallons, weighing over forty tons. Lopez made a brief inspection of his new ship—probably the last he ever saw of her—and turned her over to his captain, a sturdy Yankee named William Einglish, with the following orders:

> Sir:
> Our brig the Ann, of which you are at present the master, being loaded and ready for the Seas, Our orders to you are, That you Embrace the first fair wind and make the best of your way to the Coast of Africa; and as we have no opinion of the windward Coast trade, we think it advisable, that as soon as you procure the necessary rice that you proceed without delay to Anamoboe Road; when please God you arrive there safe Convert your cargo into good Slaves; on the best terms you can; you are not insensible that lying any considerable time on the Coast is not only attended with a very heavy expense, but also great risk of Slaves you may have on board. We therefore would recommend to you dispatch, even if you are obliged to give a few gallons more or less on each slave. . . .

Obviously, a great deal depended on the reliability of the captain, and there is no way of telling how many of these men were able successfully to cheat their owners. But Einglish seems to have been an honest man. His or-

* There was an ancient Talmudic principle involved here. For centuries the rabbinate decreed that when a Jew was involved in the human slave trade, he could not go below certain standards of humanity and decency. The Jew could deal in slaves as a business—as everyone else did—but he could not be involved in their punishment or torture. In the tenth century, for instance, there was a great vogue for blond eunuch slaves. They were used in harems and for homosexual purposes. The Jews of the Orient and Middle East were disturbed by this trade, and went to their rabbis for guidance. They were advised that it was permissible for them to buy and sell eunuchs, but that they were under no circumstances to be involved with the performance of castrations. The rabbis told them, "Let the goy do that."

ders went on to explain that a certain David Mill, governor of one of the coast castles, still owed Lopez' cousin Jacob Rivera "twenty-seven men and thirteen women slaves" from an earlier shipment which had arrived short that number. These, Lopez asserted, Mill would "immediately deliver" to Captain Einglish, and he was sure of this "from Mr. Mill's universal character." In order that these forty not be confused with the rest of the shipment, Lopez instructed the captain to "put some distinguishing mark" on those, "that we may distinguish them from those of the cargo."

The bookkeeping was then explained. Two-thirds of the regular cargo were to be bought on Lopez' account, and the remaining third were to be charged to Jacob Rivera. The forty owed slaves were to be credited to each man equally. All slaves, the orders advised, were to be sold in the slave market of Savannah La Mar, Jamaica, and the *Ann* was to return to Newport "clean of them."

It would be romantic and wrong to picture Captain Einglish as a demon. Actually, his approach to the business was crisp and dispassionate. He had a job to do. He was meticulous in his record keeping, and anything that smacked of inefficiency or wasted motion annoyed him. In his first report to Lopez, dated January 14, 1773, Einglish wrote: "After a voyage of forty days I arrived at the Islands of Deloes on the windward Coast of Africa, where I furnished myself with what rice I think will be sufficient for my voyage [rice, and a little mutton, comprised the diet of the captured slaves], and shall sail this day for the Gold Coast, wind and weather permitting." Rumors, he said, had reached him that business was "very Dull for our Trade," and that ships were being forced to move further eastward along the coast in search of slaves. "The lowest price that they asked for slaves here," he wrote, "is a hundred and fifty barrels, which is equal to two hundred gallons of Rum." He went on to report that "Various Gales of Wind" had meant that "the greatest part of my Turkeys Perished, Also Lost the 30 Bundles of Hay the Fourth day after I sail'd. I have still on board twenty-eight sheep with the greatest part of the Geese and Ducks which I expect to deliver in good order." This meant that only two sheep had been butchered and consumed during the crossing, a commendably thrifty record.

Two months later, in March, Einglish wrote to Lopez

from Anamabu, a village still standing on the Gold Coast, saying: "I arrived at Cape Corse Castle on the 12th of February, where on my arrival applied to Governor Mill and gave him the offer of my cargo on Various Terms, from one hundred and eighty gallons to two hundred for men and in proportion for women," who were always sold for somewhat less. Mr. Mill, it turned out, despite his "universal character," was somewhat overextended. He owed slaves to captains in all directions—including, of course, the forty to Lopez and Rivera—and the best he could promise Einglish, the captain reported to his employer, was that after every ship, in its proper turn, had received its share, he might be able to supply Einglish with some "in about Eighteen Months." As for the forty short from the previous order, Mill replied vaguely that he would have them for Einglish when Einglish was "ready to sail."

Anamabu that spring was understocked with slaves and overstocked with rum. Wrote Einglish: "Here is very poor times for every fort and private house is stocked with Rum . . . there is no selling of Rum nor anything else. I have not been five nights on board since my arrival but continually cruising from one fort to another striving to sell my Cargo." The more he cruised, apparently, the higher the price of slaves became and the longer the wait for delivery. From a deal which he reports "I struck with Mr. Henrick Woortman," he exchanged four thousand gallons at the rate of "two hundred gallon for men and one hundred and eighty for women, payable in three months." From "Various private traders," he was able to get a few more at a slightly lower price—"190 Gallon and 195 for men and in proportion for women"—but soon the price jumped again to 210 gallons for men slaves, and a three-month delay. He wrote to Lopez and Rivera: "Gentlemen, I have but five Slaves on board and God knows when I shall have five more for the Country Trade is so dull and Slaves scarce." He added that his supply of sheep was now down to twenty-seven, along with sixteen geese, twelve ducks, and five turkeys.

Two weeks later, Einglish wrote to Lopez that he had bought ten more slaves, bringing the total on board to fifteen, and that he was about to deliver Mr. Woortman's rum at his castle. "If Mr. Woortman pays me according to agreement," he noted somewhat nervously, "I shall sail the Beginning of June." The rum market continued depressed and, "There is no Governor, neither English Nor Dutch that will take Rum for present pay." The same went for "Lisbon wine," though the captain noted a better market for "wine that will pass for Madeira." The price of rum was driven further downward by the arrival of two more vessels, one from Boston and one "of Mr. Brown of Newport," both loaded to the gunwales with hogsheads of the stuff and, of course, when rum prices dropped, slave prices rose.

By the middle of May—Einglish had been at anchor over two months—thirty slaves were on board the *Ann.* Governor Mill had still not delivered the forty slaves he owed Aaron Lopez and Jacob Rivera, and Captain Einglish was still anxiously awaiting delivery from Mr. Woortman, which was promised for May 28. There was more bad news. Captain Einglish's chief mate, whom Einglish describes as "a worthless Drunking fellow," had, in a moment of bibulous carelessness, been responsible for the loss of the *Ann*'s longboat and a load of valuable provisions. "I dispatched him," Einglish writes, "to Cape Cord in the Long Boat for water and to settle some business there that I could not leave the vessel to tend, his boat being well fitted with everything that I thought necessary, and had in Twenty Three water casks, two barrels flour, one box soap, and fifty pounds of coffee, which goods he was to deliver and receive the Gold." However, "In one of his drunking frollicks, carrying more sail than Good Judgment would allow him, he took in a large quantity of water and stood so nigh the shore that he was almost in the breakers, whereupon the natives perceiving came off with a number of canoes and several of them boarding the boat on one side, and she already waterlogged, readily overset and Every shilling's worth lost to the Great Determent of the Voyage. For now I am obliged to hire a canoe and employ a number of Blacks that I should have had no occasion for." To add to his indignation, he noted that the price of slaves had climbed to 230 gallons a head.

By June 6, Einglish had forty-one slaves on board, and Woortman was eight days past his deadline, promising delivery now "in a few days." Mr. Mill, too, was dragging his feet, and the captain wrote to his employer in Newport: "I waited on Governor Mill two days ago for the slaves due, but did not receive them, although his promise to me was that I should have been whenever demanded."

If Mill's response seemed suspiciously evasive, Einglish's countermove against Mill was properly aggressive. He applied to Mill for payment of the sunken longboat, claiming that it was the natives, who were in Mill's charge, climbing aboard on one side that had caused the boat to sink, not the chief mate's drunkenness and poor judgment. Mill agreed that the "Natives should be made to pay," and Einglish seems to have concluded that this was quite just since "they were concerned in a most Vilanous Action in plundering and oversetting her." Einglish concludes with a prayer that no more rum might arrive from New England to further drive down the price.

On July 12, Governor Mill wrote to Lopez and Rivera explaining that he was once again sending the firm a short shipment. "I have only been able, trade being so bad," he said, "to pay Captain Einglish 30 of the 40 slaves owed . . . and hope the detention of those ten will be no loss to you. If it is I will thankfully pay you. I have paid for the stock and I hope to your satisfaction." He does not mention paying for the longboat. The same day, Captain Einglish added to the list what his hold contained: "19 men slaves, marked '0' on the right thigh, also 11 women marked ditto. Being marked and numbered as in the margin, and are to be delivered in the like good order and well conditioned at the port of Kingston in Jamaica (mortality, insurrection, and the danger of the seas only excepted)."

The Woortman delivery must have been made soon after because, on July 15, Captain Einglish set sail from Anamabu, where he had spent just over five months, with a load of ninety-five slaves comprising, in addition to the thirty from Mill, "33 men slaves, 2 boys, 27 women, and 3 girl slaves." All, he noted, "is very good and healthy at present and have not lost one slave yet. Thank God for it."

It took Einglish eighty-five days, in heavy weather most of the way, to make the westward journey across the Atlantic to Jamaica. Once there he was forced to report that he had had "the misfortune of burying six slaves on my passage," five of them from the regular cargo and one of the group marked "0"—probably by branding—on the right thigh. Of the remainder, he commented that they were "for the great part in good health and well liked by the gentleman who intends to purchase. . . . By what I can learn from several gentlemen that has seen the slaves they will sell to good advantage—the 13th Inst. is the Day for Sale." A few weeks later, however, the captain's report from Jamaica indicated that he had been somewhat optimistic in his earlier letter, as to both the state of the slaves' health and that of the market. A disorder which Einglish characterizes only as "swelling," and which was probably a form of scurvy or food poisoning, had afflicted many of his cargo during the crossing, and now Einglish wrote: "Gentlemen, I buried one man slave since my last, and the Swelling began to range so violent among the slaves that nine of them was sold for a mere trifle . . . when I arrived, there was but two slaves that had the least sign of swelling. This disorder first begun in their feet and worked upward . . . when got as far as their stomach they died in a few hours." He added gloomily that "There has been three ships' cargoes of slaves sold since my arrival, and none of their averages exceeded [ours] not five shillings in a slave. Therefor I do not think that this market is as good as the Merchants here says it ought to be."

Still, Captain Einglish was, according to the accounting he submitted, able to sell his remaining slaves for £3,620. Expenses amounted to £1,399, which meant a tidy profit of £1,259, or about 90 percent. He sailed from Jamaica in December and, after a brief stop at Môle Saint Nicolas, on the northwestern tip of Haiti, where he loaded the *Ann* with sugar, he headed home to Newport.

9.

ALLARUMS AND RAVAGES

AARON LOPEZ' ships made yearly visits to Africa in this fashion and, from his modest beginning with the *Ann*, his fleet grew to the point where, at the height of his career, just before the first guns of the American Revolution, he owned, or partly owned, more than thirty vessels in what was called the "African Trade," or, more euphemistically, the "West Indian Trade."

As his fortune grew, so did the size of his family. He seems to have been cut out to be a patriarch on the grandest scale, and doubtless envisioned each new son as a future asset to his business. His first wife, Anna, bore him eight children before she died—in childbirth—in 1762. She, of course, had been Aaron's cousin, and Aaron next married another cousin, Sally Rivera, some sixteen years his junior, the daughter of his business associate, Jacob Rodriguez Rivera. Thus his partner became his father-in-law.

Aaron's second wife proceeded to present him with nine children and when, one by one, the members of this voluminous family reached marriageable age, suitable partners had to be found among the Sephardim of Newport and New York, who, at this point, were nearly all relatives already. The web of intramural marriage drew even tighter. One Lopez daughter married a Touro, and two of Aaron's daughters married Gomez boys—who were each other's first cousins, and both nephews of Daniel Gomez—and another married a Hendricks (who were already related to Gomezes) and still another became Rachel Lopez-Lopez when she married her own first cousin. Two other Lopez girls married the same man, Jacob Levy. This happened when Mr. Levy, widowed by one Lopez girl, married her younger sister. This marriage was not so much dynastic as dizzying in the extent to which it crossed up various Levys. Since Levy had children by both his wives, his marriages made his various children first cousins. To further confuse the tangled Lopez-Gomez-Rivera bloodline, one of Aaron Lopez' daughters, Hannah, married her uncle. With this union, Aaron's brother-in-law became his son-in-law as well, and Hannah Lopez became her mother's sister-in-law.

An inevitable result of these marriages was that the two family heads, Aaron Lopez and Daniel Gomez, had close ties—family as well as business—even though they did not see eye to eye on pre-Revolutionary politics. Over the years, the two men corresponded between New York and Newport, and much of this correspondence survives. Though Daniel was more than thirty years older than Aaron, the two had much in common. Each wrote to the other in a formal, courtly style, the older man addressing his younger Newport friend as "your grace," referring to "the lady your wife," and extending best wishes to others of "your noble house."

Both Gomez and Lopez liked to gamble, and much of their correspondence concerned Gomez' purchase of lottery tickets in New York for Lopez. Neither man had much luck. In August, 1753, Gomez wrote Lopez: "According to your order, I bought in your name two lottery tickets, Nos. 1190 and 1192, which may please God to be venturous and that by that way you may obtain something of consequence. I have charged to you their cost which is £3. Your Grace orders me to send you the tickets, but I do not see fit to do it until a second order arrives because in case they are lost Your Grace will lose what they provide." Alas, a few weeks later, Daniel Gomez advised: "I sent my son to find out about the lottery tickets, but because of our sins both your tickets and mine came out blank. . . . I assure Your Grace that I am sorry that they have had such little fortune. God may please to give us a better one." Their prayers, however, seem to have gone unanswered. Years later, Gomez was writing: "According to your request I have bought, in your name, a Lottery ticket number 77 which will please Your Grace to be fortunate." And, a short while later, he was advising:

"Enclosed is your lottery ticket which I am sorry to say came out blank. God may give you a better fortune next time." Gomez' system seems to have been to buy tickets containing double numbers—1190, 77, 881, 544, 311, 2200, etc. It was as good a system as any.

The two kept each other posted on family news. When Daniel's young wife, who had been ill for many months, died, he wrote to his friend movingly: "I cannot express in words the great grief and sorrow that accompanies me as Our Lord has served to free from my company, and from this to a better life, my esteemed and loving wife, who offered her soul to the Creator on the 31st of May. . . . May the Great Majesty receive her soul with kindness and place her with the just and good . . . and that she is enjoying eternal Glory as her good heart and her being a good Jew confirm me in that certainty." And learning of the death, in infancy, of one of Aaron Lopez' children, Daniel wrote to him: "You stated your hopes that your little angel would improve in health, but [I have been informed] that God has received him and I assure you that we are in grief as if he were of our own, and I send Your Grace, the lady your wife, and the rest of the family, our sympathy, and pray to God that the life the little innocent lacked will be increased in yours."

For all his deferential manner toward Aaron Lopez, Daniel Gomez was not hesitant to give him business advice when he felt this was in order. He had little use for Lopez' candle business, which was something of a sideline, and told him: "I am sorry there is no better way in which Your Grace may occupy himself other than by making candles. My brother David invested £240 last year in green wax and tallow, his negroes made candles which he sent to all the islands, and there they stand, with no sales, and at a very low price. All of this I inform Your Grace of. . . . You will suffer great losses and if you could sell the candles I advise you to proceed." Either Lopez failed to receive this letter or he simply ignored Gomez' advice because, a few weeks later, Gomez complained because Lopez had sent them on to New York for Gomez to sell instead of selling the candles in Newport. He wrote testily: "acknowledging six boxes of spermaceti and candles which you have sent me by Captain Morrow's schooner, which I received, and am sorry you sent such merchandise to be sold here, and to exchange for tallow, when you know and everybody knows that it is very difficult to sell here and that tallow is cash money. I would appreciate your ordering me to return them to you, as I offered them to different merchants and not one is interested. I am willing to serve you in what I can, but I cannot do the impossible." His anger was quickly spent, however, for a few paragraphs later in the same letter he wrote: "Today is the last day for the Lottery. . . . I wish God is willing to give you some prize. . . ."

At the same time, the labyrinthine bloodlines that bound the Sephardim of both Newport and New York together were capable of producing weighty problems. When people are tied together by blood as well as money, the two elements fuse and cross in ways that can be painful, and already the Sephardim were showing signs of the strain. There were whole branches of certain families which —often for the most trifling reasons—no longer spoke to other branches, and the little band of Jews, who had first approached the vicissitudes of the new world with a certain unity of purpose, had spread and dispersed into touchy factions. Nearly always it was money—what some relative had done with his money, which displeased some other relative—that lay at the heart of the dispute. The more relatives there were, the more complex were the relationships.

Not only each new son, but each new son-in-law, had to be given some sort of position in the interconnected family enterprises. And, alas, not all these sons and sons-in-law possessed the talents the older generations might have wished. Both Daniel Gomez and Aaron Lopez faced this problem. Daniel's son Moses married Daniel's brother's daughter, Esther—first cousins again—but neither of their two sons (two others died in infancy) displayed any ability in the fur trade. Isaac, Jr., was always getting "stung" by the Indians. "Stung again!" he would write the patriarch, almost gaily, each time it happened. There is a suggestion that Isaac had taken to imbibing some of the firewater used in the Indian trade, a practice his grandfather had abstemiously avoided. Isaac married one of the Lopez girls.

An even more ticklish situation existed in Aaron Lopez' family. Aaron's oldest daughter, Sally, had married a young man named Abraham Pereira Mendes, a member of an old and distinguished Sephardic family that had settled in Jamaica. At the time of the engagement, Abraham Mendes' elder brother wrote to Aaron Lopez: "The choice of my brother Abraham to your daughter Miss Salle, for his consort, has merited much our Abrobation [*sic*], as also that of my honoured Mother. The Amiableness of your daughter, the Bright Character and honour of your family's, as much in these parts, as those of ancient, in Portugal, cannot but give us in general the greatest satisfaction. . . . From my brother repeated expressions of their reciprocal love must make them happy, and pleasing to you, and beg leave to return my congratulating you and all your good family, on this joyfull occasion, wishing them all the Happiness they can wish for, and pray the Almighty may crown them with his Blessings. . . ." There were other reasons for rejoicing. Sally Lopez was a rich man's eldest daughter, and the Mendeses of Jamaica, though they bore an ancient name, were sorely in need of an infusion of money. Leah Mendes, Abraham's mother, had been widowed with several children, and was described by her son as being "reduced very low, owing to the great Losses she has met with . . . the condition I found her in shocked me to the highest degree."

Abraham's brother added that he was sure Aaron had found in Abraham "such Bright Qualitys which few of his age are endowed with." He added that while Abraham's education might leave something to be desired, considering the sort of formal education available in those days on the West Indian island, his intellectual abilities were "those of Nature." He was sure, he said, that "with cultivating in your good Advice must make him a Bright Man." This, however, turned out to be wishful thinking.

Aaron decided that his new son-in-law's acquaintance with the island would make him an excellent candidate for the job of overseer of the Lopez enterprises in Jamaica, a task that up to then had been performed by a series of non-family firms. From the very beginning there were difficulties. For one thing, Abraham Pereira Mendes appears to have enjoyed poor health. A great deal of the business correspondence between father and son-in-law concerns the state of the latter's stomach, feet, or head. Abraham and Sally were married in Newport, and soon after their return to Kingston, to take up his duties, Abraham was writing Aaron: "I must now acquaint you of my safe arrival in the place. . . . I can't say agreeable being sick all the passage, and was reduced very low. At my landing I could hardly keep my legs. . . ." A few days later he was no better, writing: "My hands with weakness tremble in such a manner I can hardly write." The next year, he was complaining of "A surfeit and a fit of the Gout, which has laid me up three weeks and am now in a most deplorable condition and cannot mount my horse, which has put my business backward."

This, of course, was the most irritating result of a sickly son-in-law—business, inevitably, was put backward, and Abraham's letters back to Aaron are full of apologies and excuses for his poor performance. The news is nearly always gloomy: "We lost 10 sheep. . . . The black horse looks very bad. . . . Stepped on board to view the slaves . . . the major part of them are small things, and those that are large has age on their side. . . . The poor success I had in receiving your Outstanding Debts and not getting cash for the cargoes have not enabled me to remit until March. . . . I am much afraid your Out-Standing Debts will not be collected, not for want of my care, but the people being incapable." His father-in-law warned him about a certain slave captain named All, whom Aaron Lopez distrusted. Abraham met the man and, "To my great Surprize," found him quite satisfactory. The result was disastrous. The man turned out to be an utter scoundrel. By making private deals with Slave Coast governors, Captain All bilked Aaron Lopez out of a full year's profits.

One of Abraham's problems, in addition to his health, was his lack of education. His letters are full of eccentric spellings, their sentence structure is erratic, and at one point he apologizes: "You'll excuse the Writing being oblige to gett a Young Cousin to scrible over." It is possible that a "Young Cousin" wrote most of his letters.

His devotion to his young wife was, despite his brother's assurances, something less than complete. During the early days of his Jamaica sojourn she remained behind in Newport, and it would seem as though Abraham missed her rather little. Writing to her father, at one point, he mentioned that he had had a letter from "my dear Sally," though he has yet "not received the Sweet Meets she had promised to send." He added that he would have "no time" to write her, and quaintly urged her father to "embrace her in my behalf with all the love of a Loving Husband." His attitude may have disturbed Sally because, about a year later, she sailed to Jamaica to join him. He was probably less than happy to see her. A few months after her arrival, he did a thing that was shocking news to eighteenth-century Newport as well as to Jewish society in the West Indies. He ran off with another woman.

Obviously, this was a situation requiring delicacy and a certain firmness. Aaron Lopez was disgusted with his son-in-law's delinquency and poor performance, and he was ready to wash his hands of him. The same was true of Abraham's brothers. His father was dead, and it fell to his mother, Leah Mendes, to put her child's household in order. There was, after all, much at stake—not only Abraham's job, but the family's reputation, the possibility of future children. She set about single-handedly to repair the marriage. It wasn't easy, and took her many months, and once she had exacted her son's promise to return to his wife it was next necessary to appease his angry father-in-law. It is possible to envision this aristocratic old lady, who had been born in Spain, who had watched many of her Marrano relatives die in the Inquisition, writing this poised and elegant letter to Aaron Lopez announcing the success of her mission and begging him to forgive her son:

Honourable Sir,

It is with great pleasure and joy I now write you acquainting of the dutifulness of my son Abraham in complying to our request to return home. He has insured me of never disobliging nor never to cause you and his wife any more grievance, and will always be bound to your obedience, and he has acknowledged his fault of being so long absent, and it is with no doubt it gives him great concern in reflecting on his follies, but you are fully sensible that youthness and bad advisers are always of great prejudice, and much so when they won't be ruled. But all his transgressions will be an example for his better amendment, and I make no doubt that he will fulfill his promises to me, and he goes overjoyed to your feet to crave pardon, and which I hope you'll grant for the sake of a poor widow'd mother, who will always receive great satisfaction and contentment in knowing of his good proceedings and dutifulness to you. And as God (the best exemplar of the whole world) forgives mankind, so I hope you'll be so pleased as to pardon him, and in granting me this favour I shall forever acknowledge.

LEAH MENDES

Abraham seems to have been incapable of speaking for himself, so his mother wrote to his wife also:

Loving Daughter,
It is with great pleasure I now acquaint you of Abraham complying to our request in returning to enjoy your sweet company, and I beg of you that you'll forgive him of his misbehaving and his absence from so good a wife as you, but he has promised of never causing any more grievance, but always to be the instrument of seeking for to give you pleasure and content, therefore hope that all will be forgotten, and shall always be pleased to know of both your happiness, and remain craving you health and prosperity from, Your Loving Mother,

LEAH MENDES

All, however, was not forgotten, and the marriage continued on an unsteady course. There were a number of other separations, each of them painful for all concerned. Two years later, his brother David visited Abraham in Kingston, found him parted from his wife, and wrote to Aaron Lopez: "I found my Brother Abraham in a very poor state of health. He is just come out of dangerous fit of sickness. He seems to be very anxious of seeing his wife, and throwing himself at your feet. I shall dispatch him by the latter end of next month, in the manner I promised you, and shall write you by him more copiously on that subject." But at that point Abraham's name drops from the family correspondence. He was "dispatched" to Newport, his brother succeeded him in Jamaica, and Abraham's wife followed him home a few months later.

Aaron Lopez, meanwhile, continued to prosper until he was counted among Newport's richest men. In March of 1762 he had attempted to be naturalized but had been refused by the Newport court. His Tory leanings were making him unpopular. Since he also maintained a summer home in Swansea, Massachusetts, he petitioned the superior court of Taunton to make him a citizen of that state, and on October 15, 1762, he became the first Jew to be naturalized in Massachusetts. At his request, the words "upon the true faith of a Christian" were deleted from the oath.

He had also joined a club, established a year earlier, which was purely social and exclusively for the use of gentlemen of Newport's Jewish elite. It was the answer to Newport's Fellowship Club, which had no Jews as members. Aaron took his club with great seriousness, and was nearly always present at its gatherings, on Wednesday evenings "during the winter season." The others in the club, it might be noted, were nearly all, in one way or another, Aaron Lopez' relatives, members of the Lopez-Rivera-Mendes-Levy-Hart complex of families. The club operated under strict rules. From five to eight, members were "at liberty to divert at cards," and in order that the club not gain the reputation of a gaming club, stakes were set at "twenty shillings at whist, picquet, or any other game." If a member was found guilty of playing for higher stakes, he was to be fined "four bottles of good wines," to be enjoyed by the club at its next gathering. At eight, the rules noted that "supper (if ready)" was to be brought in. No card playing was permitted after supper, and members were to depart for their homes at ten. If any member had a matter of club business to discuss, he had to wait "till the chairman has just drank some loyal toast." The club was an excellent diversion from home, wives, children, and attendant problems. The club bylaws also specified that there should be no "conversations relating to synagogue affairs" during club evenings. Again, the punishment for mixing synagogue and club life was "four bottles of good wines."

Aaron had not joined in the nonimportation agreement, according to which a number of New England merchants had pledged to import no further goods from Britain. He could not afford to. A good standing with the British was important for business reasons. At heart, he was probably not an outright Tory. He was not as Tory as, for instance, his neighbor and fellow clubman Isaac Hart, and several other Newport Jews—a state of affairs that had begun to split Newport's Jewish club down the center. Lopez found himself in a difficult situation when the British attacked and seized Newport in 1777—moving 8,000 troops onto the island, destroying 480 houses, burning ships in the harbor, devastating fields and orchards, and in general sacking and looting the city. At this point, Aaron deemed it wise to move his large family elsewhere, to secure them, as he put it in a letter to a friend, "from sudden Allarums and the Cruel Ravages of an enraged Enemy." He chose the considerably safer inland town of Leicester, Massachusetts. All the Lopezes—including his father-in-law, Mr. Rivera—moved there in the autumn of that year.

Here, he wrote, "I pitched my tent, erecting a proportionable one to the extent of my numerous family on the summit of a high healthy hill, where we have experienced the civilities and hospitality of a kind Neighborhood." It was indeed a proportionable tent that Aaron Lopez pitched —a huge, square mansion of brick with white pilasters at the corners and tall arched windows that addressed the surrounding landscape. The Lopez mansion still stands as part of Leicester Academy. In his grand house, decorated by his young and pretty wife, Aaron Lopez became a great host, and was noted for the size and opulence of his dinner parties, receptions, and balls. He became a Jewish Maecenas, a vast patron of the arts and education, a collector of paintings, and he was still under fifty, still in his prime. There were hardly any who dared suggest to him that now, with his shipping trade cut off and his business seriously limited by the war, he might be spending too much.

He continued to keep in touch with Newport, gathering what news he could from friends who passed through the besieged city, and wrote that he had heard that "the poor inhabitants of that Town have been very much distress'd this winter for the want of fuel and provisions, those Individuals of my Society in particular, who [my informant] said had not tasted any meat but once in two months: Fish there was none at this season of the year, and they were reduced to living upon Chocolate and Coffee. These and many other Callamities and Insults the wretched inhabitants experience ought to incite our thanks to the Great Being who gave us resolution to exchange at so early a period that melancholy Spot for that we are now enjoying." To a friend he wrote: "Your dwelling house I understand has suffered much. Your neighbor Augustus Johnson was found dead at his house. My [former] neighbor Gideon Sesson's wife is crazy." What he appears to have resented most was news that the occupying British officers were spreading slanderous tales about Newport womanhood. He complained that "the vertue of several of our Reputable Ladies has been attacked and sullied by our destructive Enemys." When the chips were down, he too became a Revolutionary.

The Revolution ended the golden age of Newport as a commercial center—though of course it would flourish again as a resort—and Aaron Lopez was never to return. In 1780, he was saddened to hear of the death, in Philadelphia, of his old friend Daniel Gomez, who had reached the lofty age of eighty-five. With his death, Daniel's son Moses became a rich man. Aaron Lopez' own affairs were in a somewhat shakier condition. The situation of his oldest daughter, "my darling Sally," continued to depress him. She and Abraham Pereira Mendes had moved to Leicester with him, and the couple had taken a small house near Aaron's. Abraham continued to display his ineptitude and poor health through one or two other business ventures in which his father-in-law tried to place him. For a while he was in the candle business, and was no good at that either. Finally, which was best, Abraham was given nothing to do. Ten years after their marriage, Sally Lopez Mendes gave birth to a tiny son, on whom she doted. It began to be said that Sally was "touched," for after the baby's birth she never set foot outside her house again—a strange, unhappy woman in an unhappy marriage.

Late in May, 1782, Aaron Lopez started out for Newport in his sulky. About five miles outside Providence, at a place called Scotts' Pond, he stopped to water his horse. Suddenly the horse stepped out of its depth and the sulky came plunging after him into the pond. Aaron Lopez was flung forward, out of the sulky. He could not swim, and the servant who tried to swim after him was unable to rescue him before he drowned. He was fifty-one years old.

Learning of his death, Ezra Stiles, who was by now president of Yale, extolled him as

that amiable, benevolent, most hospitable & very respectable Gentleman Mr. Aaron Lopez . . . a merchant of the first eminence; for Honor & Extent of Commerce probably surpassed by no Merchant in America. He did business with the greatest ease and clearness—always carried about a Sweetness of Behavior, a calm Urbanity, an agreeable & unaffected Politeness of manners. Without a single Enemy & the most universally beloved by an extensive Acquaintance of any man I ever knew. His beneficence to his Family Connexions, to his Nation, and to all the World is almost without a parallel. He was my intimate Friend & Acquaintance!

The fact that much of Aaron Lopez' business was the business of slavery appears to have made little difference to the noted educator and antislavery preacher. Stiles, apparently, was against slavery in the abstract, while quite aware that a number of his intimate friends and acquaintances made their money in it. He did, however, find it quite difficult to reconcile the long list of glowing qualities he attributed to Mr. Lopez with the fact that Aaron Lopez was a Jew. His eulogy continues: "Oh! How often have I wished that sincere, pious, and candid mind could have perceived the evidence of Xtianity, perceived the Truth as it is in Jesus Christ, known that JESUS was the MESSIAH predicted by Moses and the Prophets!" He then goes on to pray that those in charge of heaven will perhaps overlook Aaron Lopez' Jewishness and admit him anyway, despite his "delusions," into "Paradise on the Xtian System, finding Grace with the all benevolent and adorable Emanuel who with his expiring breath & in his deepest agonies, prayed for those who knew not what they did."

The size of Aaron Lopez' estate was respectable for its day, but hardly what it might have been had it not been for his extensive hospitality during the Leicester years. And when it became divided between his youthful wife and that vast horde of seventeen children, his fortune began to seem a disappointing one. Each child received an inheritance of about eighty thousand dollars.

When, around 1858, Longfellow visited the old Jewish cemetery at Newport, he was so moved by the experience that he wrote a poem about it. "How strange it seems!" he wrote, "These Hebrews in their graves,/Close by the street of this fair seaport town/ . . . /The very names recorded here are strange . . . /Alvares and Rivera interchange/With Abraham and Jacob of old times. . . ." Longfellow mused:

How came they here? What burst of Christian hate,
   What persecution, merciless and blind,
Drove o'er the sea—the desert desolate—
   These Ishmaels and Hagars of mankind?
They lived in narrow streets and lanes obscure,
   Ghetto and Judenstrass, in murk and mire;*
Taught in the school of patience to endure
   The life of anguish and the death of fire. . . .

Aaron Lopez was among those who reposed there during Mr. Longfellow's visit.

* Longfellow obviously was not too clear on the living conditions of Jews in medieval Spain.

10.

MISALLIANCES AND MISUNDERSTANDINGS

As more Ashkenazic Jews trickled in from Germany and central Europe, they found that the Sephardic culture, tradition, and form were what prevailed among Jews in America. The newcomers were accepted—albeit a trifle disdainfully—into the Sephardic synagogues, and became, as it were, honorary Sephardim. The Sephardic Old Guard made it quite clear to the Johnny-come-latelys that their elevated status was being bestowed upon them without being actually earned. No small degree of social difference existed between the "new" Sephardim and the authentic Sephardim, and this was not helped by the fact that the "rough-spoken" (meaning they had foreign accents) Germans, finding themselves Sephardic blue bloods in name, if not by inheritance, often took to putting on airs and otherwise pushing themselves forward socially in a way that the Old Guard found thoroughly offensive. It was a case of titled Spaniard versus ghetto German, of third- and fourth-generation American versus foreign-born, of rich versus poor, of the cultivated versus the uncouth. In a situation like this, there were bound to be reactions.

In New Orleans, for example, the general instability of the Jewish community—still predominantly Sephardic, but with an admixture of Ashkenazic "outsiders"—was not helped by a visit from young Mathias Gomez, one of Daniel Gomez' great-nephews. Mathias got into an argument with a young man of Ashkenazic extraction over, of all things, the correct wording of a quotation from a poem. It seemed terribly trifling, but not to Mathias when his Ashkenazic acquaintance called him a "fool." Immediately,

Mathias insisted on the aristocratic privilege of challenging the man to a duel. They fought with muskets at forty paces, and each fired four times with no shot reaching a target. Normally, this is considered sufficient exercise to call off a duel, but Mathias insisted on a fifth shot, which wounded his opponent in both legs and killed Mathias himself instantly. He had made his point, however, that nobody, but nobody, should insult a Gomez.

It was said by the Sephardim, who had undergone so much horror and terror for the sake of their faith during the Inquisition, that the Jews of the rest of Europe might be Jewish, but they weren't very. They were said to lack piety, and to be easily swayed by Christian thinking and Christian methods. A case in point was certainly the New Orleans community. Everything went reasonably well in New Orleans as long as a member of one of the old Spanish families was in charge of the congregation. But when a German suddenly inherited the job of chief rabbi—well, a hundred fifty years later the New Orleans Jewish community still remembers what happened.

He was Albert J. "Roley" Marks, who described himself as a "Part-Time rabbi," and who actually earned his living as a bit player in southern traveling theatrical companies. He had earned his nickname because one of his best performances was said to be that of Rowley in *The School for Scandal*. He was also of somewhat roly-poly proportions, which made the sobriquet appropriate. He was once described by a contemporary as:

> a little *below* the middle size, measuring in his stockings, about four feet and some inches. A gleam of good humor is always beaming on his countenance, except when he experiences a twinge of the gout (unfortunately pretty often), and he is one of the best-natured fellows in existence.

"Roley" Marks's acting range was considerably limited by his size. His specialty parts were comic old men, and he was famous for a way he had of laughing on stage. "It would do your heart good to see one of his laughs," a critic of one of his performances wrote. "I say *see* one of them, for nothing in particular is heard when he laughs; a sort of turning up of his eyes, a filling up of his cheeks with wind, and suddenly letting it burst forth, at the same time giving himself a half turn, stooping as if to spit, indulging in a sly wink at the public, and swinging his cane about—and it is done." He performed in such popular dramas of the day as *Governor Heartall, Old Smacks,* and *Andrew Mucklestane.* Of his performance in the title role of the latter, the same critic wrote:

> Andrew Mucklestane! Ah! How often have I witnessed his impersonation of this character, which is nothing more or less than a sentimental Scotch fisherman, very benevolent in his feelings, and ever ready to rescue runaway countesses and drowning children! And to see Rowley sweating through the "business" of this character is a treat to all lovers of the romantic drama. Rowley introduces thirteen *falls* in his performance, and more than once has it been found necessary to prop the stage before subjecting it to his energetic manoeuvres. . . .

How did such a charming buffoon manage to become chief rabbi of the Sephardic congregation in a sophisticated city like New Orleans? Apparently his good nature won the congregation over in a weak moment, and he was given the job. He also worked as a part-time inspector at the customhouse and as a fireman. He was made a director of the Firemen's Charitable Association, helped it put on burlesques and reviews for fund-raising purposes, and composed a ditty called "The Fireman's Song," in return for which the City of New Orleans appointed him "Poet Laureate of the Firemen."

His antics, however, were somewhat differently regarded by the Sephardic elders of the synagogue, who began referring to him as "a stain on the Jewish clergy." It was reported that "Roley" Marks did not keep the dietary laws, that he had not bothered to have his sons circumcised, and that at one point, on the festival of Purim, he found himself too busy with other activities to conduct the services. At last, during a Rosh Hashanah service, an older member of the congregation rose boldly to his feet and announced to the assemblage that it was a disgrace that a man should act as rabbi "who did not have his sons initiated into the covenant of Abraham," and who "got beastly drunk on the day when his two sons died." This was too much for even "Roley" Marks's good nature. He banged his fists on the pulpit and shouted, *"By Jesus Christ! I have a right to pray!"*

It would have been easier to blame "Roley" Marks's outrageous behavior on his "low" Ashkenazic origins if it could have been claimed that the "old" Sephardic members of the New Orleans synagogue were all, to a man, acting on their best behavior. Alas, many were not. There was the case of Victor Souza, of pure Spanish bloodlines on both sides (his mother was a Pereira), who became engaged to a girl named Rose Bourdeaux, a Catholic. Nineteen days before the marriage, Victor underwent Roman Catholic baptism and the pair were married by Père Antoine in New Orleans' Saint Louis Cathedral. This did not prevent Victor Souza's being identified as an "Israelite" in the church records several years later, and the scandal of his intermarriage was as nothing compared with the announcement, not long afterward, that he and his partner, Decadie Baiz—another member of an "old" Sephardic family that had distinguished connections both in New York and on the island of Saint Thomas—had "absconded and defrauded their creditors whom they have shamefully deceived." A thousand dollars was offered for the capture of the pair, or five hundred dollars for either, and the Catholic convert was described in the "Wanted" poster:

Victor Souza, a Jew, is about 4 feet 11 inches high, has a large face, large nose and a small mouth; his face is red and his beard strong and black. D. Baiz, a Jew, about 5 feet 3 or 4 inches high, full face and pock marked, strong black beard. . . .

Victor Souza was caught, tried for fraud, convicted, and sent to prison.

The business feuds between those of Ashkenazic origins and the Sephardim were probably the worst of all, even though the men were all of one, supposedly unifying, congregation. One of the most disgraceful battles in New Orleans took place between Mr. Solomon Audler and Mr. L. A. Levy, Jr. The Audlers had come from Germany, and had made some money manufacturing something called Asiatic Lenitive, a ninety-proof patent medicine advertised "for the cure of toothaches, headaches, and other diseases." Solomon Audler also ran a leather and dry goods store. The Mr. Levy was one of several Sephardic

Levy families who were now scattered up and down the Atlantic Coast. The quarrel was over an overcoat.

It seems that a certain Mr. Phillips (also old Sephardic) was selling a consignment of linen overcoats at auction, and he had promised his friend Levy a coat, if any were left over, at the same price the coats had brought at auction. After the auction, when Levy went to Phillips' establishment to look over the remainder from the sale, he could not find an overcoat that fit him. So he—rather high-handedly, it seems—exchanged one of the remaining coats for a coat that *did* fit him out of a pile of coats purchased by Mr. Audler. Levy then paid Phillips for the coat. When Mr. Audler found out about the switch in coats he was not amused. He had, after all, made his selection of coat sizes with a reason. So he sent Mr. Levy a bill for the coat, which Levy, seeing no need to pay for his coat twice, refused to pay. Audler then sued Levy for the price of the coat, lost his suit, and, in a fury, stormed Mr. Levy at his place of business and called Levy a thief. Immediately Levy challenged Audler to a duel, but Audler haughtily refused the challenge, saying that Levy was "not a gentleman and therefore not entitled to satisfaction." Levy promptly ordered a handbill printed and distributed in the streets, which proclaimed:

> *Notice to the public.* . . . S. Audler having gravely insulted me this morning . . . I deem it my duty in justice to my reputation, to state to the public, that my friends called upon the said individual for satisfaction, which he did not grant, I hereby proclaim him to the public, as a coward, and no gentleman, and beneath the notice of the community.

The tempest in a teapot continued to escalate. Audler, not to be put down by mere handbills, took an advertisement in the newspaper in which he demanded to know:

> I have been required to give gentlemanly satisfaction, to whom? I would ask—to a man? a gentleman? No! it is to one who cannot prove himself a gentleman, for the act of which he stands charged by me cannot be termed the act of a gentleman. A man he is not; it needs but a glance to perceive it; he was well aware at the time he wrote the challenge that he could not

obtain a gentlemanly satisfaction from me, otherwise he would not have demanded it.

Audler ran his advertisement not only in New Orleans but also—doubtless to impress his friends and relatives—in the newspapers of New York and Philadelphia as well. Levy, not to be outdone, added the city of Charleston to the list of cities in which he ran *his* advertisement, which contained this sort of frenzied invective:

> This self-same Audler—this vendor of worn-out harness—this washtub dealer has the impudence and characteristic daring inherent in triflers called me . . . "a Thief" . . . Sol Audler! ! ! and who does not shrink at the very letters of his name. He *has* been *is* and *ever will be* the detestation of the honest man, the land mark for the Coward, the beacon for the Insolvent debtor, the light house for the smuggler . . . Oznaburgs, Italian silk cottonades, old swords and belts &c. &c. groan loudly a requiem for the ledger of his poor creditors . . . this blackened lump of infamy . . . the public must condemn him for calling *me* a Thief when he himself is so notoriously known as an adept in the business. . . .

Well. A good lawyer must have seen that Audler had a cause for action after being subjected to that sort of public abuse. But Audler, at this point—perhaps aware of the amusement the word battle was creating up and down the eastern seaboard—chose politely to withdraw with the calmly worded announcement that "after a long residence in this city (I flatter myself without reproach) . . . my reputation cannot suffer in the opinion of an impartial public, by the slanderous and unfounded accusations of such a worthless fellow as Levy." Therewith the battle ended, as both parties withdrew to their tents to lick their wounds.

At the same time, when an Ashkenazic Jew married one of the Sephardim, there were almost certain to be troubles, as happened in New Orleans to Samuel Jacobs (German) and his wife, Rosette (Sephardic), a Spanish-tempered lady who spoke sneeringly of her husband's "peasant" ancestry, even though Germany's Jews were somewhat worse off than the peasants. It was not long before readers of the

Louisiana Gazette were titillated to see the following paid notice:

> CAUTION. Whereas my wife Rosette has left my house without any just cause whatever, this is to caution the public not to trust her on my account, as I will not pay any debts contracted by her.

A month later, Mr. Jacobs published a retraction to the above, saying that it had all been "merely through a mistake," and adding, "I have the pleasure to let the public know that we live in perfect harmony." Despite this claim, however, the marriage continued to be a stormy one and, in less than a year, the couple were granted a legal separation, one of the first in Louisiana history and a great rarity in its days—particularly in a Jewish marriage.

When word of these scandalous goings-on in New Orleans reached the ears of Jews in such staid northern cities as New York and Newport, the reaction was one of shock and dismay. The fabric of Jewish life in New Orleans seemed to be flying apart, and this was something that Jews in the North could not accept with equanimity. Many of the New Orleans Jewish families were the northerners' close relatives. A close tie between Newport and New Orleans, for example, lay in the person of Judah Touro, the man whose celebrated will has made him something of a legend among American Jewish philanthropists.

The Touros were an old Spanish family who came to Newport by way of the West Indies, and Isaac Touro—the first to arrive—was immediately taken in by Jacob Rivera and Aaron Lopez, and made a member of Newport's exclusive Jewish club. Isaac Touro, along with Lopez and Rivera, was among those who drew up the plans for Newport's famous synagogue in 1759, and Isaac was the one selected to perform the dedication of the building when it was completed four years later. The building (which has since been renamed the Touro Synagogue and designated a national historic site) contains an architectural detail that is a haunting reminder of the Marrano past of its builders, and the dangers their ancestors faced if they wished to practice their faith in Inquisitional Spain. The plans call for "a few small stairs which lead from the altar in the center, to a secret passage in the basement"—for escape.

Isaac Touro married a Hays, another old Sephardic family,* and their daughter married one of Aaron Lopez' many sons, thus bringing the Touros, who had been merely friends, into the Lopez-Gomez-Rivera family complex.

Just what brought Isaac Touro's son Judah to New Orleans is something of a mystery. Since Judah Touro has become a legend, his life has suffered the fate of so much that is Jewish legend—distortion, and expansion out of all proportion to the facts at hand. Since he did indeed become a very rich man, and since he did write a famous will, leaving a fortune to different charities, Jewish legend makers have tended to have it that he was one of New Orleans' best-loved figures, that the entire city went into mourning when he died, and so on.

The facts indicate that Judah Touro was actually not well liked in the southern city, that he was an odd little man who may not have been even very bright, a recluse, a string saver, a nineteenth-century Collyer brother. It has been said that he left his native Newport because of blighted love, that he loved a beautiful cousin, and that his stern old uncle Moses Hays (his mother's brother) refused to let his daughter marry such a close relation. One version of the tale has it that he left Newport because of the death of this cousin, Rebecca Hays. Actually, Rebecca died nine months after he left.

Another version insists that the cousin was not Rebecca but her sister Catherine, and that Uncle Moses would not let *them* wed. And yet Uncle Moses Hays died a few days after Judah Touro arrived in New Orleans. With the opposition out of the way, wouldn't this have been the moment for him to hurry home and claim his love, or for her to run to him? It is true that neither Catherine Hays nor Judah ever married, and that they never set eyes on each other again. A romantic story exists that, throughout their lives, the two corresponded in a long series of love letters, and that in these letters the lovers never aged, that they wrote to each other as if they were both still teenagers, even in their seventies speaking of "your tiny dancing feet and glancing eyes." It may be true, but no one has ever discovered this remarkable correspondence. It is said

* The Hayses, through the mazelike tracery of Malcolm Stern's book, over the years became related or "connected" with most of the other old families, down to the recent publisher of the *New York Times*, Arthur Hays Sulzberger.

that in the delirium of his last illness Judah Touro "talked of walking in a beautiful garden with Catherine Hays, his first and only love." Perhaps, but just to whom he spoke these words is not recorded. He did, it is true, leave her a small sum of money in his will, apparently unaware that she had died a few days before he signed this document.

In any case, he did indeed, as a young man, move permanently from his native Newport to New Orleans. There *may* have been a falling out with his uncle Moses, because Judah did not come, as might have been expected, to represent his uncle's business. He came independently, as a loner, and set himself up in business as a loner. He became a commission merchant, and his earliest advertisements show him dealing in such diverse merchandise as beer, herring, lobster, butter, cigars, candles, soap, nuts, and Holland gin. He prospered, in a modest way.

The man who may have known Judah Touro best, an executor of the famous will, considered him a most peculiar man. He wrote, "Mr. Touro is the very impersonation of a snail, not to say of a crab whose progress (to use a paradox) is usually backward. . . . I must be very careful to humor him . . . he is very *slow*. . . . You know he is a strange man." In business Judah Touro was hesitant, indecisive, never adventuresome or imaginative. And yet he was successful. He was by no means the most successful commission merchant in New Orleans. He was not even the most successful Jewish commission merchant. And yet, little by little, he was becoming very rich, and, little by little, the rest of New Orleans began to suspect this fact and to study him with new interest. What was his formula to riches? It was simply that he didn't spend. The fortune Judah Touro was amassing was coming to him penny by hard penny, and he was squirreling it away in banks. As a rabbi acquaintance explained it:

Mr. T. was not a man of brilliant mind; on the contrary, he was slow, and not given to bursts of enthusiasm, as little as he was fond of hazardous speculations; and he used to say that he could only be said to have *saved* a fortune by strict economy, while others had spent one by their liberal expenditures . . . he had no tastes for the wasteful outlay of means on enjoyments which he had no relish for. He had thus

the best wines always by him, without drinking them
himself; his table, whatever delicacies it bore, had
only plain and simple food for him. . . .

His existence was solitary. For most of his life he lived
in a series of cheap rooming houses on the wrong side of
town, at a time when other New Orleans rich men were
trying to outdo each other by building elaborate mansions.
Only late in life did he permit himself the luxury of buying a small house. When he bought real estate, it was as
an investment. He never sold anything, and his real estate,
in a growing city, tended to appreciate over the years. He
was a hoarder, but only of the barest necessities of life. He
shunned possessions to such an extent that, when he died
and his estate was appraised, only $1,960 was assigned
to personal property. This included silverware valued at
$805 and $600 worth of wine—wine seems to have been
his sole personal indulgence—and $555 worth of crockery,
glassware, office furniture, his carpets, hat stand, bed-
spread, and chairs. His personal estate was valued at $928,
774.74—doubtless an extremely low appraisal. Though
the sum is not staggering by today's standards, there were
probably only ten Americans in Judah Touro's day who
were worth as much.

Judah Touro, according to the legend, gave away a fortune in private philanthropies during his lifetime. If true,
he must have given anonymously, adhering to the Talmudic exhortation that "Twice blessed is he who gives in
secret." He also, according to the legend, gave away the
entire $80,000 fortune he inherited from his sister, Rebecca
Touro Lopez, who died before him. This appears not to
be true since no record of any such bequest exists in the
various papers pertaining to Mrs. Lopez' estate. The plain
fact is that, during his lifetime, Judah Touro evinced no
interest in philanthropy whatever, and seemed obsessed
only with the making and saving of money.

What prompted him, in the end, to give it all away remains another puzzle. But two weeks before his death he
sat down and wrote his famous will. In sixty-five separate
bequests, Judah Touro gave away money, in sums ranging
from three thousand to twenty thousand dollars, to a long
list of charitable causes throughout the eastern United
States, from the orphans of Boston to the Ladies Benevolent Society in New Orleans. The Jewish congregations of

Philadelphia, Baltimore, Charleston, Mobile, Savannah, Montgomery, Memphis, Louisville, Cincinnati, Cleveland, Saint Louis, Buffalo, Albany—and, of course, New York and Newport—all received bequests.

In Boston, Touro's name is now associated with Massachusetts General Hospital, the Asylum for Indigent Boys, the Female Orphan Asylum, the Humane Society, and many other charities. To New Orleans he left funds to combat yellow fever, which was in those days endemic, and a hospital—the Touro Infirmary—was established in that connection. A bequest to Newport's "Old Stone Mill," also known as the Newport Tower, saved that venerable structure from demolition by the city fathers, and he also left funds to the City of Newport for a public park to be laid out around the tower. This plot is now known as Touro Park.

All in all, a grand total of $483,000 went to charities. It was, indeed, the greatest display of philanthropic largesse the new world had ever seen. Thus, his death being the most significant act of his life, Judah Touro entered history, and legend.

The balance of his estate, after all the charitable bequests were paid, was directed to go to "my dear, old and devoted friend," Mr. Rezin Davis Shepherd. When serving in the Louisiana Militia during the Battle of New Orleans, Judah Touro had been wounded in the thigh by a shell, and it was Shepherd who carried him off the field to a doctor, and whom Touro always credited with saving his life. Shepherd, whose great-great-grandson is Senator Leverett Saltonstall of Massachusetts, received between $500,000 and $750,000 under Touro's will—again a huge sum at the time—and this windfall is one of the cornerstones of the Boston Saltonstalls' family fortune.

One of the elements of the Judah Touro legend is that he was an early pioneer for civil rights, and frequently bought Negro slaves only to set them free. Alas, there is no proof of this, either, although there is evidence that he did not trade in slavery as extensively as his southern contemporaries, and that he had a genuine aversion for the trade in which his sister's husband's family, the Lopezes, had made so much money. On the other hand, a timid trader, he didn't trade in *anything* extensively.

There are, however, two quite intriguing pieces of information in this regard that turned up after Judah Touro's death. One was the discovery that a certain Ellen Wilson, identified as an "F.W.C." (Free Woman of Color, in southern parlance), had had a house purchased for her in Judah Touro's name. Among his effects, a note to this same woman in the amount of $4,100 was found. Ellen Wilson, who may have already died, never came forward to claim her inheritance, and has never been identified.

The second fact is that Pierre André Destrac Cazenove, appointed by Judah as one of the executors of his will, and one of its beneficiaries—Cazenove received a $10,000 gift—was a mulatto. Little is known about Cazenove, except that he was some forty-eight years younger than Judah Touro, that he had once worked for Judah as a clerk and was described as a great "pet" of Mr. Touro's. At the time of Touro's death, young Cazenove was reportedly worth some $20,000, quite a lot for a black man in the antebellum South. By the time of the Civil War, Cazenove and his four sons were operating a funeral parlor and livery stable, and were said to be worth $100,000. The Cazenove family were described as "Quadroons—Creoles, more properly now called colored persons."

It is astonishing that when the contents of Judah Touro's will were made public—and made headlines in newspapers all over America—no mention was made of the startling fact that Touro had named a "colored person" as one of his executors, yet none was. Was this a fact deliberately suppressed, in order that the good Judah had done through his bequests should not be sullied by some sort of interracial scandal? Was Ellen Wilson actually Judah Touro's mistress? Such alliances were certainly not unheard of, but would have been considered by the press unsuitable for public consumption. Was the romantically named Pierre André Destrac Cazenove, then, of whom Judah Touro was so fond, one of the few men he could trust to execute his will, actually Judah Touro's son? And who was *John* Touro, who appeared in New Orleans between 1855 and 1865, not long after Judah Touro's death? None of his known relatives ever followed him there. All these questions can now be only the subject of speculation.

With all the embellishments of the legend that have grown around this odd little man, Jews today proudly point out to their children that America's first philanthropist on any important scale was a Jew. Sephardim today remind *their* children that Judah Touro was a Sephardic Jew, "one of us," with all his credentials in order. Judah Touro rests, along with all the puzzles and questions about his life, in the Jewish cemetery in his native Newport, with all his relatives. But what the purveyors of the legend do not tell their children—what many of them, in fact, do not know —is that many of Judah Touro's benefactions were to Christian causes. At one point, for example, when the First Congregational Church of New Orleans was having financial difficulties, and was about to be torn down, Judah Touro bought the church for $20,000 and then gave the building back to the congregation.

But Congregationalism was never quite his cup of tea. Quite early on, after his arrival in New Orleans, he rented a pew at Christ Church, and became an Episcopalian.

Meanwhile, farther north, in Philadelphia, another Sephardic Jew was becoming the center of a storm of controversy and the basis of a legend. Haym Salomon, his family and other admirers were claiming, had actually "financed the American Revolution" by presenting General George Washington with a large personal loan at a crucial moment. Salomon's detractors, meanwhile, were saying in loud voices that he had done no such thing. Once more, as in the case of Judah Touro, the extent of Jewish contribution to the course of American history was under examination.

From the beginning, of course, the spirit that guided the American Revolution had strong Judaic overtones. The Old Testament had become, in many ways, a Revolutionary textbook. For one thing, the Puritans of Colonial New England considered themselves the spiritual offspring of Old Testament characters. Like the Jews, they gave their children Old Testament names. It was to the Old Testament that the Puritans turned to find God. They regarded the New Testament as merely the story of Christ. In England, the Puritans had been called "Jewish fellow travelers," and they had compared their flight to America with the Jews' escape from Egypt. They called the Massachusetts Bay Colony "the New Jerusalem." There was a proposal that Hebrew be made the official language of the Colonies (it was on the regular curriculum, along with Latin and Greek, when Harvard was founded, a knowledge of the language being considered part of the equipment of a cultivated man). John Cotton had suggested that the Mosaic Code be used as the basis for Massachusetts laws. There is a manifestation of the Code, meanwhile, in the wording of the American Constitution.

Under the oppression of George III, the American colonists likened themselves to the Jews, and the king to the pharaoh. They quoted Samuel, who, when the people of Palestine came clamoring to him for the creation of a Hebrew royal family, raised strong objections to this notion, and the colonists found in his arguments a Biblical authority for their refusal to submit to the doctrine of the Divine Right of Kings. In 1775, the Reverend Jonathan Mayhew, a Boston preacher, announced from the pulpit —the most effective medium of communication of the day —that the American colonists were like the people of Israel who resisted the unjust taxation of Solomon's successor, and the Reverend Samuel Langdon, president of Harvard, preached that just as ancient Israel was wrong to take a king for itself, so were the colonists wrong to accept a king who was a tyrant. Aaron Lopez' friend President Ezra Stiles of Yale delivered a sermon in which he traced the evolution of the democratic form of government from Palestine to America. He called America "God's American Israel," and George Washington "the American Joshua," called forth by God to set His people free.

The first Independence Day was something very close to a Jewish holiday. On July 4, 1776, the day that the great Declaration was officially published, the Continental Congress appointed a committee of three—Benjamin Franklin, Samuel Adams, and Thomas Jefferson—and asked them to prepare a seal for the United States of America. The design chosen by the committee depicted Pharaoh, crowned, in an open chariot, with a sword in his hand, passing through the divided waters of the Red Sea in pursuit of the Israelites. On the opposite shore stood Moses bathed in light from a pillar of fire, extending his hands toward the sea and bidding the waters to close and swallow Pharaoh. The legend emblazoned upon the seal was: "Rebellion against tyranny is obedience to God." The theme, of course, was freedom, and this first Great Seal of the United States seems somewhat more appropriate than the present, more warlike seal, with its fierce eagle clutching a handful of arrows.

Haym Salomon, meanwhile, who may or may not have "financed" the Revolution, was a member in good standing of two Sephardic congregations—Shearith Israel in

New York and, later on, when his activities were centered there, Mikveh Israel in Philadelphia. He had, however, been born in Poland—around 1740—and this fact, of course, made him Sephardic second class. In America, after his arrival in 1772, he made an auspicious marriage, to Rachel Franks, daughter of Moses Franks of Philadelphia. Frankses—the name had been Franco in Spain—were a prominent mercantile family in both Philadelphia and New York, and families such as the Gomezes, Lopezes, and "old" Levys considered the Franks family "one of us." At the time of his marriage to Miss Franks, Haym Salomon was thirty-seven. His bride was fifteen. Still, this alliance considerably elevated his social position in the Jewish community.

He also had acquired, before leaving Europe, a university education, which was unusual for a young Polish Jew in the late eighteenth century. He spoke a number of languages, including, as he once mentioned offhandedly in a letter, "French, Polish, Russian, Italian, etc. Languages." He also spoke Hebrew, and Yiddish—a tongue the old Sephardic families had only vaguely heard of.

Despite his educated tastes, he first set himself up in New York as a dry goods merchant and, in 1776, Leonard Gansevoort, himself a prominent store owner, recommended young Salomon to Philip Schuyler, who commanded the troops of the Northern Department in upper New York State, and asked that Salomon be allowed "to go suttling to Lake George," that is, to accompany the troops and provide them with clothing, provisions, whiskey, and such. Gansevoort wrote to Schuyler: "I can inform the General that Mr. Salomon has hitherto sustained the Character of being warmly attached to America." He followed the troops through most of that summer, returned to New York in September, and when, on September 15, 1776, the British captured New York, Haym Salomon was one of a group of men who formed a dangerous plan to send fire ships into the Narrows of New York harbor to destroy the British fleet. The plan was discovered, and Haym Salomon was arrested as a spy.

Whether or not he was sentenced to be shot by a firing squad is another point widely disputed within and without the now extensive Salomon family, and among historians of the Revolution. Salomon's son, who may have had reasons to exaggerate certain aspects of his father's career, always insisted that the threat of death was there. In the only existing description of the event by Haym Salomon himself, he makes no mention of this. He became, however, a valuable prisoner. With his knowledge of languages he was able to communicate with a motley assortment of other prisoners, which included mercenary soldiers Britain had hired from all over Europe to fight its war, and Salomon was assigned the job of prison interpreter.

He must have done his job well, for he was eventually released. In 1778, threatened with arrest again, he fled to Philadelphia, where he decided to remain since he possessed "principles repugnant to British hostilities," as he put it in his somewhat flowery style.

In Philadelphia, he wasted no time before appealing to the Continental Congress for a job, citing in his letter his past services to the Revolution, and informing the Congress that he had left behind him all his "Effects and credits to the amount of five or six thousand pounds sterling and [a] distressed Wife and Child of a month old at New York, waiting that they may soon have an opportunity to come out from thence with empty hands." Robert Morris, the Philadelphia financier who had founded the Bank of North America—and whose personal credit at one point during the war was better than the government's —took Salomon on and assigned him to negotiate war loans. What this amounted to was going out into the market and selling the infant government's bonds. He was so good at this that soon he was being called "the most successful of the war brokers," and, though he charged only a modest ¼ of 1 percent for his services, his account at the Bank of North America grew until it was nearly as large as Robert Morris'. With hands no longer empty, he sent for his wife and child, and the family settled comfortably on Philadelphia's Front Street.

He dealt in other goods than government securities, as is apparent in a letter that survives, written to a merchant in Virginia and advising that "The hats are so much higher than you judged that I shall defer sending them till I hear from you. They cannot be got for less than 10½ dollars. Silk stockings are also high and scarce, and am afraid shall not be able to send the quantity you want. Goods are grown scarce, and from the number of vessels we have lost, and our capes now swarming with enemy cruisers, we expect they [the goods] will rise considerably." Wartime inflation was on, but still the amounts Salomon dealt in were not impossibly large. In this same letter he adds: "The forty dollars in favor of Robert B. Chew I have paid."

In 1781, he was prosperous enough to send off a draft in the amount of a thousand pounds to his family in Poland. This turned out to have been an unwise move. The minute his relatives in Europe discovered that they had an affluent kinsman on the other side of the Atlantic, they descended upon him in droves, hat in hand. Haym Salomon found to his dismay that he had more aunts, uncles, nephews, nieces, and cousins in more corners of the Continent than he had ever imagined, and that they all expected to be put on allowances. Furthermore, as Jewish relatives have always tended to do, they did not simply *ask* for their share of their cousin's wealth. They demanded it as their right, and were highly indignant when they were turned down. By 1783, Haym Salomon had clearly begun to weary of their petitions, and we see him writing to an itinerant uncle in England: "I have ordered fifty guilders to be paid you by Mr. Gumple Samson in Amsterdam, which letter giving that order you must already have rec'd, and I now send you an order for six guineas." As patiently as possible he tries to outline his financial situation to his uncle:

> Your bias of my riches are too extensive. Rich I am not, but the little I have, think it my duty to share with my poor father and mother. They are the first that are to be provided for by me, and must and shall have the preference. Whatever little more I can squeeze out I will give my relations, but I tell you plainly and truly that it is not in my power to give you or any relations yearly allowances. Don't you nor any of them expect it. Don't fill your mind with vain and idle expectations and golden dreams that never will nor can be accomplished. Besides my father and mother, my wife and children must be provided for. I have three young children, and as my wife is very young may have more, and if you and the rest of my relatives will consider things with reason, they will be sensible of this I now write. But notwithstanding this I mean to assist my relations as far as lays in my power.

His uncle had mentioned coming to America, where, without doubt, he expected to be put on the payroll. Haym wrote him indignantly:

> I am much surprised at your intention of coming here. Your *yikes* [family background and education] is worth very little here, nor can I imagine what you mean to do here. I think your duty calls for your going to your family, and besides these six guineas you will receive in Amsterdam fifty guineas from Mr. Gumple Samson. . . . *I desire no relation may be sent.* Have I not children, are they not relations? When I shall be fully informed of all the young people of our family and their qualifications explained, I may then perhaps advise sending one or two to this country. I will explain to you the nature of this country: *vinig yidishkayt* ["little Jewishness"].

He had a sense of humor, and was capable of writing gossipy letters, too, as he did to a friend whom he accused of not keeping him posted, twitting him that doubtless "your whole time is devoted to the ladies, and can't spare time to inform a friend of your welfare. . . . I doubt if the ladies here have the same reason to complain of your neglect. Am certain you would not make it long before your return, was you to know how desirous the ladies are of your presence. And one in particular who wishes that no pecuniary views may get the better of the partiality you always entertained for her. . . ."

He was proud of his position as the Revolution's leading—and best—banker, and he guarded this position jealously. Other Jewish brokers were doing what Haym Salomon was doing, buying and selling government notes. These included Isaac Franks, Benjamin Nones, and Lion Moses, but Salomon did the biggest amount of business and, in 1782, he asked Robert Morris for permission to advertise himself as "Broker to the Office of Finance." Morris gave him permission to use this prestigious title, noting in his diary: "This broker has been usefull to the public interest, and requests leave to publish himself as broker to the office which I have consented, as I do not see that any disadvantage can possibly arise to the public service but the reverse, and he expects individual benefits therefrom"—benefits, of course, in respect to his competition. In his advertisements, Haym Salomon frequently made such statements as one which announced that the advertiser "flatters himself that his assiduity, punctuality, and extensive connections in business, as a broker, is well established in various parts of Europe, and in the United States in particular." He continued to buy and sell on commission tobacco, sugar, tea, silk stockings, and ladies' bonnets. But he summed himself up in a letter to a London merchant when he said: "My business is a broker, and chiefly in bills of exchange, and so very extensive that I am generally known to the mercantile part of North America." All this is most certainly true.

On Yom Kippur eve, 1779—it is said—Washington's armies were in desperate straits. His soldiers had not been paid for several months, they were at the point of mutiny, and battle was at hand. Washington pleaded with his men, then threatened, but they were adamant; they would fight no more without their wages. At last a desperate Washington sent a messenger on horseback through the night to Philadelphia with instructions to obtain, from Haym Salomon, a loan of $400,000, an enormous sum in those days, to pay and provision his troops. The messenger found Salomon in the synagogue, and a hasty whispered conference took place. Salomon rose and quickly moved about the synagogue, collecting certain friends. A small group left together, and that night the money was raised. Did Haym Salomon *himself* contribute $240,000 of the money? So the legend, perpetuated in many accounts, insists.

It is at this point, alas, that the story of Haym Salomon dissolves into speculation and controversy. Did he, as his son later claimed, loan "vast sums" to the government, personally pay soldiers' salaries, and pay for the Revolution? There is no proof of it. He did, however, extend personal loans to many prominent individuals of the Revolution and members of the Continental Congress, including James Wilson, General St. Clair, Edmund Randolph, and many Philadelphians, and often charged them no interest. Presidents Jefferson, Madison, and Monroe were all aided by him at one time or another when short of ready cash. Poor Madison was perennially in financial difficulties and in 1782 wrote to his friend Edmund Randolph: "I cannot in any way make you more sensible of the importance of your kind attention to pecuniary remittances for me than by informing you that I have for some time past been a pensioner on the favor of Haym Salomon, a Jew broker." A few weeks later, Madison was in as bad shape as ever, and Salomon had come to be something more to him than "a Jew broker." He wrote, again to Randolph:

> I am almost ashamed to reiterate my wants so incessantly to you, but they begin to be so urgent that it is impossible to suppress them. The kindness of our little friend in Front Street, near the coffee house, is a fund which will preserve me from extremities, but I never resort to it without great mortification, as he so obstinately rejects all recompense. The price of money is so usurious that he thinks it ought to be extorted from none but those who aim at profitable speculations. To a necessitous delegate he gratuitously spares a supply out of his private stock.

Salomon's son claimed that his father also aided the Polish patriots Pulaski and Kosciusko with enormous loans, but there is no proof of this either. He did, however, when the British fleet cut off all communication with Europe, maintain the Spanish ambassador to the Revolutionary government, Don Francesco Randon, out of his own funds. And it can be argued, from this, that a vital service was performed, since, had Salomon not done so, Spain *might* have damaged American prestige—such as it was—abroad. And it is known that he did sell hundreds of thousands of dollars' worth of American bonds, which found their way to the bourses of Paris, London, and Frankfurt, and which certainly did much to establish American credit in the world market.

Does the United States government still owe Haym Salomon a huge amount of money? His son, Haym Moses Salomon, always said so, and his many descendents—he had four children, and a multitude of grandchildren—who are scattered about the country in such places as New Orleans; Galveston; Houston; Saint Louis; Ardmore, Oklahoma; and Canton, Kansas, would like to think so, and grow wistful dreaming of the fortune they might split if only they could prove that it existed.

His son's story is this: Between the years 1778 and 1782, Haym Salomon loaned the United States government money in the neighborhood of $700,000, more than half of which was never repaid. On January 5, 1785, the government sent Haym Salomon a full and complete accounting of all the money it owed him. But it was a Sabbath day and, pious Jew that he was, Salomon refused—though a few years earlier he had supposedly been willing to interrupt high holy day services to help George Washington—to sign the papers until the day of rest and prayer was over. On the next day, Sunday, January 6, before he had a chance to examine the government's statement, he died —a victim of the heart disease he had contracted while a prisoner of the British in New York.

The figure of $700,000, his son claimed, represented money that had gone through Haym Salomon's bank account, payable to the government of the United States, and this same figure has been given authority in such publications as the *Dictionary of American Biography,* in its sketch on Salomon, as the amount he "loaned" the government. It would have been an extraordinarily large sum in 1782. Salomon *can't* have been that rich. If he had— and, on top of that, supported his family and all his European relatives—he would have been by far the richest man in America. In 1778, he had escaped from New York and arrived in Philadelphia without a penny to his name. How, in four short years' time, would he have possibly amassed so staggering a fortune? It is hard to credit, too, that, just a year after his escape, he could personally have come up with $240,000 to loan George Washington. His wife's family, the Frankses, was rich, but Rachel Franks Salomon descended from the poor branch.

How reliable was his son? It was from him, too, that biographers learned that Haym Salomon's parents in Poland were "wealthy." But still Salomon thought it needful to send them a thousand pounds when at last he became successful, and in his letter he spoke of his "poor father and mother." In his will, he provided that his mother be bequeathed a gold chain, and his aged father enough money to purchase a burial plot.

Several years ago, the Federation of Polish Jews of America attempted to have a statue erected in Haym Salomon's memory, citing, among other sources, the *Dictionary of American Biography* account of his services to the Revolution, and saying: "America failed to repay the money he advanced, and now men seek to rob him of his posthumous fame." What the Federation wanted to demonstrate, of course, with their statue, was that there had been Polish Jews in America long before the Czarist pogroms of 1881, and that they had contributed mightily. The chief "robber" of Salomon's posthumous fame as the late historian Max J. Kohler. Kohler called the Poles' project ridiculous, and there was a great deal of angry talk. Kohler was a German Jew, and the mutual antipathy that has existed between the earlier-arrived Germans and the later-arriving Poles and Russians was at the heart of most of it. The project sputtered, with much acrimony, to no conclusion.

Haym Salomon was, in his own words, a broker, a trader of government bonds, an agent. The $700,000 that may have gone through his account over the four years in question was not his money; it was the government's and represented funds from securities he had sold, deposited, and then turned over to Robert Morris. On these moneys Morris now paid him a tidy commission—½ of 1 percent. Haym Salomon was also a generous man. Even the remote uncles got their guineas. He was generous, too, to his friends in Philadelphia, offering unsecured loans, loans without interest—generous to a fault. After his death, merchants to whom he had loaned money could not pay. His estate was found to be insolvent. His chief creditor was the Bank of North America, Robert Morris' bank.

His son claimed that the United States government owed Haym Salomon $354,000—which today, with interest, would be worth in the tens of millions of dollars. His son said the government had come with a detailed statement to that effect. True, his son waited decades after his father's death to make this claim, and after all records had inconveniently been destroyed when the British captured Washington during the War of 1812. Mysteriously, the government never came around with that statement again. The money has never been paid. The papers are gone.

But the Polish Americans did get their statue—not in New York, where they wanted it, but in Chicago. And it is a memorial not to one but to three men. Haym Salomon shares the marble pedestal—and perfectly properly, it would seem—with George Washington and Robert Morris. At the time of the statue's dedication, President Franklin D. Roosevelt turned to an aide and, in full innocence, asked: "I know who the other two are, but *who . . . ?*"

To those of the Old Guard Sephardim who had questioned the importance of Haym Salomon's Revolutionary role, there was always the point that he was "not really Sephardic," something of an interloper and stealer of Sephardic thunder. Now, however, that his statue stands proudly in Chicago, and in such illustrious company, for all the world to see, most Sephardim prefer to claim him —it seems too bad to give him to the Poles—and Sephardic parents tell their children, "And he was one of us!"

11.

FIRST LADIES

IT comes as a surprise to many people that there are Jewish Daughters of the American Revolution—just as there are Sons—though of course there are. Some of the Old Guard Sephardic families are a little sheepish about being DAR members, to be sure, since that organization has gained a reputation of making members of minority groups feel less than welcome. At the same time, these people keep their little certificates of membership, and show *these* to their children and grandchildren as well.

While men like Haym Salomon were raising and supplying money for Revolutionary coffers, and while Judah Touro was saving his money in New Orleans, a number of Sephardic women were gaining reputations as Revolutionary heroines. There was Mrs. David Hays, for example. Esther Hays and Judah Touro were second cousins by marriage; that is, Esther's husband, David, was a first cousin of Judah's mother. By the time of the Revolution, branches of the Hays family were well established in Newport, New York, Philadelphia, and Richmond, where they can still be found. Esther Hays was an Etting, of the Philadelphia Ettings—a Sephardic family that had come to that city as early as 1758, and Ettings can still be found *there* (including the painter Emlen Etting, a seventh-generation Philadelphian). Esther Etting had met David Hays through Philadelphia connections, and theirs was the first Hays-Etting union (there would, of course, be others). It was considered an event of great social importance, creating as it did an even stronger tie among the Jewish communities of Philadelphia, New York, and Newport.

David Hays took his bride north to an extensive farm he operated in New York's Westchester County, near what is now the town of Bedford, and here the Revolution found them. The Hayses backed the Revolutionary cause and, one night in the winter of 1779, David Hays received word that a company camped not far from his farm had been surrounded by the British. Food and supplies were running low, and unless help reached them soon, the men would be forced to surrender or starve. With one of his young sons as a helper, Hays volunteered to try to drive a herd of seventy-five of his cattle through the enemy lines to the imperiled troops. He chose a moonless night for his mission. The cows were blindfolded, their jaws tied closed with rope so they could make no noise, and their hoofs wrapped in heavy sacking to muffle the sound of their march through the snow. The greatest risk came from the Hayses' own neighbors, many of whom were Tory sympathizers, and the exploit had to be carried out in utmost secrecy.

Nonetheless, somehow word of what David Hays was up to leaked out. He and his son had no sooner left the house than a group of angry and suspicious Tories gathered outside it, shouting for his wife. Esther Hays, still weak from the birth of her sixth child, had been in bed with a fever, but she rose and went to the door. When asked where her husband was, she refused to say. Even when the Tory group threatened to kill her small children, she refused to give the mob any information. She was then forced back inside her house; the windows and doors were barricaded, and the house was set afire. Fortunately, the Hayses' Negro slaves, who lived nearby, were able to rescue Esther and her children, and carry them to safety in the slave quarters. But when David Hays and his son returned the next morning—after successfully completing their delivery of the cattle—the farmhouse had burned to the ground.

Esther Hays was a woman not easily daunted. She showed her patriotic zeal on another occasion when she calmly walked through enemy lines in broad daylight. Ostensibly on a routine shopping errand, she was actually purveying a vital commodity to the Revolutionary soldiers. Her plump petticoats were heavily quilted with salt. Before the war was over, both Esther's husband and her eldest son had fought at the front, as had her brother, Reuben, who died as a prisoner of war of the British. A volunteer the moment he learned of the first shot at Lexington, Reuben Etting had left his bank clerk's job to join the American forces. After his capture he refused to eat pork, which, of course, was the chief staple supplied. He must have been as strong-willed as his sister, for his death was attributed to starvation.

A gaudier Revolutionary role, though more social than military, was meanwhile being played by the women of Philadelphia's Franks family, into which the entry—by marriage—had been such an important step for Haym Salomon. It had, in fact, by the time of the Revolution begun to seem as though Philadelphia's Sephardim were taking themselves even more seriously than their relatives in New York and Newport, even though the Philadelphia community was newer than—and in many ways an offshoot of—the other two. Philadelphians generally had begun to think of themselves as superior to New Yorkers, as, of course, they still do. New York and Newport were looked down on as "commercial" cities; Philadelphia was a city more devoted to culture, the arts and graces. Sephardim in the more northerly cities had already begun to speak with a certain awe of their Philadelphia kin, and on one occasion Mrs. Aaron Lopez wrote one of her daughters a long letter (or memorandum, since the girl was living at home at the time) on how to behave: "Not to forget yr. curtsies, how d'you dos and thank-yous," when meeting "our Philadelphia cousins."

The Franks family had settled in Philadelphia early in the eighteenth century, along with the Levys, to whom they were distantly related. The family, during its passage from fifteenth-century Spain to eighteenth-century Philadelphia, had been prominent elsewhere. Aaron Franks, grandfather of the first American Franks, had been a banker in Hanover, and, under the aegis of George I, who discovered his talent there, was brought to England as the king's personal financial adviser. He was known as "the Jew Broker of London." The Levys, meanwhile, could trace their lineage back to a number of prominent early American Jewish families. The two families became even more tightly entwined with each other when, in what was considered a dynastic union, Abigail Levy married Jacob Franks in 1712, and both families moved with great ease (certainly with more ease than the Jews of New York and Newport, who, socially, still kept to themselves) into the purlieus of Christian Philadelphia society. Both David Franks and his cousin, Samson Levy, were on the original list of the Assembly, Philadelphia's most exclusive social event and one of the oldest balls in America, when it was composed in 1748.

By the 1750's, Philadelphia's Jewish elite had added the Gratz family, along with the Ettings, and of course the Philadelphia branch of the Hayses. The Gratzes, like the Ettings and the Frankses, had come from Inquisitional Spain by way of Germany. In Spain, the name may have been Gracia, or Garcia. It was Philadelphia's large German-speaking population that attracted these Sephardim with German-sounding names, who had taken the German route out of Spain, and knew the language. By the mid-eighteenth century, no good Philadelphia club was without its Gratz, Etting, Franks, Levy, or Hays. They were members of the Philadelphia and the Rittenhouse clubs, the Union League, the Racquet, the Rabbit, and the City Troop, and their names decorated the membership lists—and the lists of officers and directors and sponsors—of such august institutions as the Historical Society, the Philosophical Society, the Academy of Art, the Academy of Science, and the Atheneum.

The Frankses and Hayses and Gratzes and Ettings not only married "within the group" but, by the time of the Revolution, had begun making brilliantly social marriages to members of Philadelphia's non-Jewish elite. In the cities to the north, where the Sephardim remained more strait-laced and orthodox, the Philadelphia Jews' behavior was looked on with something close to horror. "The German influence" was blamed for this sort of laxity—the same Christianizing influence that would lead to the Reform movement in Judaism, in both Germany and in the United States. But these intermarriages of Philadelphia's Christian and Jewish families have meant that "Jewish blood," as they say, flows in the veins of many an old American family, from Philadelphia Morrises and Newbolds and Ingersolls to the New York Verplancks.

Abigail Levy Franks, meanwhile—she was one half of the first Franks-Levy marriage—was not at all sure she approved of these developments, as she watched them unfold in Philadelphia. Abigail regarded herself as an eighteenth-century aristocratic lady. But in many ways she was also a prototype Jewish mother, so familiar in fiction of modern times. She was forever wrapping up and sending off to her sons packages of preserved relishes and "smoakt fish," urging them not to forget to bathe regularly and eat three good meals daily. In correspondence to her son Naphtali Franks, covering the years 1733–1748, she repeatedly scolds him for his failure to write, or for spending too much money on gifts and "entertainments." Addressing him always as "Heartsey" (not only a term of endearment, but also a play on her son's middle name, which was Hart), she was fond of delivering Polonius-like pronouncements and advice. "You are now launched out amongst strangers," she told him upon his arrival in England on a business trip. "You must be exceeding circumspect in your conduct, be affable to all men but not credulous, nor too soon be led away by fair speeches. Be likewise a very just observer of your word in all respects, even in ye most trivial matters." She was a woman from whom it was not difficult to obtain an opinion, whether it was on the quality of a certain medicinal water or which was the "best Scotch snuff." She deplored the split between the Sephardic and the Ashkenazic Jewish communities (in New York, she had heard, Sephardic Jews were all in the East Ward, and Ashkenazic Jews were in the less fashionable Dock Ward). She disliked the noise of eighteenth-century horse-drawn traffic in the city, and complained of the gaming and drinking that went on "from Sunday night to Saturday morning." She called the ladies of her synagogue a "stupid set of people." She was literate, and fond of quoting, often inaccurately and in the erratic spelling that was typical of the age, advice from the contemporary novels of Fielding and Smollett, and from the essays of Dryden, Addison, and her favorite, Pope. She directed "Heartsey" that "Two mornings a week should be entirely untill dinner time dedicated to some useful book besides an hour every week to that purpose."

She was preoccupied with finding a suitable mate for each of her seven children, and marital matters take up much of the space in her letters to her son. She quotes Heartsey the little verse, the source of which is unknown:

Man the first happy favourite above,
When heaven endowed him with a power to love.
His God ne'er thought him in a blessed state
Till Woman made his happyness compleat.

And one of her great disappointments seems to have been the failure of her daughter Richa to complete a marriage alliance with David Gomez, and thereby with the illustrious Gomez family, even though David, Daniel's brother, was almost forty years Richa's senior. She adopts a sour-grapes attitude, speaking of David as "such a stupid wretch," and adds to Heartsey that even if David had proposed, she and Richa would not have accepted him anyway, probably, not even "if his fortune were much more and I a beggar." Better no marriage at all than marriage to *that* scoundrel, she seems to say, and Richa did indeed remain unmarried all her life, a heavy burden to her mother. Heartsey himself married his first cousin, Phila Franks, in a most satisfactory intramural manner.

Another marital calamity involved the marriage of Abigail's eldest daughter, also named Phila, to General Oliver De Lancey—who not only eloped with Phila but had her baptized. "Good God what a shock it was," she wrote Heartsey, "when they acquainted me she had left the house and had bin married six months, I can hardly hold my pen whilst I am writting. . . ." She wrote that "Oliver has sent many times to beg leave to see me, but I never would. . . . Now he sent word that he will come here. . . . I dread seeing him and how to avoid I know no way." It would be difficult, since the Frankses and the De Lanceys lived next door to each other. Abigail announced that she had instructed her errant daughter never to darken her door again and said: "I am determined I never will see nor let none of ye family go near her," but she added in almost the next sentence that "Nature is very strong, and it would give me a great concern if she should live unhappy, though it's a concern she does not merit."

Abigail Franks's distress appears to have been entirely over the fact that Oliver De Lancey was a Christian, and to have had nothing to do with what might seem to have been certain deficiencies in the young man's character. Present-day members of the De Lancey family take their pre-Revolutionary ancestry very seriously but, from contemporary reports, Oliver De Lancey emerges as a scapegrace, a bounder, a drunk, and—if we are to believe the source—a murderer. It was said, at the time, that he married Phila Franks for her money—a considerable inheritance left to her by her uncle Isaac. Shortly after the marriage, on November 3, 1742, Oliver was indicted for assaulting one of his wife's relatives, Judah Mears, who was the brother of Abigail Franks's stepmother. He and his friends were accused of attacking "a poor Dutch Jew and his wife," of breaking their windows, and "swearing that they would lie with the woman." Using foul language, they warned the couple not to bring charges since De Lancey and his friends were members of prominent New York families. Later the same year, according to a report from Governor George Clinton, Oliver stabbed and killed a Dr. Colchoun in a drunken brawl. This, however, may be an exaggeration or even an untruth. The De Lanceys and the Clintons were bitterest enemies, the Montagues and Capulets of early New York. It is known that Oliver De Lancey was something of a dandy and spent much of his time, and money, at the barber and at the wigmaker's.

After a while, Oliver seems to have settled down. He brought his wife to the De Lancey "country seat," which was located on what is now West Twelfth Street, west of Hudson Street, in Greenwich Village.* Oliver and Phila had seven children, all of whom made socially important marriages, three of them to titled Englishmen. Susannah married Sir William Draper, Phila married the Honorable Stephen Payne-Gallwey, and Charlotte married Sir David Dundas. Stephen De Lancey married Cornelia Barclay, of another old New York family, and *their* son became Sir William Howe De Lancey. In the next De Lancey generation there appeared, in addition to a flock of Episcopal clergymen, Count Alexander Balmain. †

Meanwhile, intermarriage—the thing which, despite her certain sophistication and attitude of tolerance, Abigail Levy Franks dreaded the most—occurred to the good Jewish mother a second time, when her son David, barely six months after his sister's marriage to De Lancey, married Margaret Evans of Philadelphia. His mother died convinced that she had been a failure as a parent.

It was the Franks-Evans union that produced the beautiful Franks sisters, Rebecca and Abigail, named after her grandmother. We see them in their portraits—Rebecca's

---

* Alexander Hamilton, a frequent traveler, wrote in the summer of 1744: "At twelve o'clock we passed a little town, starboard, called Greenwitch, consisting of eight or ten neat houses, and two or three miles above that on the same shore, a pretty box of a house with an avenue fronting the river belonging to Oliver De Lancey."
† Kin, though distantly, of the Paris couturier Pierre Balmain.

by Thomas Sully, who later became Philadelphia's most popular society portraitist—pale, dark-haired, with high cheekbones, long thin noses, and arresting eyes, white and swanlike necks, white bosoms swelling over low-cut dresses. They were unquestionably belles. Rebecca, the younger and probably the more beautiful of the two, was one of the stars, along with Peggy Shippen (who married Benedict Arnold), of one of the most extraordinary affairs in the annals of American entertaining, Philadelphia's "notorious Meschianza."

The Meschianza was an altogether curious event. Just why, in the middle of a great war, British-occupied Philadelphia should have decided to treat itself to a lavish party has never been entirely clear. Perhaps everyone was tired of battles and torn loyalties, and a fancy-dress ball seemed the answer. In any case, appropriate or not, a group of British officers decided in the spring of 1779 to put on the most extravagant social entertainment the new world had ever seen. The party was to honor the British General Sir William Howe, who was returning home to England.

Within the family, to say nothing of within the Jewish community, the situation must have seemed grotesque. Cousins David and Esther Hays in Westchester were risking their lives and losing their home in order to smuggle provisions through to Revolutionary soldiers. Here, right in Philadelphia, Haym Salomon, whose wife was the Franks sisters' first cousin, was working to fill the Revolution's coffers—and all the while the two giddy girls were planning a party to toast an enemy general. Feelings must have run strong, to say the least.

The men in charge of arrangements for the party were Major John André and Captain Oliver De Lancey, Jr. Both were close friends of the Franks girls. De Lancey, of course, was another first cousin, and Major André had been a suitor, of sorts, of Rebecca's. After being captured at Saint John's in 1775, André had been paroled in Philadelphia. He had been a frequent guest at the Franks mansion, where he spent a long summer of infatuation with Rebecca, then a girl in her middle teens. Dreamily, he passed the warm afternoons reading love poetry to her, and painting a delicate miniature of her face. Rebecca, like her De Lancey cousins, had already become decidedly Tory in her politics. Perhaps her affinity for kings had something to do with her ancestor whom George I had made "the Jew Broker of London." Certainly Major André's attentions can only have bolstered her sentiments.

For weeks before the Meschianza was to take place, Philadelphia was caught up in a flurry of preparations. One London firm reported that it had sold more than £12,000 worth of costly silks and laces for the Philadelphia ladies' dresses. For the British officers, Savile Row shipped red-coated dress uniforms, powdered wigs, cutlasses in bejeweled scabbards.

The party was held at Walnut Grove, the country home of Joseph Wharton, a sedate Quaker, but the party was un-Quakerish in every detail. It turned out that what Major André and Captain De Lancey had in mind was a sort of medieval tournament-festival, along the lines of the one held at the Field of the Cloth of Gold. The Philadelphia replica may well have outdone the original. There were jousts, duels, contests, and feats of strength among the young officers. There was a water festival, a regatta of brightly decorated sailboats on the river. There were parades and processions under triumphal arches. Blackamoor slaves in Oriental garb served nearly a thousand guests with fifteen varieties of champagnes and other wines, and buffet tables set up throughout the house and gardens offered an "indescribable assortment" of exotic foods, according to one report of the affair. No expense was spared, obviously, for what had been billed as "a medley of extravagance"—which it most certainly was.

The height of the gala was the moment when fourteen "knights"—young British officers—in fancy costumes were divided into two teams of seven men each for a tourney. One team was called "the Knights of the Blended Rose," the other "the Knights of the Burning Mountain." After the tilting and jousting—which was all in a lighthearted spirit, and in which no one was even slightly bruised—each side of the tournament selected its "Queen of Beauty." The Knights of the Blended Rose chose a Miss Auchmuty. The Knights of the Burning Mountain chose Rebecca Franks. She was gowned for the occasion in what was described as "a white silk gown, trimmed with black and white sashes, edged with black. It was a polonaise dress which formed a flowing robe and was open in front to the waist. The sash, six inches wide, was filled with spangles, as was the veil, which was edged with silver lace. The headdress was towering, in the fashion of the time, and was filled with a profusion of pearls and jewels." She was nineteen years old.

After the tournament, there was a climactic grand ball with fireworks and a "royal repast." The late spring weather—the date was May 18—was perfect for a party. It had started at four in the afternoon, and lasted all night long. It was midmorning the next day before the last of the revelers turned wearily homeward.

Not many miles away, in Valley Forge, a particularly harried and hard-pressed division of Continental troops was encamped where it had spent a parlous winter with heavy loss of life from disease and starvation.

A month later, the British left Philadelphia, and marched across New Jersey, to be met and defeated at Monmouth. But the memory of the lavish Meschianza rankled for a long time in the minds of the Continental generals, including General Anthony Wayne, who wrote sarcastically:

> Tell those Philadelphia ladies who attended Howe's assemblies and *levees,* that the heavenly, sweet, pretty red-coats, the accomplished gentlemen of the guards and grenadiers, have been humbled on the plains of Monmouth. The Knights of the Blended Roses and the Burning Mount have resigned their laurels to rebel officers, who will lay them at the feet of *those* virtuous daughters of America who cheerfully gave up ease and affluence in a city for liberty and peace of mind in a cottage.

Rebecca Franks had admirers on both sides of the Revolution, though she did seem to favor those with pro-British leanings or those who, intentionally or not, did things that helped the British cause. One rebel officer who fancied her was General Charles Lee. His conduct at Monmouth had been somewhat less than glorious. He took his orders from General Washington oddly lightly, and failed to do as he was told, which was to lead an attack on the British from the rear. Was this because Lee had originally been on the British side, and his loyalties still lay in that direction? Was he actually in collaboration with the enemy? There was that possibility. In any case, his behavior caused Washington to suspend him for twelve months. During this time, he engaged in a spirited correspondence with Becky Franks. Occasionally, however, General Lee overstepped himself in his letters, and he had a tendency to use double entendres in such a way that it was often possible to infer a vulgar, if not downright off color, meaning from his words.

Once, for instance, Lee wrote Rebecca a long letter about his trousers. In it, he said that she might have accused him of theft, of getting drunk, of treasonable correspondence with the enemy—had he actually done things of this sort?—or of "never parting with his shirt until his shirt parted with him," but that it had been unpardonably slanderous of Rebecca to say that he had worn green riding breeches *patched* with leather instead of green riding breeches *reinforced* with leather. "You have injured me in the tenderest part," he wrote to her, "and I demand satisfaction." He went on to say: "You cannot be ignorant of the laws of duelling. . . . I insist on the privilege of the injured party, which is to name his hour and weapons. . . . I intend it to be a very serious affair."

This sort of coarse talk—"tenderest part" indeed!—was too much for a properly bred Philadelphia lady like Rebecca Franks. She wrote him tersely to say that she considered his innuendos excessively vulgar, and that she wished to have no further correspondence with General Lee. He, however, quickly apologized and Rebecca eventually took him back into her circle.

Meanwhile, Rebecca's Tory and Tory-oriented friends were not doing her father any good at all, nor does Rebecca's behavior give any evidence that she was aware in the slightest of the trouble she was causing him. The British had left Philadelphia. The extravagant display of the Meschianza had left a poor impression. Public opinion associated David Franks with his party-loving daughter, and his business began to suffer. As one of Philadelphia's most important merchants, David Franks had been a logical choice for commissary to the British prisoners quartered in the city. Now the fact that he had fed and supplied the British—even though they were prisoners of the United States—began to be held against him. In September of 1778, for lack of cash, he was unable to deliver the prisoners their monthly rations and, this excuse being all they needed, the federal authorities promptly arrested David Franks and threw him in prison. The charge was treason against the United States of America.

A mysterious letter, which, if it ever existed, never appeared during the trial, and has never been seen since, was the chief piece of evidence against him. Allegedly written to his brother Moses in England, the letter was said to have contained "intentions inimical to the safety and liberty of the United States." David Franks may well have been in an inimical frame of mind about the United States and about England as well. The arrangement for him to be paid for feeding and quartering British prisoners had been a quaint one. He had been given the job by the Continental Congress. But he was to have been paid, his orders stipulated, by the British. The British, however, who had perhaps not been consulted in the matter, showed a certain reluctance when it came down to actually reimbursing Mr. Franks for his expenditures and, by December, 1778, Franks was in the dismaying position of owing his creditors for over 500,000 meals supplied to British prisoners in American hands. He had written to the British about this pressing matter. In a series of anxious letters to the Lords of the Treasury, he had outlined his plight; the Lords simply referred him back to Sir Henry Clinton in America, who did nothing.

With her father languishing in prison, Rebecca Franks went right on going to parties. At one ball, a high-ranking American officer made an entrance wearing a bright scarlet coat, and Rebecca Franks was overheard to comment sarcastically, "I see certain animals will put on the lion's skin." The story was printed in the paper, noting that Rebecca was "a lady well known in the Tory world." Though she might have done well to ignore the report, she instead decided to issue a snappy rejoinder, and in a succeeding issue of the newspaper she commented:

> There are many people so unhappy in their dispositions that, like the dog in the manger, they can neither enjoy the innocent pleasures of life themselves nor let others, without grumbling or growling, participate in them. Hence it is we frequently observe hints and anecdotes in your paper respecting the commanding officer, headquarters, and Tory ladies. This mode of attacking characters is really admirable, and equally as polite as conveying slander and defamation by significant nods, winks, and shrugs. Poor beings in-

deed, who plainly indicate to what species of animals they belong, by the baseness of their conduct.

To have defended her "innocent pleasures" at this particular moment, and in the public press, seems callous indeed. Soon after, however, her father's case was thrown out of court for lack of evidence, and he was released.

David Franks continued to try to collect his money from the British, and begged to be allowed to go personally to British-held New York to see what he could do. His daughter, he wrote, would like to accompany him and "would be very happy in taking a view of the Mall, or having a ramble under the holy old trees in the Broadway." In October, 1780, he was arrested again for corresponding with the enemy in New York—which he had most certainly been doing in an attempt to resolve his financial problems—and this time his punishment was exile to New York, which was exactly what he wanted. He and Rebecca left Philadelphia late that year in high spirits.

Rebecca not only had her ramble on Broadway. She also had more parties with British officers. A captain's barge, she wrote, was ready down at the wharf to carry guests to General Robertson's summer home, up the river, for a gala weekend. Her letters were filled with chatter about her beaux. There was Captain Montague, for instance—"Such eyes!"—and she was always most impressed with a suitor who had a title. At one point she was being wooed by no less than three Honorables, one with an income of "£26,000 a year!" Her view of New York was somewhat condescending. She was irked to find that in New York it was impossible for her to step out unchaperoned by an older woman, that this was considered unsafe. "We Philadelphians," she wrote, "knowing no harm, fear'd none." The quality of New York entertaining, she felt, was beneath Philadelphia standards, and she found New York ladies short on conversation and addicted to card playing. In a long letter to her sister Abigail, Rebecca wrote:

Few N. York ladies know how to entertain company in their own houses unless they introduce the card tables. . . . I don't know a woman or girl that can chat above half an hour, and that's on the form of a cap, the color of a ribbon, or the set of a hoop stay or *jupon* [petticoat]. I will do our ladies, that is Philadelphians, the justice to say they have more cleverness in the turn of an eye than the New York girls have in their whole composition. With what ease I have seen a Chew, a Penn, Oswald, Allen, and a thousand others entertain a large circle of both sexes, and the conversation without the aid of cards not flag or seem the least strained or stupid.

Here, or more properly speaking in N.Y., you enter the room with a formal set curtsy and after the how do's, 'tis a fine or a bad day, and those trifling nothings are finished, then all's a dead calm till the cards are introduced when you see pleasure dancing in the eye of all the matrons, and they seem to gain new life.

Rebecca also had salty comments to make on the courting habits of young New York ladies and gentlemen:

The misses, if they have a favorite swain, frequently decline playing [cards] for the pleasure of making love, for to all appearances 'tis the ladies and not the gentlemen that show a preference nowadays. 'Tis here, I fancy, always leap year. For my part, that am used to quite another mode of behavior, cannot help showing my surprise, perhaps they call it ignorance, when I see a lady single out her *pet* to lean almost in his arms at an assembly or play house (which I give my honor I have too often seen both in married and single), and to hear a lady confes a partiality for a man who perhaps she has not seen three times. These women say, "Well, I declare, such a gentleman is a delightful creature, and I could love him for my husband," or "I could marry such and such a person." And scandal says with respect to most who have been married, the advances have first come from the ladies' side. Or she has got a male friend to introduce him and puff her off. 'Tis really the case, and with me they lose half their charms; and I fancy there would be more marriage was another mode adopted. But they've made the men so saucy that I sincerely believe the lowest ensign thinks 'tis but ask and have; a red coat and smart epaulet is sufficient to secure a female heart.

Her appraisals of female contemporaries were frank and gossipy. Of a Miss Cornelia Van Horn, Rebecca wrote:

> She is in disposition as fine a girl as ever you saw, a great deal of good humor and good sense. Her person is too large for a beauty, in my opinion (and yet I am not partial to a *little* woman). Her complexion, eyes, and teeth are very good, and a great quantity of light brown hair (*Entre nous,* the girls of New York excell us Philadelphians in that particular and in their form), and a sweet countenance and agreeable smile. Her feet, as you desire, I'll say nothing about; they are Van Horns' and what you'd call Willings.* But her sister Kitty is the belle of the family, I think, though some give preference to Betsy. . . . Kitty's form is much in the style of our admired Mrs. Galloway, but rather taller and larger, her complexion very fine, and the finest hair I ever saw. Her teeth are beginning to decay, which is the case of most New York girls after eighteen—and a great deal of elegance of manners.

But it was the men and the parties that received most of Becky Franks's attention. "Yesterday," she wrote, "the grenadiers had a race at the Flatlands (Long Island), and in the afternoon this house swarmed with beaus and some very smart ones. How the girls would have envied me could they have peeped and seen how I was surrounded." Six months after the above was written, Rebecca married one of her handsome, titled swains, Sir Henry Johnson. The American Revolution ruined her father. He never succeeded in obtaining a fraction of the money the British owed him and, in later years, David Franks appears to have survived by obtaining a series of small loans from Michael Gratz, one of his fellow Sephardim in Philadelphia.

But his daughter had made a brilliant marriage and, in later years, she also appears to have changed her politics. In 1816, after England had lost both the Revolution and the War of 1812, Rebecca, now Lady Johnson, was visited in London by General Winfield Scott, the dashing hero—

* The Willings, partners of Robert Morris, apparently had big feet.

a general at the age of twenty-eight—of the latter war. She had lost her looks, but not her enthusiasm, and she said to Scott, "I have gloried in my rebel countrymen! Would to God I, too, had been a patriot!"

Rebecca and her sister Abigail were responsible for elevating the Franks family name into the highest society on both sides of the Atlantic. Rebecca's descendants, the Johnsons of Bath, stud Burke's Peerage as well as the officer corps of the British Army. Of her nine grandsons, three were generals, one was a major general, one a lieutenant general, two were colonels, one a captain. The ninth became an Episcopal clergyman.

Abigail, meanwhile, married Andrew Hamilton, the jurist of whom it is said that "All Philadelphia lawyers look on him as their exemplar." In addition to the American Hamiltons, not to be sneezed at, her family tree has become decorated with such imposing names as Sir Thomas Whichcote; the Honorable Henry Campbell Bruce, Lord Aberdare; Orlando Bridgeman, fifth earl of Bradford; Sir Robert Edward Henry Abdy, fifth baronet; Algernon Henry Strutt, third Baron Belper; Albert Edward Harry Mayer Archibald Primrose, sixth earl of Rosebery; and Edward Kenelm Digby, eleventh Baron Digby. The list of descendants of Abigail Franks is topped off by the former Mrs. Randolph Churchill, and by the actual entrance of the blood royal, which occurred when Lady Lavinia Mary, the earl of Rosebery's daughter, married Bernard Marmaduke Fitzalan Howard, sixteenth duke of Norfolk.

It seems a respectable enough collection of descendants for an eighteenth-century Philadelphia Jewish mother whose greatest ambition was for her daughter to marry a Gomez.

In retrospect, Becky Franks appears to us as a vain, frivolous, fickle woman, single-mindedly dedicated to her "innocent pleasures" and little else, committed to taking the center of the stage and getting what she wanted. Her contemporary in Philadelphia society, Rebecca Gratz— also renowned for her beauty—was a very different sort of person: serious, a do-gooder, a premature Victorian, a little stuffy, something of a bluestocking. The Gratzes were "connected" with the Franks family, via the Hayses and the Ettings. One of Rebecca Gratz's sisters, for example, had married Reuben Etting II (Esther Etting Hays's first cousin, named after Esther's brother who had died as a

British prisoner), and another sister was Mrs. Samuel Hays. The Gratzes rather disapproved of the high-living Franks family, particularly the girls, and the Gratzes found it rather comforting to remember that David Franks, whose family had carried on in such a purse-proud manner, had had to turn to a Gratz—Rebecca Gratz's father—for financial help in his latter years.

The Gratzes also disapproved of intermarriage, and they disapproved of what they heard about the Jewish community of New Orleans, of the loose and backsliding ways that seemed to prevail in that southern city. In 1807, Rebecca Gratz wrote her brother Joseph a cautioning letter before he set out for a trip south:

> . . . At New Orleans, there are many who call themselves Jews, or at least whose parentage being known are obliged to acknowledge themselves such, but who neglect those duties which would make that title honorable and then respected—among such as [you] my dear Jo, I hope you will never make one; be asured the worthy and the thinking part of the community will ever estimate a man, by his attention to the serious, domestic duties which speak more truly his character than the external forms in which he presents himself to the world; who would depend on a man's engagements with his fellow men, if he violates his more important engagements with God?

She may well have had in mind just such men as Judah Touro, about whom it was already being said that he paid little attention to his religion. If Rebecca Franks liked to fill her days with party-going and flirtation, Rebecca Gratz preferred more serious pursuits. She was literary, and enjoyed the company of painters and writers, including William Cullen Bryant, James Fenimore Cooper, Henry Tuckerman, and Washington Irving. She was philanthropic. In her Sully portrait, we see a demurely smiling beauty: olive-skinned, with soft dark brown eyes, black hair under a heart-shaped hat from which falls a bit of white lace draping. Her yellow mantle is lined with white fur. John Sartain, in *The Reminiscences of a Very Old Man*, described a visit to Rebecca Gratz: "Her eyes struck me as piercingly dark, yet mild of expression, in a face tenderly pale. The portrait Sully painted of her must have been a remarkable likeness, that so many years after I should recognize her instantly by remembrance of her." Meanwhile, according to her relative Gratz Van Rensselaer: "The Gratz family mansion was known far and wide as the home of a refined and elegant hospitality. Gifted and distinguished guests—illustrious statesmen, and eminent persons from abroad whom choice or vicissitude brought to this country—found there an appreciative welcome."

A particularly close friend of Rebecca Gratz's was Matilda Hoffman. It was in the office of Matilda's father, Judge Ogden Hoffman, that Washington Irving studied law, and presently Miss Hoffman and Washington Irving became engaged. But before the pair could marry, Miss Hoffman became ill with "wasting disease," a common affliction of the day, and Rebecca went to live at the Hoffmans' to help nurse her friend. Rebecca was there to close Matilda's eyes at the end.

This devotion of one young woman to another impressed Irving. When he went to England to try to forget his sweetheart's death, Rebecca Gratz and her kindness to Matilda became almost an obsession with him. He could talk of little else but the Jewess' services to her Christian friend. One of the people he told the story to was Sir Walter Scott, and from this the legend has descended that Scott—who never met Rebecca Gratz—used her as his model for the character Rebecca in *Ivanhoe*. It is probably true, but the evidence is not as clear-cut as it might be. It has been said, for example, that when Ivanhoe was published, Scott sent Irving a first edition inscribed: "How does my Rebecca compare with yours?" Actually, Scott wrote Irving a letter saying, in somewhat different words: "How do you like your Rebecca? Does the Rebecca I have pictured compare well with the pattern given?"—a small, possibly insignificant, difference.

Rebecca Gratz, meanwhile, was clearly pleased to think that she and Rebecca in *Ivanhoe* were the same person. She read the novel in 1820 and immediately wrote to her sister-in-law: "Have you received Ivanhoe? When you read it tell me what you think of my namesake Rebecca." A few weeks later she wrote again:

> I am glad you admire Rebecca, for she is just such a representation of a good girl as I think human nature can reach. Ivanhoe's insensibility to her, you must re-

collect, may be accounted to his previous attachment
—his prejudice was a characteristic of the age he lived
in—he fought for Rebecca, though he despised her
race—the veil that is drawn over his feelings was necessary to the fable, and the beautiful sensibility of
hers, so regulated yet so intense, might show the
triumph of faith over human affection. I have dwelt
on this character as we sometimes do on an exquisite
painting until the canvas seems to breathe and we believe it is life.

In later years, when asked—and she frequently was—
whether she was Rebecca of Scott's romance, she would
merely smile primly and change the subject.

One aspect of Rebecca Gratz's story that must have ap-
pealed to Scott's sentimental nature—so much so that he
may easily have been tempted to borrow it for his tale—
was that Rebecca, in life, like Rebecca in fiction, had had
an unhappy love affair with a Christian. He had been
young Samuel Ewing, the son of the Presbyterian provost
of the University of Pennsylvania. He had escorted Rebecca to the Assembly ball of 1802. But Rebecca's parents,
and Rebecca herself, had always opposed intermarriage
with non-Jews. Rebecca's and young Ewing's love was
star-crossed from the beginning. Faith, as she put it, had
to triumph over affection.

Rebecca Gratz was nearly forty when she read *Ivanhoe*.
She could look back on events of twenty years before with
equanimity. In time, Sam Ewing had made a proper Philadelphia wedding, to one of the Redman girls. But it was
not a happy union, and he died young. When he was lying in his coffin there was a sudden hush in the church as
the heavily veiled figure of Rebecca Gratz appeared in the
doorway. She moved swiftly to the coffin, placed a small
object on his breast, and just as swiftly departed. The object was a miniature portrait of herself. With it were three
white roses, crossed to form a six-pointed star.

She never married. She devoted her life to good deeds.
She founded the Philadelphia Orphan Society, in 1815.
She became secretary of the Female Association for the
Relief of Women and Children in Reduced Circumstances.
She founded the Hebrew Sunday School Society, the first
of its kind in America. She helped found the Jewish Foster
Home. She began and ended each day with prayer. When

her sister, Rachel Gratz Moses, died in 1823, Rebecca helped raise Rachel's nine small children. Her spirit showed in her face. After painting her, Thomas Sully said that he had "never seen a more striking Hebraic face. The easy pose, suggestive of perfect health, the delicately turned neck and shoulders with the firmly poised head and its profusion of dark curling hair, large, clear black eyes, the contour of the face, the fine white skin, the expressive mouth and the firmly chiselled nose, with its strength of character, left no doubt as to the race from which she had sprung. Possessed of an elegant bearing, a melodiously sympathetic voice, a simple and frank and gracious womanliness, there was about Rebecca Gratz all that a princess of the blood Royal might have coveted." What better description of a heroine of fiction?

The religious school she founded still operates, and Rebecca Gratz foundations continue to dispense funds in Philadelphia. In later Gratz generations, family strictures against marrying Christians relaxed considerably. Collateral Gratz descendants today are named Wallace, Rowland, Taylor, Brewster, Marshall, McClure, and Gillette. Her brother's great-granddaughter is the present Mrs. Godfrey S. Rockefeller of Greenwich, Connecticut.

Helen Gratz Rockefeller is a handsome, cheerful woman in her sixties who recalls, of the Gratz relatives whom she knew: "We were a rather tempestuous, almost violent family. Life was hardly ever placid. My grandfather, Henry Howard Gratz, had a terrible temper and was something of a despot. He used to terrify us. He'd do things like throw his cane at you if he caught you eating an apple. He had three wives. The third one he married when he was seventy, and she was only thirty. She adored him, but when he was cross with her he'd throw all of her flowerpots out the window. But we had a terribly strong sense of family obligation. We stuck together through thick and thin."

Mrs. Rockefeller says: "The Gratz family fortune was pretty well diminished by the time it reached my grandfather's generation. My father, Benjamin Gratz III, left home with two dollars and fifty cents in his pocket when he was in his early twenties. The two dollars was stolen, but with the fifty cents he built up a whole new fortune for himself, and took care of everybody in the family—aunts, uncles, relatives from miles around. We all lived together in Saint Louis. There was a great deal of singing together and reading aloud." Though Mrs. Rockefeller is proud of her Jewish heritage, the Gratzes she descends from have been Episcopalians from her grandfather's generation on, if not from even before. It strikes her as quaintly ironic that her collateral ancestor Rebecca Gratz should have remained unmarried for life because she loved a Christian, whereas Gratzes in subsequent generations have displayed a tendency to marry several times—her grandfather three times, and her father twice. As a child, growing up in Saint Louis, she recalls her parents as stalwart churchgoers, and Bishop Tuttle of Saint Louis was a regular guest at the Gratz Sunday dinner table. Mrs. Rockefeller remembers her mother asking the deaf old bishop, "Do you like bananas, Bishop?" and the bishop cupping his ear to inquire, "What was that?" *"Do you like bananas, Bishop?"* Mrs. Gratz asked in a louder voice. "No," the bishop replied, "I prefer the old-fashioned nightshirt."

There is no question that the social distinction, and the charm, of early American Jewish women, as well as the financial assistance and business probity of the men, all helped George Washington—who, after all, was an aristocratic Virginian and something of a snob—to look with favor on Jews as a whole, as a people, as a valuable part of the new nation. Jewish officers, including two cousins of the Franks sisters, served on his staff. Colonel David Salisbury Franks—Haym Salomon's brother-in-law—was Washington's emissary to Paris, where he carried dispatches between Washington and Ambassador Benjamin Franklin; he also delivered copies of the 1784 treaty of peace with England to the American embassies in Europe. Colonel Isaac Franks, called "the boy hero of the Revolution" (he was only sixteen when he enlisted), rose in the ranks until he was attached to headquarters as General Washington's aide-de-camp.

But at the war's end, the still relative minority of Jews in the country looked at their new government with a certain apprehensiveness. After all, not all had backed the Revolutionary cause. And for three hundred years, under a variety of monarchs and colonial leaders, under many flags, these ancient, proud, and highly bred families from Spain and Portugal had received treatment that had been, at best, uneven and, at its worst, calamitous. Which way would the winds blow now?

When George Washington was inaugurated as first President of the United States of America, the heads of the Jewish communities in Philadelphia, New York, Richmond, Charleston, and Savannah all wrote cautious letters to the new chief executive. They reminded him, as politely as possible, of the kind of country they hoped the United States would be. Moses Seixas, head of the Newport congregation, put it best. Would the world now see, he asked, "a Government which to bigotry gives no sanction, to persecution no assistance, but generously affording to all liberty of conscience and immunities of citizenship, deeming everyone of whatever nation, tongue and language, equal parts of the great government machine?"

Seixas' letter obviously impressed the President, for he actually borrowed some of Seixas' rhetoric in his reply:

Gentlemen:

While I receive with much satisfaction your address replete with expressions of esteem, I rejoice in the opportunity of assuring you that I shall always retain grateful remembrance of the cordial welcome I experienced on my visit to Newport from all classes of citizens.

The reflection on the days of difficulty and danger which are passed is rendered the more sweet from a consciousness that they are succeeded by days of uncommon prosperity and security.

If we have wisdom to make the best use of the advantages with which we are now favored, we cannot fail, under the just administration of a good government to become a great and happy people.

The citizens of the United States of America have a right to applaud themselves for having given to mankind examples of an enlarged and liberal policy worthy of imitation. All possess alike liberty of conscience and immunities of citizenship.

It is now no more that toleration is spoken of as if it were by the indulgence of one class of people that another enjoyed the exercise of their inherent natural right, for, happily, the Government of the United States, which gives to bigotry no sanction, to persecution no assistance, requires only that they who live under its protection shall demean themselves as good citizens in giving it on all occasions their effectual support.

It would be inconsistent with the frankness of my character not to avow that I am pleased with your favorable opinion of my administration and fervent wishes for my felicity.

May the children of the stock of Abraham who dwell in this land continue to merit and enjoy the good will of the other inhabitants, while everyone shall sit in safety under his own vine and fig tree, and there shall be none to make him afraid.

May the Father of all Mercies scatter light, and not darkness upon our paths, and make us all in our several vocations useful here, and in His own due time and way, everlasting happy.

G. WASHINGTON

In his sometimes jawbreaking prose, he was uttering almost dreamily noble sentiments, painting a picture of America's future that was close to utopian. But the heart of "G. Washington" was in the right place.

12.

LEGENDS AND LEGACIES

EACH of the old families has its favorite legend, and Aunt Elvira Nathan Solis knew them all. Some of the most romantic, to be sure, involved members of the Solis family who, through the vellum pages of Dr. Stern's book, can be seen to have evolved into present-day New York and Philadelphia Solises out of a series of dynastic marriages in fifteenth- and sixteenth-century Iberia. It all began when a certain Marquesa Lopes (undoubtedly a distant ancestor of Aaron Lopez) married Fernao Jorge Da Solis and, at roughly the same time, Beatrice Pinto married Duarte Da Silva. The Da Silvas' son married the Da Solises' daughter, bringing the two houses together, and from then on— making use of the Spanish practice of appending the mother's name to the surnames of the children—the family fell heir to the double name of Da Silva Solis or, as it was used in certain branches, Da Silva y Solis. This was all in the sixteenth century, and is remarkable in that the practice has been continued to this day. (Emily Nathan's full name, for instance, is Emily Da Silva Solis Nathan.)

Dr. Stern's book reveals such peripheral information about the Solis family as the fact that one Joseph Da Silva Solis, a London gold broker, was so good at his job that he earned the admiring nickname "El Dorado." In one branch of the family, for several generations, the male heirs bore the hereditary title of Marquis de Montfort. Next to another name in the voluminous Solis family tree, Dr. Stern has made the sinister notation: "Murdered at Murney, Friday, October 17, 1817."

The Solises, Aunt Ellie Solis liked to remind the children, were noted for producing strong-minded ladies. A number of Solis women, through history, have let their husbands retire to intellectual pursuits while the women ran the family business—or the country. A fifteenth-century example of this breed was Isabel de Solis, otherwise romantically known as "Zoraya the Morning Star." Isabel, or Zoraya, was captured as a slave by Suley Hassan, the Moorish sultan of Granada, who made her his concubine. But so strong was her will, and so powerful was her allure, that she was soon running both the sultan and the sultanate. All American Solises also descend from Dona Isabel de Fonseca, a daughter of the Marquis of Turin and the Count of Villa Real and Monterrey, and Solomon da Silva Solis. In a plan masterminded by Dona Isabel, the pair escaped from Portugal disguised as Christians and were married as Jews in Amsterdam in 1670.

By the time Jacob da Silva Solis arrived in New York from London in 1803, the family fortunes were somewhat diminished. Jacob made an auspicious in-the-group marriage to David and Esther Hays's daughter Charity, and took her with him to Wilmington, Delaware, where he opened a store. Jacob's theory was that Wilmingtonians were doing too much of their shopping in nearby Philadelphia, and would save time and money by buying their dry-goods nearer home. Apparently he was wrong, for five years later, when this venture failed, he himself was in Philadelphia, looking for a job. He applied to one of his wife's relatives, Simon Gratz, for the humble position of shohet, or ritual slaughterer, and was rather summarily turned down by Mr. Gratz. Leaving his wife and children behind, he went south to New Orleans, where an earlier Solis, Joseph, had made a fortune developing Louisiana's sugar cane industry. But Jacob, alas, had no such luck. One of the stories Aunt Ellie Solis used to tell was that in the spring of 1827 in New Orleans, Jacob da Silva Solis was so poor that, unable to purchase matzos for his Passover festival—and horrified that New Orleans Jews seemed to care so little for Passover that they had none to give him—he sat down and ground the meal and made his own. As other good orthodox Sephardim had before him, Jacob deplored the laxity, when it came to religious matters, of the New Orleans Jews. He determined to establish his own congregation, and at this he was successful. Though Jacob Solis' personal congregation never achieved any sort of dominance in the community, it did get a New Orleans thoroughfare named Solis Street.

Probably Jacob da Silva Solis' greatest moment came when it was discovered that the *Converso* line of the House of Solis had become extinct in Portugal. The Portuguese ambassador, himself of Marrano descent, journeyed to New Orleans to advise Jacob that he could succeed to the Solis titles and properties in Europe, provided, of course, that he would become a Catholic. Jacob da Silva Solis gazed stonily at the ambassador for a moment, and declined the offer. The ambassador could not believe his ears. "You fool!" he is said to have cried. "It is one of the greatest dignities in Europe!" Mr. Solis, secure in his own dignity, replied: "Not for the whole of Europe would I forsake my faith, and neither would my son Solomon." It was one of Aunt Ellie's favorite tales. How Jacob Solis' poor wife back in Philadelphia—she had borne him seven children—felt about this gesture is not recorded.

Two of Jacob Solis' children managed to redeem the family name, and handsomely at that. His son David married Elvira Nathan (Aunt Ellie's mother), and brought the American Solises into the Seixas-Nathan-Mendes family complex. The Nathans, of course, were New York-based. Jacob Solis' daughter Judith married Myer David Cohen, of Philadelphia, and produced nine children. At Judith's insistence—she was another strong-willed lady—her children bore the hyphenated name Solis-Cohen, their mother's name placed *first*. Solis, she explained, was after all a more important name than Cohen; Mr. Cohen, furthermore, had been born in southern Germany. Solis-Cohens are still prominent in Philadelphia, and continue to be loyal to da Silva when it comes to middle names.

Both the da Silvas and the Solises are connected with the Peixottos—another old Sephardic family—and the Peixottos are similarly name-proud. The Peixotto family crest depicts two ovals, one containing two fish, the other a hand pouring water from a pitcher into a bowl. The ovals are surmounted by a very regal-looking crown, and the entirety is circled by an elaborate wreath. The word *peixotto*, in Portuguese, means "little fish," explaining the first oval. The hand pouring water is the symbol of the Levites, or priests of Israel. Though present-day Peixottos are not sure just how, they are convinced that the crown and the wreath cannot stand for anything less than royalty.

In 1634, one Don Diego Peixotto and his two brothers
—Antonio Mendes Peixotto and Joshua Peixotto—were
imprisoned for high treason. They were accused, no less,
of "governing an armada which caused the downfall of
Pernambuco," and the motive ascribed to them was ven-
geance against the Inquisition. The Peixottos also were
fond of hyphenated names. When, in the eighteenth century, a Miss Cohen Peixotto married Mr. Levy Maduro,
their descendants used the name Maduro-Peixotto, the
wife's name last.

The Peixottos were noted for their hot tempers and, as
happens in any tight-knit family, feuds developed. There
are branches of the Peixotto family that have not spoken
to each other for generations. At a Peixotto family funeral in the 1830's, hardly any of the mourners were on
speaking terms with the others. Peixottos have been quick
to cut their heirs out of their wills for the slightest breach
of loyalty, but then so have the Seixases. When Abraham
Mendes Seixas, patriarch of the American branch of the
family (who, to confuse things somewhat, also used the
name Miguel Pacheco da Silva), died in London in 1738,
he left a will—written in Portuguese—in which he left the
bulk of his considerable estate to his two daughters. To
his only son—who later emigrated to New York—he left
"only fifty pounds for reasons known to myself." It was
possibly because the young man had reached the advanced
age of thirty without marrying to produce an heir. (He
eventually succeeded in performing both duties.)

(Equally testy in his will was Judah Hays. When he
died in New York in 1764, he cut off his daughter Rachel
with only five shillings for marrying against his wishes, and
another daughter, Caty, received her inheritance in an
elaborate trust because, as her father put it in his will, he
had little opinion of the business ability of her husband,
Abraham Sarzedas, with whom she had gone off to live
in Georgia. Later, Sarzedas distinguished himself as a Revolutionary officer of the Light Dragoons—too late, however, to redeem himself with his father-in-law.)

Peixottos were also determinedly civic-minded. When
the Shearith Israel congregation lost its pastor of fifty
years, Gershom Mendes Seixas, when he died in 1816,
there was difficulty finding a rabbi who could fill his place.
Moses Levy Maduro-Peixotto, a prosperous merchant, was
a Judaic scholar, though not a rabbi, and he offered to

fill the vacancy until a permanent replacement could be found. So well did he fill the post that the congregation voted to keep him. He gave up his mercantile career to devote himself to the parish, and continued to do so until his death in 1828. Because he was rich, furthermore, he turned over his salary throughout these years to Rabbi Seixas' widow.

All these strains—Seixas, Peixotto, Maduro, Hays, Solis, and a good many others—and, no doubt, their accompanying characteristics, come together in the Hendricks family. Perhaps the quickest way to see how this happened is to realize that when Uriah Hendricks arrived on American shores in 1755, he married, first, Daniel Gomez' niece Eve Esther Gomez. Widowed a few years later, he married, second, Aaron Lopez' daughter Rebecca. From then on, the pattern of intramural marriages became so bewilderingly complex that even Dr. Stern slips and stumbles now and then as, under the Hendricks family name, all the old names gather, weaving the whole into an ever tightening bundle.

The Hendrickses had a knack for making money. Uriah Hendricks opened a small store in Cliff Street, in lower Manhattan, selling dry goods—underwear, suspenders, shoelaces, cheap watches, handkerchiefs—anything that could be stored in a small place, sold quickly and for a little profit. Soon he was prospering, and able to move to a larger store in Mill Street, now South William Street. He embarked upon the creation of a large family. Eventually there were ten children. Uriah may also have been something of a philanderer, if we are to take the implications contained in an early letter to Uriah from his wife's brother Isaac Gomez, who, in a scolding tone, took Uriah to task over an "infatuation." Gomez wrote that "To support my character as a gentleman and for no other reason, I would wish you to enquire of the company [you are keeping] who must displease her ladyship [Mrs. Hendricks] as much as I and my family." The warning may have worked, for subsequent letters contain no mention of the matter.

Uriah Hendricks supplied the Colonies in the French and Indian wars and laid the groundwork for a fortune. But it was his second-eldest son, Harmon Hendricks, born in New York in 1771, who brought the Hendricks business to success on a national and even international scale. Harmon Hendricks took his father's business and began expanding it. From undershirts and watches, he moved into spangles, looking glasses, umbrellas, and tablecloths. He sold snuff boxes, gilt frames, ivory combs, beads, and brass kettles. He traded rice for pianos, and pianos for shipments of German glass, gold leaf, knives, forks, and brooches. He dealt in wire, tinplate, Spanish dollars, and lottery tickets—even tickets described in his books as "enemy lottery." His business correspondence is filled with notations such as: "Bicycle horns are no use in New England," and "Epaulets too high in price," and "Large kettles not salable in Hartford." He established for himself a variety of buying and selling agents in London and Bristol, England; in Kingston, Jamaica; in Boston, Hartford, Newport, Philadelphia, and Charleston. He was, in short, a trader. He could trade with equal ease in any commodity.

There were, of course, deals that were less profitable than others, as is apparent in a revealing series of letters between Harmon Hendricks and one Abraham Cohen of Philadelphia. Late in 1797, Harmon had sent Mr. Cohen a sizable shipment of cigars, or "segars," as they are referred to in the correspondence that ensued. In March, 1798, Mr. Hendricks wrote Mr. Cohen a carefully worded letter in which he expressed "surprise" at Mr. Cohen's "silence of four months without remittance" in payment for the shipment. Mr. Cohen's reply to this was disturbingly vague. He explained that he had been "every day expecting of making a remittance and thought I would wait [before writing] until then." No remittance was made, and six months of further silence went by. In November, Mr. Cohen wrote to say that he would pay "when Isaac Pesoa goes to N.Y.," the plan apparently being to have Mr. Pesoa deliver the money. Cohen added an encouraging note that he had opened a retail-wholesale grocery store at 44 South Fourth Street in Philadelphia, "An excellent place for smoking segars—no less than 4 tavern [sic] in the neighborhood!" Two weeks later, however, Mr. Cohen wrote to Mr. Hendricks to express his own indignant "surprise" that Hendricks should himself have sent Isaac Pesoa to collect, or try to collect, the owed money. Cohen added that he "cannot sell the segars"—despite the four taverns.

On December 10, Cohen wrote that he could still not pay for the cigars due to "unforseen circumstances." A month later, on January 16, 1799, obviously feeling under pressure, Mr. Cohen wrote to Hendricks that a certain John Barnes had collected $52.40 in partial payment for the shipment, but a month later this turned out to be untrue. Mr. Barnes swore that he had received no money at all from Mr. Cohen. By summer of 1799, Harmon Hendricks was clearly losing patience with Cohen and wrote to Isaac Pesoa, saying: "this segar article is so very uncertain on acct. of the many various deceptions," and added that he would certainly like to collect from Cohen but "will not protest it." In August, Pesoa replied that there was nothing to be gained, in his opinion, from Hendricks' suing Cohen for the money. "I have no doubt," said Pesoa, "that if any of his creditors sue him he will be oblige [sic] to take the benefit of the Act"—that is, for indigents and insolvents. And there the matter ended. Harmon Hendricks was never paid for his "segars."

He was, in the meantime, dealing in a more lucrative commodity. Though he continued to trade in combs, snuffboxes, spangles, mirrors, and pianos, he had been steadily focusing more and more of his time and attention on the copper trade. Copper has been called "the poor man's metal," and "the ugly duckling of metals," despised for its very abundance. There are copper deposits in virtually every part of the globe, from Cape Horn to Siberia. Copper is easily mined, cheaply milled. Historically, little value has been attached to it, and it has been used for the cheapest coins, the meanest utensils, kitchen pots and pans. But in the eighteenth and nineteenth centuries, the booming African slave trade created, indirectly, a new and important need for copper. Copper was needed in New England and in the West Indies for the bottoms of the huge stills that turned out the hundreds of thousands of gallons of rum that occupied such an important point of the three-cornered pattern of the slave trade. In 1812, Harmon Hendricks moved westward into the town of Belleville, New Jersey, and built what was the first copper-rolling mill in the United States. Within a few years, most of the rum produced in the Americas was coming from stills made of Hendricks copper.

Both Harmon and his father had been Tories during the Revolution, but that did not prevent Harmon from doing business with Paul Revere a few years later. In fact, as early as 1805, the two copper titans had reached an in-

formal agreement by which they intended to corner the
American copper market and set its price. Let us, Revere
proposed, buy "the whole block of copper in our single
name"—or in the names of friends and relatives, depending on how sales went—and then, as he put it, "equalize
between us the quality and the price." Both men were firmly against the imposition of an import duty on foreign
copper, particularly from Britain, brought into the United
States. As Hendricks expressed it in a letter to Revere:
"There will be more honor in beating John Bull out of
our market by low price and superior quality than by
duties which may tempt new manufacturers to operate
more to our prejudice." The two men wanted, in other
words, no further domestic competition, and for several
years they were able to have the American copper pie
fairly evenly divided between them. They were also opposed to the administration of James Madison, whose pur-
chasing agents they frequently accused of supplying fishy
figures.

"We have observed Mr. Smith's report," Revere wrote
Hendricks early in 1806. "It is all of a piece with the present administration of government. His report has $56,8
worth of sheets, bolts, spikes. . . . Now we know ther
in store in Charlestown more than $120,000 worth. . . .
Less than half, in other words, of what had been shipped
was being acknowledged as received. But apparently the
men got their money, for the Revere-Hendricks accounts
show more than half a million dollars received in payment
for government orders that year.

In 1803, a young man named Robert Fulton succeeded
in demonstrating that a water-going vessel could be pro-
pelled by steam. Fulton's steam boilers were made of copper, and Fulton became another important customer of
Harmon Hendricks. Hendricks boilers went into the *Fulton*
—the first steam warship—the *Paragon*, the *Firefly*, the
Nassau, and the *Clermont*, which for years plied up and
down the Hudson River between New York and Albany.
Soon, selling copper for Fulton's boilers—Fulton had a
monopoly on the manufacture of steamboats for thirty
years—became more lucrative than selling copper for stills.
Harmon Hendricks' partner (and brother-in-law), Solomon Isaacs, became so identified with boilers that he was
nicknamed "Steamboat" Isaacs. In 1819, when Fulton was
fitting out the S.S. *Savannah* to be the first oceangoing

steamship, the craft was labeled a "steam coffin" by various nay-sayers in high places, who insisted it would never work. When the ship completed its triumphant voyage across the Atlantic in record time, Harmon Hendricks modestly announced that his copper was in the *Savannah*'s boilers.

The *Savannah*, however, was not one of his firm's more profitable undertakings. Harmon Hendricks had cousins in the city of Savannah—the Henrys and the Minises—who were important stockholders in the Savannah Steamship Company, and Hendricks had sold them his copper at family prices. One boiler, twenty by eight and a half feet in size, had cost $30,000 for the *Fulton* five years earlier. For the *Savannah*'s two larger boilers, each twenty-six by six feet, he charged only $1,237.72. Also, for some reason, Hendricks' relatives never paid him in full. He received only $1,115.05—$122.67 short.

Success and riches were, of course, a mixed blessing when, as word of Harmon Hendricks' wealth reached them, distant kin from all over the globe began writing him for what they felt was their proper share of the bounty.

It is clear that a good part of each day was taken up dealing with these demands. There were, for instance, some of his stepmother's Lopez cousins in Newport who continually wrote to declare themselves "destitute," asking for money in sums small and large. To a typically tearful Lopez note, asking for thirty dollars, Harmon Hendricks would append the curt notation of his own: "Sent her $20." A few months later, another relative of his stepmother's, Samuel Lopez, wanted two hundred dollars, promising "with the honor of a Mason" to repay it. To a nephew of Gilbert Stuart, Harmon Hendricks loaned $12,000, and when Stuart heard of this he cautioned Hendricks: "If you have patience, he will repay you, but if, like a hard master, you attempt to cast him into prison you may lose all." At the same time, money was coming into the Hendricks firm at a gratifying rate, from sales of copper as well as from such items as turpentine, pigs, pumpkins, gin, and garden seed. In 1807, Hendricks' brother-in-law Jacob de Leon noted to Hendricks that he had sold "upward of $70,000 in black birds"—a euphemism for Negro slaves—and would be paid in November. His good luck continued. On July 22, 1814, Harmon bet one Jack Cohen "a beaver hat" that there would be peace within four months—and won the bet, for hostilities of the War of 1812 ended before November.

But relatives continued to pester him. From England a widowed aunt, Rachel Waag, wrote to him to explain that her late husband's estate had not yet been settled; until then she needed money. Hendricks appointed one of his London representatives to supply her with cash. A cousin, Benjamin Da Costa, whose wife had died, sent his young son, Moses, to live with the Hendrickses, who already had twelve children of their own, and Da Costa kept Harmon Hendricks busy with instructions as to what sort of an education the boy should receive. Harmon had him studying Spanish and French, but Da Costa preferred that the boy study English, "the Mother Tongue," and even suggested that Hebrew be dropped from his curriculum, "As I daresay he knows his prayers in that language by now, which is as much as I wish."

There was also the painful problem of Harmon Hendricks' sister Sally, one of those whom Malcolm Stern's book adjudges to have been "insane." Insane or not, she was certainly a trial to her family, never content to be where she was, always wanting to be somewhere else. She spent her life being shuttled back and forth among relatives, none of whom was ever particularly overjoyed to see her. She was referred to as "our unfortunate sister," and described as being "of a very unsettled disposition." Her condition must have been particularly unsettling to Harmon Hendricks, three of whose children had already shown signs of being, as it was said, "peculiar." One son, for example, made a fetish of cleanliness, and would eat nothing that had not been scrubbed with hot water and strong soap. He washed his hands as often as a hundred times a day. A daughter was "melancholy," and lapsed into alarming depressions that lasted for days. Sally Hendricks' obsession was with her money, which, she insisted, many enemies were determined to take away from her and put to dark uses. Her father had left her a comfortable inheritance but, since she considered the money to be in such a hazardous position, she refused to spend any of it and filled her time moving her accounts—no one but she knew how many she had—from bank to bank. For a while, Sally lived with her brother-in-law Jacob de Leon in Charleston, but she was unhappy there and insisted on returning to New York "to see after her money." She set sail from Charleston on a ship called the *Rose-in-Bloom*, and it was an agonizing voyage. She was mistreated at sea, she claimed, by the ship's captain, was given short rations and bad food, and, instead of a private stateroom, was placed in a cabin with another woman and a child. The woman, Sally complained, was "of a certain character." In New York, Sally—and her complaints—went to live with Harmon Hendricks and his brood, a large and not entirely happy family.

There were difficulties of other sorts. By 1793, yellow fever had become an annual blight in both Philadelphia and New York, and, when it made its summer appearance, Harmon Hendricks was forced to close his copper mill and all business came to a standstill. "It carries off 60 a day," he wrote in 1805. New Yorkers were baffled by the disease, and a variety of theories as to its cause were advanced. Harmon Hendricks wrote that he believed "trade with the French Islands of the West Indies" was indirectly responsible, and that beef stored in warehouses for this trade had putrefied and somehow made the air contagious and unfit to breathe. He pointed out that people in the neighborhoods of the warehouses—which, of course, were not located in the tidiest parts of town—fell victims first. He was able to make a convincing argument of this, and, that same year, during the height of the plague, five thousand barrels of beef were dumped into the Hudson River. Those New Yorkers who could afford to fled north to the "Village of Greenwich" each year when the fever began to rage and, of course, those who were already infected by the mosquito that caused it took the disease with them.

But, for all his business and family ups and downs, Harmon Hendricks was able to establish himself as one of the East's most important merchant-manufacturers. By 1812, he was rich enough to make his celebrated offer of a loan to the government to finance its war with the British. By 1825, he had his own bank and was also a director of the Hartford Bank (which would tactfully ask "for a reply by Sunday mail if not trespassing on your Sabbath"). He also acquired considerable real estate. In addition to the New Jersey plant, he owned from Twentieth to Twenty-second streets between Sixth and Seventh avenues in Manhattan, and also thirty acres along Broadway. He continued to sell copper for the bottoms of stills and the boilers of ships, and to the United States mint for coins, while making loans in the hundreds of thousands of dollars. He also established the Hendricks family socially, and was a member of the elite Union Club. Harmon Hendricks died in 1838. Several years later, Joseph Scoville, in *The Old Merchants of New York City,* wrote:

> Mr. Hendricks was a born New Yorker, of the Jewish persuasion—honest, upright, prudent, and a very cautious man. . . . He died immensely rich, leaving over three millions of dollars. . . . His heirs are worth at least seven millions. . . . With all the revulsions in trade, the credit of the house for half a century has never been questioned, either in this country or in Europe, and today in Wall Street their obligations would sell quite as readily as government securities bearing the same rates of interest. No man stood higher in this community while he lived, and no man left a memory more revered than Harmon Hendricks.

He also left three strong sons—Uriah II, Henry, and Montague—all eager to carry on his scattered enterprises.

And he left a more important heritage in terms of values that would come to be a preoccupation among the Jewish first families as they moved to positions of money and social acceptance. As Harmon Hendricks' little daughter Roselane put it in 1834, when she was fourteen years old, in her copybook of "Daily Compositions," written in a careful schoolgirlish hand: "Education is one of the most important subjects to which our attention can be directed. It is to education alone that we are indebted for the formation of our minds, the improvement of our understandings, and the developing of our faculties. . . . It is education which elevates our mind towards that Great Being from whence every good flows."

13.

THE FIREBRAND

WHAT the American Jewish community required was a man to serve as its conscience. At least this was the contention of young Uriah Phillips Levy of Philadelphia, who seems to have decided at a very early age that he would fill that role. To him it was a question of assimilation—and loss of all that it meant to be a Sephardic Jew—or of continuity, and he placed tremendous value on the latter. He thoroughly disapproved of what he had heard was going on in cities such as New Orleans, and of men such as Judah Touro, who were Jews with only half their hearts. He disapproved of fellow Philadelphians such as the Franks girls, who seemed not only to care nothing about their country but to care less about their faith, being bent apparently only on marrying titled Englishmen. He disapproved of his Levy cousins Samson, Benjamin, and Nathan—the latter had been David Franks's partner—who danced at the Assembly, joined Christian clubs, and paid only lip service to their noble heritage. Their children were all marrying Christians and converting. Uriah Phillips Levy believed that American Jews needed Great Men—the kind who would stand up foursquarely as *Americans,* and just as foursquarely as *Jews,* who would assume positions of leadership in American institutions, but on their own Jewish terms. It was a large order to give to an already seriously fragmented and disunified group of people, but Uriah Levy gave it. He was small in stature, but his ego was more vast than the whole of the new republic. Equally sizable was the chip that Uriah Levy carried, through most of his life, on his diminutive shoulder.

To be a crusader, a setter-to-rights, he regarded as part of his birthright. He was, after all, a Philadelphia Levy. His family, Uriah Levy felt, were in no way to be taken lightly. After all, George Washington had been at his grandparents' wedding. His great-great-grandfather had been the personal physician to King John V of Portugal. The Levy family had made all the proper in-the-group marriages. One of Uriah's sisters had married a Hendricks, another a Lopez—one of Aaron Lopez' West Indian cousins. Though Uriah's family was sometimes referred to as "the poor branch" (the Samson Levys were considerably richer), the Levys were nothing if not proud.

In 1806, when Uriah Levy announced that he intended to embark upon a naval career, he was barely fourteen years old. He had already learned to identify, from their silhouettes, the names and flags of all the ships that entered and departed Philadelphia harbor. He first signed on as a cabin boy, with duties, among other things, of making up the captain's bunk. By autumn of the following year, pressures were building toward the War of 1812, and President Jefferson declared an embargo on all American trade with Europe. This meant that the shipping industry fell idle, and Uriah used this time to attend a navigation school in Philadelphia, where it was quickly apparent that he was brilliant.

The American Navy, at this time, was closely modeled after the British. Its officer class consisted of men with old-school ties, who all "knew" each other, who regarded themselves as "gentlemen." U.S. naval officers, in other words, constituted a kind of club, with rules and rituals and membership requirements that were inflexible. No Jew had ever been a U.S. naval officer, and it was unthinkable that one should ever wish or try to be. Uriah Levy had chosen for his arena the institution of American life where the Jew's role had always been the weakest, the most capitulating, where Jews had traditionally been given the least power and the meanest jobs.

In 1809, the Embargo Act was lifted, and Uriah Levy —now a naval school graduate—was back in service. It wasn't long before he had his first run-in with the power structure.

In the years between the two wars, British impressment gangs prowled the streets of American port cities looking for susceptible young men whom they could literally shanghai into the British Navy. American men who carried the proper documents were usually immune from this sort of danger, however, and Uriah Levy had naturally taken pains to have his "protection certificate" up to date and in order. As a result, when the cry of "Press gang!" rang through a Philadelphia tavern one afternoon—and most of the young men in the place headed quickly for the back door—Uriah Levy remained calm, sipping his coffee.

A squad of British marines, in white breeches and blue coats, with tall red plumes sprouting from fat shakos, marched into the room with rifles at port, and demanded to see Uriah's credentials. Uriah withdrew his certificate from his breast pocket. One of the marines took the certificate, scanned it, looked at Uriah, and said, "You don't look like an American to me. You look like a Jew."

Uriah replied coolly, "I am an American and a Jew."

"If the Americans have Jew peddlers manning their ships, it's no wonder they sail so badly," the sergeant said.

The Levy temper took over. Uriah immediately doubled his fist and struck the British sergeant in the jaw. A second member of the press gang promptly raised his rifle butt and felled Uriah with a single blow. When he regained consciousness, Uriah Levy was in the brig of a British cutter named the *Vermyra,* bound for Jamaica.

Uriah spent several miserable weeks slaving as a deckhand on the British ship. He was repeatedly ordered to be sworn into His Majesty's Navy, and each time refused with the polite and formal statement: "Sir, I cannot take the oath. I am an American and I cannot swear allegiance to your king. And I am a Hebrew, and do not swear on your testament, or with my head uncovered." Obviously, the commander of the *Vermyra* realized he had a somewhat unusual situation on his hands. Possibly his uncertainty as to what a Jew actually was caused him to treat Uriah Levy with some deference. The young man's stiff and haughty attitude, and carefully phrased responses, hinted that the captain was in the presence of a Personage. At Jamaica, Uriah was permitted an audience with Sir Alexander Cochrane—the Briton who, a few years later, would order the city of Washington, D.C., put to the torch. Uriah, however, found Sir Alexander sympathetic and disapproving of the practice of impressment. Sir Alexander looked over Uriah's papers, said that they appeared to be authentic, and announced that Uriah could be released provided he made his own way back to the United States. Within a few weeks, he was back in Philadelphia again.

In 1811, Uriah Levy had saved enough money to purchase a one-third interest in a 138-ton schooner named the *George Washington*—from the first names of his other partners, George Mesoncort and Washington Garrison. Levy was designated the ship's master. "By this time," he wrote, with unfailingly breezy self-confidence, in his memoirs, "I had passed through every grade of service—cabin boy, ordinary seaman, able-bodied seaman, boatswain, third, second, and first mates, to that of captain. By means of my eight years' experience and instruction afloat and ashore, I had become familiar with every part of my profession—from the sculling of the compass to the taking of the altitude of the sun; from the splicing of a rope to the fishing of a mainmast; from the holding of a reel to the heaving to of a ship in a gale of wind." He was perhaps the first commander in the history of American shipping to nail a mezuzah outside his cabin door; it was a gift from his proud Jewish mother. When he took command of the *George Washington*, Uriah Levy was only nineteen years old.

His first command involved a cargo of corn, which Uriah carried to the Canary Islands and sold for 2,500 Spanish dollars. He then took on a second cargo of Canary wine and headed for the Cape Verde Islands, off the coast of Africa.

When he arrived at the Isle of May in the Cape Verde group, Levy anchored and began what turned out to be an extended stay. He remained at anchor offshore nearly three weeks all told, and in his copious memoirs he never satisfactorily explained the reasons for his stay—nor why, inexplicably, he never attempted to unload his wine. Did he spend these weeks studying the slave trade? Possibly. The Cape Verde Islands lie off Africa's western coastal bulge, along which was strung the chain of slaving "castles." During his stay, Levy became friendly with another American captain, Levi Joy, and the two men spent considerable time together. Captain Joy was definitely involved in the slave trade, and might have been regarded as a certain kind of expert at it. He and Uriah Levy met frequently ashore for meals and exchanged visits on each other's ships. What did they talk about? It is impossible to say, and hard to know what Uriah's feelings about the slave trade might have been, because his visit to the Isle of May was terminated in dramatic fashion.

At dinner one night aboard Captain Joy's ship, Uriah was suddenly interrupted by an excited pair of his crewmen, who clambered on board from the *George Washington*'s dinghy, crying, "Sir, your ship has been stolen!" Uriah rushed to the rail and watched as his ship, under full sail, disappeared over the horizon. It was the last he ever saw of her. A treacherous first mate and a couple of accomplices among the crew had plotted the piracy. With them went all of Uriah Levy's Spanish dollars, and all his casks of Canary Island wine. By the time he made his way home, an impoverished maritime hitchhiker, America was at war with England for a second time.

For his war service, Uriah Levy had two choices. He could sign on a privateer—an often lucrative occupation, particularly if one was successful at capturing enemy ships and splitting up the booty—or he could join the United States Navy as a sailing master, at a modest forty dollars a month. Though it afforded "little prospect of promotion and little gain," as he put it, the Navy "furnished the best proof of love to my country." Also, this was clearly where he was aiming. On October 21, 1812, after a visit to a Boston tailor, Uriah Phillips Levy made his first appearance in the full uniform of the United States Navy as it was in the War of 1812: "A dark blue double-breasted coat, with a rolling collar with two loops of gold lace on each side; blue woolen pantaloons and white stockings; black silk cravat with a white shirt, and a black cocked hat."

He cut a dashing figure, for he was slim and well built, with dark hair, curling sideburns, and a perfectly clipped and curled handlebar moustache. His earliest naval assignments took him frequently to Manhattan, where he attended synagogue at Shearith Israel, was entertained at the best teas and dinner dances, and was frequently seen strolling with well-placed young ladies along State Street and Battery Walk. In New York he heard rumors that the brig *Argus,* which had been anchored in the bay for several months, was preparing to break the British blockade. Uriah borrowed a rowboat, rowed over to the *Argus,* and presented himself to her commander. "Knowing that the cruise of the *Argus* could not fail to be a stirring one," he wrote, "and hoping she might meet the enemy in such circumstances as to permit a battle, I sought and obtained permission to join her as a volunteer."

The career of the *Argus* has become one of the greatest in the annals of U.S. naval history. Her first task, with Uriah aboard, was to carry—through the blockade—America's new minister to France, William H. Crawford. During the crossing, Levy was able, as he put it, "to gain the confidence and friendship of this eminent and most upright man." This friendship was to stand Levy in good stead later on.

After depositing Crawford on the coast of France, the *Argus* went on to become "the dreaded ghost ship," the raider that haunted the English and Bristol channels, that cruised the English and Irish coasts, attacking and destroying much larger ships, the ship whose very name was said to strike terror in the hearts of British sailors. At one point, with Uriah Levy at the helm, the *Argus* found itself—at dawn, in heavy fog—in the middle of a British squadron. Ghostlike, it made its way through and was not spotted until it was out of reach of the enemy cannon. In its many gory encounters, the decks of the *Argus* were spread with wet sand so that the fighting crew of the "phantom raider" would not slither in the blood. When the *Argus* was finally captured, the ship was held in such respect that its crew was greeted with three cheers by the British. The final battle was "kept up with great spirit on both sides," and when the captain, who lost his leg in the encounter, was captured and taken to Britain, he became a kind of folk hero during the several months before he died of his wounds, uttering to his men, "God bless you, my lads, we shall not meet again."

Unfortunately, Uriah had no part in these final glories. One of the ships that the *Argus* had overtaken carried a cargo of sugar, which was considered a bit too valuable to be put to the torch at sea. Uriah Levy was assigned to take her and her sugar across the channel to France. A day later, the new ship, heavy with sugar, virtually unarmed, encountered a British merchantman with eight gun carronades on each side and long guns forward and amidships. To defend the little ship was hopeless. Uriah surrendered and was carried off to England, and to Dartmoor Prison.

Charles Andrews, a prisoner at Dartmoor for three years, wrote:

Any man sent to Dartmoor might have exclaimed:
"Hail, horrors! Hail, thou profoundest hell!
Receive thy new possessor."
For any man ordered to this prison counted himself lost.

A Philadelphia gentleman by upbringing, a Jewish aristocrat by instinct, Uriah worked at keeping up his health and his spirits. The winter of 1813–1814, which he spent at Dartmoor, was one of the hardest in British history, and the Thames froze solidly to the bottom. Levy was confined at Dartmoor for sixteen months and, by the time he was released, in an exchange of British and American prisoners, the war was over.

At Dartmoor, he had accomplished a few things. He had taught himself French, with the help of French prisoners. He had learned to fence. He had had a book, the *New American Practical Navigator,* which he read over and over again. But one thing he had most wanted to do in prison he had been unable to do. He had tried to organize a Jewish congregation. But Jewish law requires that there be a minyan, or quorum, of at least ten Jews before the Sabbath or any public prayer can be celebrated. Uriah could find only four at Dartmoor.

Back home again in Philadelphia, a friend took Uriah Levy aside and counseled him not to continue his Navy career in peacetime. "Nine out of ten of your superiors may not care a fig that you are a Jew," the friend warned him. "But the tenth may make your life a hell." Uriah, however, was by now a man with a mission. He struck a pose and replied, according to his memoirs: "What will be the future of our Navy if others such as I refuse to serve because of the prejudices of a few? There will be other Hebrews, in times to come, of whom America will have need. By serving myself, I will help give them a chance to serve."*

* Uriah Levy's style of speech, which sounds a little pompous, is, we must remember, the speaker's recollection—and reconstruction—of it years later, when he could devote himself to his memoirs. He may not have spoken in precisely these words, but doubtless they express his true sentiments at the time.

He was ready for his next round with the Establishment, and he did not have long to wait. Dancing in full uniform at Philadelphia's Patriots' Ball, he brushed shoulders accidentally with a young naval officer, Lieutenant William Potter. Or was it an accident? A few minutes later, Lieutenant Potter collided with him again, this time with more force. Moments later, the lieutenant crashed into Levy and his partner a third time. Uriah turned and smartly slapped the lieutenant across the face. An enlisted man had struck an officer. "You damned Jew!" Potter cried. A crowd gathered, and several of Potter's fellow officers, murmuring that Potter had had too much to drink, led him off the floor while he continued to shout insults and obscenities. The music resumed, Levy and his partner returned to the floor, and Uriah assumed that the incident was over. The next morning, however, an emissary from Lieutenant Potter appeared on board Uriah's ship, the *Franklin*, carrying a written challenge to a duel.

Dueling had become extremely fashionable in the United States. Duels were fought for the slightest of excuses, and an elaborate framework of rules and ritual grew up around them. Technically against the law, dueling existed in a kind of limbo within the law, with its own, unwritten set of statutes.

Law cases involving deaths through dueling had also to contend with the mystical duelists' code. And, meanwhile, all the best people dueled. In the fifty years between 1798 and 1848, deaths from dueling were two-thirds the number of those from wars, and 20 percent of those who fought in duels were killed. Perhaps one of the charms of dueling was that when a duel was over, both combatants—the victor and the loser—were elevated to the rank of heroes. To have fought a duel—whether to have won or lost— was one of a man's surest ways to achieve social success.

Uriah Levy was not at all anxious to fight a duel over the matter of a dance-floor insult from a drunken lieutenant. But when he demurred, offering to shake hands with Potter and forget the whole thing, he was warned that if he did so he would be labeled a coward. And it was true, according to the code duello, that "a man who makes arms his profession cannot with honor decline an invitation from a professional or social equal." Uriah wrote later that he "wanted to be the first Jew to rise to high rank in the Navy, not be the first Jewish officer killed in a duel." But the code left him no way out. A date was selected, seconds were chosen. The weapons were agreed upon: pistols.

When the date and hour arrived, a sizable audience had gathered. There were a number of Uriah's shipmates off the *Franklin*, an equal number of friends and fellow officers of Potter, the two men's seconds and their friends, the mandatory physician, a judge, and a crowd of Philadelphians who had come out to see the show. Thus what happened is well attested to by witnesses. A distance of twenty paces was chosen. This was somewhat farther apart than most duelists elected to stand. Ten paces was a commoner stand-off distance, and even shorter distances—of two paces, or even one—were frequently selected, with the result that both duelists, firing at each other from arm's length, were virtually guaranteed death. But both Levy and Potter were rated as excellent shots, and so the greater stretch of ground between them may have been regarded as a test of marksmanship. The judge asked each man whether he had anything to say. Uriah Levy asked permission to utter a Hebrew prayer, the Shema, and then in a characteristic gesture said: "I also wish to state that, although I am a crack shot, I shall not fire at my opponent. I suggest it would be wiser if this ridiculous affair be abandoned." "Coward!" Potter shouted in reply. "Gentlemen, no further words," the judge instructed, and began his count.

Both men turned to face each other. Potter fired first, missing Uriah widely. Uriah then raised his arm straight up and fired a bullet into the air. The duel might have ended there, for Potter could have considered his honor satisfied, but Uriah's gesture clearly had enraged him. He began reloading his pistol for a second round and Uriah, according to the code, was required to do the same. The second volley ended with the same results, Potter missing his mark and Uriah firing skyward. Now, like a man possessed, Lieutenant Potter began reloading a third time and, perhaps because his fury was affecting his aim, the third series of shots was a repetition of the first two. But clearly the affair had gone too far for sanity, and the seconds and a number of Potter's friends rushed in to try to persuade him to abandon the duel "with honor," but he would have none of it. For a fourth time he reloaded and fired at Uriah, missing again. On Uriah's side of the field, his friends shouted to him to kill Potter, but once again Uriah merely reached into the air and fired. He then cried out to Potter's aides, "Gentlemen, stop him or I must!"

But Lieutenant Potter was at this point beyond control. He reloaded for a fifth shot and, screaming, "Stand back! I mean to have his life!" fired again, nicking Uriah's left ear. Blood spurted across his face and shoulder. This time, Uriah held his fire altogether. Then, as Potter reloaded for a sixth shot, Uriah's limits of patience and temper were reached. Shouting, "Very well, I'll spoil his dancing," Uriah for the first time took aim and fired at his opponent. From his remark about dancing, the audience assumed that Uriah Levy intended to shoot the lieutenant in the leg. But the bullet struck him in the chest, Lieutenant Potter fell to the ground without a word, and was immediately pronounced dead by the doctor.

It was, everyone agreed, an extraordinary duel. Potter had behaved extraordinarily badly, and Levy had conducted himself extraordinarily well. There were, however, some unfortunate realities to be faced. In the eyes of the law, Uriah Phillips Levy had committed a murder. In the eyes of the United States Navy, an important bylaw of the club had been breached. An enlisted man—a mere sailing master—had not only slapped, but now had killed, an officer. No one, least of all Uriah Levy, was sure how this might affect a man whose ambition was already "to rise to high rank in the Navy," and to set an example for future Jews to follow.

The affair created a stir of major proportions in Philadelphia. The press praised him for the way "Levy fired shots in the air, and then for the first time fired at his antagonist, and with the unerring certainty of a true marksman, made him bite the dust." Uriah was particularly idolized by his fellow crew members on the *Franklin.* But there was an element, and a strong one, in Philadelphia that was less than happy with the outcome of the duel, and said so. Lieutenant Potter might have been a boor and a drunk, but he had been a popular young man about Philadelphia parties. Levy might have been astonishingly coolheaded and brave, but he was, despite his proper connections, nonetheless—to some—an "outsider." It was, after all, a case of a Jew having killed a Christian. The Navy commodore investigating the episode decided that Uriah had been neither the provocator nor the aggressor in the case, and dismissed it without action. But the Philadelphia grand jury felt otherwise, and handed down an indictment for "making a challenge to a duel."

Almost immediately, Uriah was in another difficulty. One Sunday morning shortly after the duel, he walked into the wardroom aboard the *Franklin* for breakfast. In one corner of the room sat a certain Lieutenant Bond, breakfasting with two other officers. Uriah seated himself at a table on the opposite side of the room. The table was cluttered with used crockery and partly filled coffee cups, and Uriah asked a passing cabin boy to please clear it for him. Instantly, Lieutenant Bond was on his feet shouting that Uriah had no right to give orders to cabin boys. Uriah replied that he had given no orders, but had merely asked that the table be cleared. Bond answered that he had heard Uriah order the cabin boy to bring him breakfast. Uriah replied that he had not, and suddenly, amid shouts of "Liar!" "No gentleman!" and "Dictator!" the fight was on. Both men were on their feet, and it took the other two officers in the room plus two cabin boys to prevent them from coming to blows. And presently Bond was calling Uriah a "damned Jew."

In the lengthy transcript of the court-martial that followed—a trial which, in Navy history, has been called "the Breakfast Court Martial" and "the Tempest in the Coffee Cups"—there is endless testimony not only about who accused whom of what, but also about how many dishes were on the table at the time, their degree of dirtiness, whether soiled coffee cups or tea cups were involved, and what the various participants in the fracas were wearing. It is hard to see why all this was taken so seriously, and yet it was. Uriah made a long and impassioned speech in which he added patriotism, honor, manliness, and duty to the other issues in the case. It ended at last in a draw. Both Uriah and Lieutenant Bond were ordered reprimanded by the Secretary of the Navy for un-naval behavior.

But while all this trivial and generally undignified business was going on, things were looking up for Uriah Levy again. In Philadelphia, the dueling case had come to trial in the civilian court and, despite the fact that public sentiment had been running against him, Uriah had been acquitted by the jury. The foreman, in fact, had risen from the jury box to add to its decision that "any man brave enough to fire in the air and let his opponent take deadly aim at him, deserved his life."

And so, despite the fact that naval court-martial proceedings were under way against him, Uriah took the unusual step of applying for a commission in the Navy. He was applying under the rule which stated that "Masters of extraordinary merit, and for extraordinary services, may be promoted to Lieutenant." His friends who saw him as a man involved in two actions—one civil and one military —begged him to wait until the fuss had died down. But Uriah, confident of his extraordinary capabilities, plunged ahead. His commission was signed by President Monroe on March 5, 1817. The U.S. Navy had a Jewish officer at last.

The first thing Uriah did when he had donned his gold-fringed lieutenant's epaulets was to have his portrait painted by Thomas Sully. Sully always romanticized his subjects—which was certainly the key to his great popularity—and generously overlooked their physical shortcomings. So we must not take the Sully portrait of Uriah Levy entirely at face value. But it portrays a striking figure. Uriah's face in the portrait is the face of a boy—he was twenty-five that year—clean-jawed, with a straight nose, wide forehead, large and arresting black eyes, a mop of dark curly hair, and dashing Rhett Butler sideburns. Sully exaggerates Uriah's slight build so that his figure appears almost girl-like, frail and delicate, the slim legs almost spidery. Yet as he stands in the portrait, arms folded across his chest, the picture pulses with haughtiness, arrogance, defiance. The picture has been described as making Uriah Levy look "a little vain, more than a little handsome, and very determined."

The officer corps of the United States Navy was not at all sure how it wished to treat this brash young upstart. The first few months of Uriah's lieutenancy were particularly difficult for him aboard his ship, the *Franklin*. A former enlisted man was, after all, now an officer. A man who had taken commands was now giving them. The *Franklin*'s other officers, with whom Uriah had once worked cheerfully, as well as the enlisted men, who had once been his equals, all looked at him now with distrust and disdain. The friends who had cheered him in his duel and in the ordeal after it were suddenly chilly and aloof. Uriah had a long voyage to England, and then to Sicily, in this hostile atmosphere, before he was notified that he was to be transferred to the frigate *United States.*

The *United States* was one of the Navy's most prestigious addresses. The ship had been the heroine of several important battles in the 1812 war and she had, in the process, become known as a "gentlemen's ship." Nowhere was the clublike nature of the Navy more apparent. The great Stephen Decatur ("our country, right or wrong") had been the *United States'*s commander when the ship had overcome and captured H.M.S. *Macedonian,* and now she was captained by the equally aristocratic William Crane, a man of whom it was said that he "believed his blood ran bluer than all the rest."

The day before Uriah was to report, Captain Crane dispatched a long letter to Commodore Charles Stewart, in charge of the Navy's Mediterranean Fleet. In it, Captain Crane argued vaguely about Uriah being a "disturbing influence," and suggested that he might create "disharmony" among the ship's other officers. In concluding the letter he said flatly: "Considerations of a personal nature render Lieutenant Levy particularly objectionable, and I trust he will not be forced on me."

It is seldom in the Navy that an officer attempts to tell a superior what to do. But Captain Crane's letter displays a great deal of confidence, and it is likely that he thought he stood a good chance of getting his way. And he may have. Though the commodore is said to have been "boiling mad" at Crane's note, his reply—signed "Your obedient servant"—is both a lengthy and a mealymouthed affair, when one would have thought that a terse note of reprimand would have been in order. It is clear that Commodore Stewart realized that he was involved in a ticklish situation, and that Lieutenant Levy's Jewishness was what it was all about. In his reply, Commodore Stewart "regrets exceedingly" having to disappoint his captain and, after several conciliatory paragraphs, he adds: "Should you be possessed of a knowledge of any conduct on the part of Lieutenant Levy which would render him unworthy of the commission he holds, I would at the request of any commander represent it to the government. As your letter contains no specific notice of his misconduct, I can find nothing therein whereupon to find a reason for countermanding the order for changing his destination."

The commodore showed both Crane's and his own letter to Uriah, assured him that "everything would be all right," and the next morning Uriah set off to present himself to his new commander. Navy protocol required that an arriving officer pay two visits to his captain—the first, briefly and formally to present his orders, and the second, a longer social visit to be carried out within forty-eight hours. But when Uriah was admitted to his cabin, Captain Crane, without even looking up from his desk, said, "The *United States* has as many officers as I need or want." He ordered that Uriah be escorted off his ship and back to the *Franklin*. Now Crane was not merely advising, but defying, a superior officer.

This, it turned out, was too much for the commodore, who now wrote:

Sir:
    Lt. U. P. Levy will report to you for duty on board the frigate *United States* under your command.

    It is not without regret that a second order is found necessary to change the position of one officer in this squadron.

CHARLES STEWART

In humiliating fashion, Uriah was rowed back to the *United States* to present his orders a second time. Crane kept him waiting outside his cabin for over two hours. Then, ordering him in, Crane glanced at the letter, handed it back to Uriah, and muttered, "So be it." He returned to his paperwork. He did not so much as rise, offer a handshake, or even return Uriah's salute. Uriah carried his gear to the wardroom. There he was told by another officer—there were only eight others aboard—that theirs had been "a very pleasant and harmonious officers' mess," until now.

It was aboard the *United States* that Uriah was required to witness his first flogging. The practice was commonplace. American naval regulations were based on the British Articles of War, which dated back to the earliest days of the Restoration, when they had been formulated by the Duke of York, Lord High Admiral of the British Navy, who later became King James II. Flogging was advocated as the most practical way to maintain discipline and order on shipboard, and its benefits had been touted by commanders for generations. "Low company," Commodore Edward Thompson had written, "is the bane of all young men, but in a man-of-war you have the collected filth of jails. The scenes of horror and infamy on board are many." Thus, the horror of flogging was merely another to be endured. By the nineteenth century, when sailors stripped to the waist to work, it was not remarkable to see that the backs of many of them were solidly ridged and bubbled with scar tissue.

Often a flogging was so severe as to destroy the muscle tissue of a man's back and shoulders, thus making him unable to work and useless to the Navy. A captain was given great latitude in terms of meting out the penalty and, needless to say, the practice was often abused by sadistic commanders. It was prescribed for such misdeeds as "keeping low company"—a euphemism for drunkenness—for profanity, and "For Unlawful Carnal Knowledge."* Flogging could also be ordered for such relatively minor offenses as "spitting in the deck," or for "looking sullen." There were also more severe punishments available. Keelhauling was still practiced in the Navy and, for the crime of murder, a man might be tied to the mouth of a cannon. Then the cannon was fired.

Uriah had been aboard the *United States* only a few weeks when Captain Crane issued the order for all hands to appear on deck. A middle-aged gunner's mate had come back from shoreleave drunk, and had been noisy and abusive. Thirty lashes had been ordered, a relatively moderate sentence. Uriah now saw how, over the centuries, flogging had been perfected to the point where it was almost an art form of its own. The first few blows of the lash softened the muscles of the back. The fourth or fifth blow broke the skin. Then an expert with the lash could direct his blows so that they fell in a symmetrical crisscross pattern, so that the flesh of the back was cut in equal diamond-shaped pieces. An alternate stood by in case the first man wielding the lash grew tired. Also, several extra "cats" were provided so that when one of them grew too slippery from blood to be gripped, another could be substituted. Men had been known to remain standing through as many as sixty strokes of the lash, but the gunner's mate, not young, fainted several times during his ordeal, and was

---

* The phrase "For Unlawful Carnal Knowledge"—abbreviated with the letters "F.U.C.K." in ships' logbooks, next to records of punishments—thus contributed a vivid four-letter word to the English language.

unconscious when it was over. He was at last cut down from the rack where he had been tied, spread-eagled, and pails of salt water were poured over his raw and bleeding flesh.

Uriah, sickened by the hideous spectacle, nonetheless forced himself to watch it, never once diverting his eyes. For weeks after the experience, he could talk of nothing else but the brutality of flogging as a punishment. This did little to further endear him to his fellow officers. Not only was he a Jew, but there was also something subversive about him. It was whispered that Uriah Levy disapproved of Navy discipline, but Uriah had found another crusade.

Uriah had been able to make only one friend on the ship, its executive officer, a young man named Thomas Catesby Jones, who had counseled him: "Do your duty as an officer and a gentleman. Be civil to all, and the first man who pursues a different course to you, call him to a strict and proper account." It was good advice, but advice that was difficult for Uriah to follow. One night, for example, when Uriah was standing watch on deck, he saw two young cabin boys dash up a companionway, pursued, it appeared, by a boatswain's mate named Porter, who held what looked like a whip in his hand. When Uriah halted Porter, and asked him why he was whipping the boys, Porter answered him in what Uriah considered an "insolent and mocking" tone. Uriah slapped Porter across the cheek with the back of his hand. Within an hour, Uriah was called before his superior officers and—in the presence of Porter—was asked to explain his actions. Uriah considered *this* a severe breach of Navy etiquette, and cried out, "Sir, I am not to be called to account in this way in front of a boatswain!" Warned that he was being disrespectful, Uriah replied, "And you, sir, are treating me in an equally disrespectful manner." Uriah was then ordered to his cabin and warned, "You will hear more of this." He did—his second court-martial, in which he was charged with disobedience of orders, contempt of a superior officer, and unofficerlike conduct. The president of the court-martial was Captain Crane, a circumstance not likely to benefit the defendant. He was found guilty on all three charges and sentenced to be "dismissed from the U.S.S. Frigate *United States* and not allowed to serve on board."

Actually, such a sentence—over such a petty matter—was so unusual as to be considered irregular, and when the case was reviewed by the naval commander in chief, President James Monroe reversed the sentence. But when' this news reached Uriah Levy he was already in trouble again over a matter that was, if anything, even more trifling. This time it was a rowboat. Lieutenant Levy had ordered a boat to row him ashore. Told that his boat was ready, he arrived on deck. When he was about to board the boat, another lieutenant, named Williamson, told him the boat was not his. Uriah insisted it was. Williamson repeated that it wasn't. Presently both men were shouting epithets at each other, including "Liar!" "Scoundrel!" "Rascal!" "Coward!" and so on. In a rage, Uriah went back to his cabin and dashed off the following note to Williamson:

Sir:
The attack which you were pleased to make on my feelings this afternoon, in saying I prevaricated, thereby insulting me in the grossest manner without any cause on my part, demands that you should make such concessions as the case requires before these gentlemen in whose presence I was insulted—or to have a personal interview tomorrow morning at the Navy Yard, at which time, if you please, I expect a direct answer.

Uriah delivered the note to Williamson's cabin in person. The lieutenant flung the note, unread, in Uriah's face and slammed the door.

Brandishing his letter, Uriah went ashore that night, according to subsequent testimony, into "taverns and divers places," reading the letter to anyone who would listen, giving a high-pitched account of the rowboat incident, and, in the process, he "wickedly and maliciously uttered and published false, slanderous, scandalous, and opprobrious words concerning Lt. Williamson, including poltroon, coward, and scoundrel, as well as rogue and rascal." This was very bad Navy form. Lieutenant Williamson took action the following morning, and court-martial number three was under way. Uriah was charged with "using provoking and reproachful words, treating his superior officer with contempt, and teaching others who chose to learn from his example to make use of falsehood as an easy convenience, with scandalous conduct tending to the destruction of good morals, and attempting to leave the ship without permission from the officer of the deck." These were much more serious charges than any that had been leveled against him before, and to these was added an even graver one. He was accused of "being addicted to the vice of lying."

For his defense, he turned to the only course that seemed open to him. He accused his fellow officers of anti-Semitism. At the end of his trial, he took the stand and said:

> I am of the faith which has never been endured in Christendom 'til the Constitution of the United States raised us to a level with our fellow citizens of every religious denomination. I need not apprise you that I have been designated in the language of idle scorn "the Jew!" Perhaps I have been thus reproached by those who recognize neither the God of Moses nor of Christ. May I not say that I have been marked out to common contempt as a Jew until the slow unmoving finger of scorn has drawn a circle round me that includes all friendships and companions and attachments and all the blandishments of life and leaves me isolated and alone in the very midst of society. . . .
>
> To be a Jew as the world now stands is an act of faith that no Christian martyrdom can exceed—for in every corner of the earth but one it consists in this, to be excluded from almost every advantage of society. Although the sufferers of my race have had the trust and confidence of all their Christian Revilers as their commercial agents throughout the world, they have been cut off from some of the most substantial benefits of the social company in Europe. They cannot inherit or devise at law, they could not 'til lately sit as jurors or testify as witnesses. They could not educate their children in their own faith. Children were encouraged to abandon their parents and their God, to rob a father of his estate—a rich Jewess might have been ravished or stolen and the law afforded no remedy—these heart-rending cruel distinctions have been gradually and imperceptibly worn down by the resistless current of time, but they have

in no instance been voluntarily obliterated by an act of Christian charity.

But I beg to make the most solemn appeal to the pure and heavenly spirit of universal toleration that pervades the constitution of the United States in the presence of this court; whether before a court-martial in the American Navy, whoever may be the party arraigned, be he Jew or Gentile, Christian or pagan, shall he not have the justice done him which forms the essential principle of the best maxim of all their code, "Do unto others as ye would have them do unto you."

With its references to "the social company in Europe," and to ravished Jewish maidens, Uriah's speech must have seemed completely beside the point. Though everything he said was true, and though his remarks reveal much of what he was feeling at the time, certainly none of this sank in with the officers of the court-martial. After all, in early-nineteenth-century America, the concept of anti-Semitism, or even of religious prejudice, was such an exotic one—so removed from what most Americans thought about and talked about and read about—that, to the judges hearing Uriah's case, a charge of prejudice seemed a non sequitur.

The court reached a quick and unanimous verdict: guilty. Uriah was sentenced "to be cashiered out of the Naval service of the United States."

It was early spring, 1819. He was only twenty-seven years old, and his Navy career appeared ended. He entered a long period of funk, and for many months he disappeared from sight, refusing to go back to Philadelphia, where he would have to face his family, disgraced. For nearly two years he wandered about Europe. At one point, his widow wrote many years later, he lived in Paris, where "he met a lady of title in whom he became very much interested, and they were very much in love with each other. Lieutenant Levy would have married her, only she refused to return with him to America. But as his one ambition in life was to rise in the navy, he returned to his beloved country unmarried."

He returned to America because an astonishing thing happened. It took twenty-three months for the court-martial proceedings to reach the President's desk for review, but when they did, Monroe once more reversed them, noting that: "Although Lieutenant Levy's conduct merited censure, it is considered that his long suspension from the service has been a sufficient punishment for his offense. The sentence of the court is therefore disapproved, and he is returned to duty."

Once again his honor had been satisfied. On the other hand, he found now that wherever he went his reputation as a hothead had preceded him, and that now he was *expected* to throw tantrums and slap senior officers with gloves. Instead of becoming the conscience of American Jews, the "terrible-tempered Lieutenant Levy" was becoming something of a legendary Navy figure. Uriah found himself good-naturedly teased and goaded about his dueling and multiple courts-martial, and egged into arguments. And so, not surprisingly, it wasn't long before he erupted again.

This time his adversary was a lieutenant named William Weaver. In the presence of one of Uriah's friends, Weaver had called Uriah a "great scoundrel" and a "thoroughgoing rascal." His friend reported these slurs to Uriah, who was typically enraged and who immediately dashed off one of his indignant letters to Weaver. The letter was not answered. A few days later, however, an article, heavy with suggestive italics, appeared in a Washington newspaper:

> If convicted of charges proved, the leniency of naval courts-martial has become proverbial—so that the sitting of a court-martial generally eventuates in a reprimand. If, however, and what is very common, the guilty officer should be *cashiered,* as in a recent *case,* he sets himself to work with *political friends of his tribe,* and loaded with papers, presents himself at Washington, the strong arm of the executive is palsied. *He dare not approve the justly merited sentence;* the culprit is retained.

The allusion was obviously to Uriah. The article was unsigned, but Uriah was able to discover that its author was Weaver.

Uriah's first assignment on being reinstated was to the *Spark,* on duty in the Mediterranean. He boarded the *Spark* in June, 1821, and remained aboard her until the following March, when the ship docked at Charleston, South Carolina. In those intervening months, it seemed, Uriah had done nothing but vilify the character of Lieutenant Weaver, making, to anyone who would listen, such comments as: "Weaver is a coward, a damned rascal, a scoundrel and no gentleman," "Weaver is an errant bastard," and "If I ever run into the damned rascal, I'll tweak his nose." These remarks had made their way to Weaver, now stationed at the Charleston Naval Yard. Uriah, upon debarking, was met with a summons to a court-martial, his fourth, charged with "scandalous conduct—using provoking reproachful words—ungentlemanly conduct—forgery and falsification."

Forgery, of course, was a new charge. It related to the fact that Uriah had carried around a copy of his indignant note to Weaver, with its challenging accusations, had shown the note to many people, whereas Weaver now maintained that he had never received the note, and that it was a forgery. The court found Uriah guilty of scandalous conduct, and noted that "he did suffer others to read a note purporting to be a challenge." The other charges were dropped. The court ordered that Uriah be "publically reprimanded." But the court also scolded Lieutenant Weaver. "The court," the judges wrote, "in passing this sentence, cannot, however, forbear expressing their disapprobation of the behavior of the prosecutor toward the prisoner in so far as the circumstances thereof have come before them in evidence." So Uriah's court-martial number four ended more or less in a draw. But it began to seem as though sooner or later either he or the United States Navy would have to change its ways.

In 1823, Uriah was assigned as second lieutenant on the *Cyane*, which was being transferred from the Mediterranean to the Brazil Squadron. The ship made a slow crossing of the Atlantic, putting in at various West Indies ports before heading for the northern coast of South America. At Rio de Janeiro, the ship anchored for repairs to its mainmast, and Uriah was put in charge of these. Normally, it seemed, such repairs were handled by the executive officer, but the captain had casually commented that Uriah could supervise the repairs as well as anyone. This angered the *Cyane*'s executive officer, William Spencer, and presently word had reached Uriah that Spencer was "out to bring him to his knees."

One afternoon while the repairs were going on, Uriah came aboard carrying a wide slab of Brazilian mahogany with which he intended to build a bookshelf for his cabin. A certain Lieutenant Ellery, a friend of the wounded Spencer, commented in "a sneering tone" that he thought rather little of officers who stole lumber from ships' stores. Uriah replied that he had bought the wood in town, and had the bill of sale in his pocket. Ellery said that he doubted this, since Uriah was known by everyone to be a liar. In a rage, Uriah challenged Ellery to a duel, to which Ellery answered that he would not fight a duel with a man who was not a gentleman. He would, furthermore, report the challenge to the commanding officer.

For several days, the affair simmered, and seemed about to die down until it bubbled up again in another burst of pettishness. In the officers' mess someone said loudly that "some damned fool" had dismissed the steward. "If you meant that for me . . ." Uriah put in quickly, always the first to detect an insult. "Don't speak to me, Levy," said Executive Officer Spencer, "or I'll gag you." Instantly Uriah was on his feet, crying, "If you think you're able, you may try!" And there it was, all over again—shouts of "No gentleman!" "Coward!" "Jew!" In the morning, court-martial number five had been ordered started, with the drearily familiar set of charges against Uriah: "Conduct unbecoming an officer and a gentleman, using provoking and reproachful words, offering to waive rank and fight a duel with Lieutenant Frank Ellery, and, in the presence and hearing of many of the officers of the *Cyane*, inviting William A. Spencer to fight a duel."

Once more the findings were against Uriah, with the curiously worded verdict that he was "Guilty of conduct unbecoming an officer, *but not of a gentleman.*" The sentence was humiliating. He was to be reprimanded "publically on the quarter deck of every vessel of the Navy in commission, and at every Navy Yard in the United States." Uriah retaliated by bringing a counter-suit against William Spencer—and won, with the result that Spencer was suspended from the Navy for a year for "insulting and un-officer-like and ungentlemanly expressions and gestures against the said Uriah P. Levy."

Uriah may have felt himself vindicated. But this action did nothing to endear him in the eyes of his fellow officers. To bring a superior officer to court was something that was not done. At the Philadelphia Navy Yard, Uriah Levy was put "in Coventry"—ostracized and ignored by everyone. Restless and bitter, Uriah applied for a six-month leave of absence. The request was quickly granted and, in granting it, his commanding officer said to Uriah with a little smile, "We would be happy to extend your leave indefinitely."

When his words had sunk in, Uriah said, "It's because I'm a Jew, isn't it, sir?"

"Yes, Levy," the officer said—he did not use "Lieutenant," or even "Mr." "It is."

He had been asked to leave the club. In his long battle with the Navy Establishment, he seemed to have lost the final round.

14.

THE NEW JEWS VERSUS
THE OLD

THERE may have been some in the American Jewish community who approved of Uriah Phillips Levy's well-publicized squabbles with the Navy, and the focus he had managed to bring to bear on the fact of anti-Semitism in the New World. But most did not approve, and felt that Levy's behavior had done the Jews more harm than good. As it is with any problem, it had been easier for Jews to pretend that it did not exist. The Jewish community was still small, and news and opinions within it traveled rapidly. Some of Levy's contemporaries praised him for his insistence on Old Testament justice to the bitter end. To the younger generation, however, he was merely old-fashioned and excessively "stiff-necked." Uriah Phillips Levy had, among his other accomplishments, helped define the split between "old Jews" and "new Jews."

The split was more than generational. The prejudice of the old against the new was also directed at newer immigrants, who were now being looked on as troublemakers. There was nothing new about this particular form of *Jewish* anti-Semitism. Jews have always resented, and looked askance at, Jewish newcomers. "A few of us," to the world's scattered Jewish communities, has always seemed just about enough. In Philadelphia, for example, as early as the 1760's, the Jewish congregation had swelled to such a size, from eager immigrants, that it was considered in "grave danger." Jews rolled their eyes and muttered dark thoughts about an "infestation of Jews" from other lands. Mathias Bush was a partner of David Franks in the candle business, and both men were immigrants to Philadelphia. Yet when Franks traveled to London on business in 1769, he received a letter from Bush bemoaning that "These New Jews are a plague," and beseeching his partner, "Pray prevent what is in your power to hinder any more of that sort to come." Mr. Bush clearly considered himself an Old Jew. He had come to America exactly twenty-five years earlier. And the scale of his alarm can be judged by noting that, at the time of the "infestation," there were no more than thirty Jewish families in Philadelphia.

Quite naturally the newcomers resented the snobbery of the older group—and its prosperity—and so the battle lines were drawn. At one point the squabble in Philadelphia grew to such proportions that families of the refractory new migration held separate services during the high holy days. At the same time, it was charged that the more recent arrivals were not being properly loyal to their faith, and it was certainly true that the newcomers—hungrier, more eager to get on with the business of earning livelihoods for themselves—had less time to spend on piety.

Older families of Philadelphia looked with disapproval at newer Jewish communities springing up in other cities. New Orleans was getting a particularly bad reputation for religious laxity. Why was it, for example, that New Orleans' Jews were having to come, hat in hand, begging for funds to build a synagogue, to the Jewish communities of Philadelphia, New York, and Newport? Why weren't wealthy New Orleans businessmen such as Jacob Hart and Judah Touro—both of whom were sons of great Jewish leaders—willing to contribute money to this cause, and why were they giving instead to Christian philanthropies?

The newer immigrants were poor, they needed baths, they worked as foot peddlers, they spoke with accents. They lacked the social status that the Jewish first families had achieved, the breeding, the education, yet they called themselves brethren. They judged a man by the success of his enterprises rather than by his "engagements with God," as pious people such as Rebecca Gratz would have preferred, yet they called themselves Jews. They were an embarrassment. By the early 1800's, they were threatening to fling the fabric of Jewish society in America apart, threatening the "tribal" feeling that is at the heart of all feelings of Jewishness.

But the real trouble was that most of the "new Jews" were Ashkenazic Jews, from central Europe. They could not trace their ancestry back to Spain and Portugal. The Sephardim pointed out that the Ashkenazim used a different ritual, and they did—somewhat. The pronunciation of Hebrew was slightly different. The Sephardim spoke with a Mediterranean inflection, the accent often falling on the last syllable. (The Sephardim say Yom Kip*pur*, for example, not Yom *Kip*pur, as the Ashkenazim do.) Sephardic ritual also included some Spanish prayers, and Sephardic music—bearing traces of ancient Spanish folk music, reminiscent of flamenco—was distinctive. These differences, which may seem very slight, began to loom as all-important in the 1800's.

The Ashkenazim spoke "heavy, ugly" languages su[ch] as German, and an "abominable garble of German a[nd] Hebrew" called Yiddish, instead of "musical, lyrical" Spa[n]ish and Portuguese. They even looked different, and it w[as] pointed out that German Jews had large, awkward-looki[ng] noses, and lacked the elegant refinement of the high[ly] bred, heart-shaped, olive-skinned Spanish face. But the[ir] greatest difference of all, of course, was that the As[h]kenazim came from countries where to be a Jew was a [dis]grace. The Sephardim descended from lands where, fo[r a] while at least, to be a Jew had been to be a knight i[n] shining armor, a duke or duchess, the king's physician—the proudest thing a man could be. From the beginning, the two groups were like oil and water.

In 1790, a Savannah gentleman named De Leon Norden, of Sephardic stock, had written in his will that "None of the Sheftalls need be present" at his funeral. The Sheftalls were German. Even before that—in 1763, across the sea in France—the Spanish and Portuguese Jews of Bordeaux had succeeded in persuading the king to sign an edict expelling all German and Avignonese Jews from Bordeaux. In America, many of the new arrivals had names containing combinations of the word "schine" or "schien," and so the label "sheeny" was attached to them —an epithet of Sephardic origin. The word was picked up and used generally in the press, and when a fight broke out right in the synagogue in Montreal—with top-hatted gentlemen having at each other with walking sticks and furniture—between old and new Jews, a Montreal newspaper headlined an account of the battle with the words *"Bad Sheenies!"*

Three things were happening, all interconnected, and all at the same time. The Ashkenazim were beginning to out-number the older Sephardim, and it was only a matter of time before majority rule would mean that Ashkenazic ritual would have to prevail in synagogues in most American cities—while the Sephardim who insisted on retaining the old would withdraw into their own tight groups, with doors closed to the Germans. Also the first stirrings of the Reform movement were being felt in the land. Reform—with rebuke for existing forms inherent in the very word—was by its nature incompatible with traditional Sephardic orthodoxy. Reform, an attempt to bring Judaism "up to date," to make Judaism appear to be at home with exist-ing American religious patterns, was attacked by tradi-tionalists as a subversive attempt to "Christianize" Judaism. Under Reform, women would come down from their se-cluded balconies in synagogues, and worship side by side with their husbands. Men would take off their tall silk hats. Synagogues would look more like churches. English would replace Hebrew.

And while all this was happening, the oldest Jewish families were watching with dismay as their children and grandchildren seemed to be slipping away from the faith. It is an ironic fact that the heirs and assigns of men and women who had made such an arduous journey to America in order to preserve their faith should have begun to abandon it once they were here. But that was happening. Grandchildren of old Sephardic families had begun, by the early 1800's, to marry into the Ashkenazic group, but some of them were doing something even worse than that. They were marrying Christians, and converting to Christianity.

The granddaughter of a wealthy Jewish businessman was suing to break her grandfather's will, which provided that she could not partake of a large family trust if she married a non-Jew. She wanted her share of her grand-father's money, none of the clumsy entanglements of his religion, and her Christian fiancé. It might have happened yesterday in Manhattan. It happened in Charleston in 1820. She won her case.

And was something else happening to the Sephardim? Were the long inbred centuries exacting a quirky genetic toll? Certainly, by the nineteenth century, eccentrics were no rarity among the Old Guard, and few families were without their "strange" members. More and more, moving down the laddered generations in Malcolm Stern's huge book, the notation "Insane" appears next to various names, as does the comment "Unmarried." Spinster aunts and bachelor uncles were becoming the rule now, rather than the exception. The families, once so prolific, seemed on the verge of becoming extinct.

15.

THE U.S. NAVY
SURRENDERS AT LAST!

URIAH P. Levy, in the meantime, had been continuing with his crusade to have Jews treated as the equals of Christians. He had gone on with his lecturing and scolding of fellow Jews who took insults lying down, who responded to slurs by turning the other cheek. He was a frequent writer of peppery letters to the editor, and was otherwise securing his reputation as a firebrand. He had also decided—since he no longer had Navy duties to occupy him—that it was time for him to make some money.

New York in the early nineteenth century had become a more important seaport than either Newport or Philadelphia. The completion of the Erie Canal, "linking East to West," in 1825, secured New York's position as the maritime—hence commercial, and hence money—capital of the United States. In that year alone, five hundred new businesses were started in the city, and twelve banks and thirteen marine insurance companies opened their doors. The population topped 150,000, and—an unheard-of thing in America—one of the city newspapers announced that it would publish on Sundays. The Park Theatre declared that it would present grand opera, and number 7 Cherry Street became the first private house in America to be lit by gas.

Maiden Lane, four blocks north of Wall Street, had been the division between the commercial and residential sections of the city. South of Maiden Lane, the city was abustle with business; to the north lay houses with gardens, estates, and farms. Greenwich Village had been a separate village, approached by crossing a stone bridge at

Canal Street, but, by 1825, the commercial part of the city had encroached so far north that it was pointed out that no more than "the width of one block" separated the city from the suburban Village, and the most daring of the speculators prophesied that Broadway would one day extend as far north as Tenth Street. Today, of course, it continues on through the length of Manhattan, through the Bronx, Yonkers, and into Tarrytown. Washington Square, at the northern edge of Greenwich Village, had been the city's potter's field until 1823, when its development into a park was begun and the tall red-brick mansions were built on its perimeter. This helped establish Fifth Avenue—which sprouted from the northern side of the park—as the fashionable residential address it was to become. When Washington Square Park was completed in 1827, it was felt that the city would never reasonably be expected to grow north of Fourteenth Street. Within a year or so, even a Fourteenth Street boundary seemed too constricting. It did not take especial real estate shrewdness to see that Manhattan island, shaped like an elongated footprint and growing upward from the toe, had no way to expand except to the north. It was in this northern real estate that Uriah Levy decided to invest his Navy savings. He bought, in 1828, three rooming houses, two on Duane Street and one on Greenwich Street.

It was quickly clear that his unofficial discharge from Navy duty had put him in the right place at the right time. Within a few months, he was able to sell one of his Duane Street houses for nearly twice what he had paid for it. He bought more real estate, sold it, and bought more, parlaying each deal into something bigger than the last. Such was the booming state of Manhattan real estate that, within just four years, Uriah Levy was a rich man. He began to cut a considerable figure in New York's fledgling society—which had never been the "set thing" it had been in Philadelphia—and was able to afford to turn his affairs over to a staff of assistants and to take off for Europe, where he acquired, among other things, a Savile Row tailor and "a broadcloth frock coat with velvet collar; white satin stock shaped with whalebone; pantaloons of wool and silk jersey; two linen suits; white pleated shirts with gold buttons; light colored fawn gloves, a walking stick with ivory knob," according to his tailor's bill.

Rich almost overnight, still a bachelor—and, it began

to seem, a confirmed one—Uriah was now able to indulge himself in personal whims and fancies, and, after his rejection from the Navy, this must have given him a certain amount of personal satisfaction. One of his enthusiasms was Thomas Jefferson, whom he regarded as "one of the greatest men in history. . . . He did much to mold our Republic in a form in which a man's *religion* does not make him ineligible for political or governmental life." In the summer of 1833, he conceived the idea of personally commissioning a statue of Jefferson and presenting it to the United States government. It was a totally new concept. Individuals had never before given statues of American heroes to the public. Perhaps Uriah felt that by celebrating Jefferson—the champion of tolerance—in this public way he could get back at the United States Navy for its snubs. In any case, in Paris Uriah gave the assignment to Pierre Jean David d'Angers, considered one of the greatest sculptors of his day, who used a Sully portrait of Jefferson, which Uriah borrowed from General Lafayette, as a likeness. It took d'Angers nearly a year to complete the sculpture, a massive bronze which depicts Jefferson standing astride two books, a quill pen poised in his right hand and, in his left, a scroll on which the Declaration of Independence is inscribed in its entirety. Uriah arranged for the statue's shipment to Washington, and wrote a formal letter of presentation to Congress.

In its customary fashion, Congress did a certain amount of hemming and hawing over the unusual gift, and there was a good deal of debate over whether it should be accepted or not. What sort of "precedent" would be set by accepting a gift like this? Congress wondered. And from an expected quarter—the Navy Department—came disgruntled noises to the effect that it was "presumptuous" for a "mere lieutenant" to present a statue of a great President. Once more, Uriah was being called pushy and over-assertive. But at last, when Representative Amos Lane of Indiana said bluntly that he saw no reason why the statue should be turned down simply "because it had been presented by a lieutenant instead of a commander," the Congress seemed to recognize the silliness of its behavior, and the Jefferson statue was accepted by a substantial majority. It was placed in the Capitol Rotunda. Several years later, it was moved to the north front lawn of the White House, where it stood for thirty years. Then it was returned to the

Capitol, where it presently stands, to the right of Washington's statue, the only statue in the Rotunda ever donated by a private citizen.*

Uriah Levy may, in a way, have begun to identify himself with his hero at this point in his life. Like Jefferson, Uriah possessed a certain genius and had experienced command. But now the great moments of his life must have seemed past. Like Uriah, Jefferson had been rich, but, Uriah may have remembered, he died penniless and heavily in debt. Uriah's thoughts turned next to Monticello, the extraordinary manor house Jefferson had designed and built for himself on a mountaintop near Charlottesville, Virginia.

When Jefferson died, Monticello went to his daughter, Martha Jefferson Randolph, along with 409 acres, all that remained of what had been a 10,000-acre estate. By 1828, she could no longer afford to run the great house, and she advertised it for sale at $71,000. But Monticello proved itself something of a white elephant. In design, it was revolutionary for its day, built like a temple and topped with a huge octagonal tower and dome. Guests had complained that for all the aesthetic pleasure the place provided, it was not really comfortable. Inside, it contained innovative oddities. There were no bedrooms in the conventional sense. Sleepers used platforms in curtained-off cubicles. In 1830, Mrs. Randolph's asking price had dropped to $11,000. A year later, she announced she would accept $7,000. At that price, Monticello was bought by a Charlottesville man named James Barclay, an eccentric who cared nothing about Thomas Jefferson's house; the house did not figure in his plans at all. Barclay had a grandiose scheme to plant the mountaintop with mulberry trees and grow silkworms, in order to corner the world's silk market. By the time Uriah Levy made what he described as a "pilgrimage" to Monticello in 1836, the silkworm program had been abandoned. The house, left empty, had been attacked by vandals and the weather. Uriah rode on horseback up a rutted roadway that had once been a gracious drive and found the house almost in a state of ruin. He bought the house and land for $2,700, from a grateful Barclay.

* A copy of the Jefferson statue stands in the council chamber of City Hall in New York City.

Because he did indeed get Monticello at a bargain price, and because he was regarded somewhat coolly by his new neighbors—who resented him more for being a Yankee than a Jew—rumors began, in Charlottesville, about Uriah's obtaining Monticello through some sort of chicanery, and these stories persisted and have been perpetuated in history texts. In one tale, Uriah, having learned that a wealthy Bostonian had decided to buy Monticello for a considerably higher figure, hurried to Charlottesville and put in his low bid before the Bostonian's bid arrived by mail. Another story, even more unlikely, is that Uriah—who never drank—engaged a prospective buyer (from Philadelphia) in "a drinking bout," and then bought Monticello while the Philadelphian was recovering from a hangover. None of these stories is remotely true, and the purchase was carried out in a perfectly straightforward and orderly manner. Uriah immediately began a long and costly program of renovation and restoration, paying particular attention to the cherry and walnut parquet floors, the room that Jefferson had used for his study, the area he had used as a sleeping room, and the place where President Madison had slept. He tried to recover, wherever he could, Monticello's original furnishings, most of which had been sold and scattered about the country, and he hired gardeners to restore the grounds in accordance with the elaborate plans drawn up by Jefferson. In 1837, Uriah bought 960 adjoining acres to protect the property, and a few months later he added 1,542 acres more. In the middle of this happy—if at times lonely—activity, a surprising thing happened. Suddenly, in a commission signed by President Andrew Jackson, Uriah learned that he had been promoted—after twenty years as a lieutenant—to the rank of commander. All at once things were looking up again.

Though Uriah certainly didn't need the Navy pay, he immediately applied for sea duty and—again—was delighted and surprised to receive orders assigning him to proceed "with as little delay as possible" to Pensacola, Florida, where he was to report to the war sloop *Vandalia* as its commanding officer. When he arrived in Pensacola, however, and went aboard the *Vandalia,* he must have wondered whether his old enemies in the Navy Establishment weren't after him again and giving him this assignment as a cruel joke. The *Vandalia* was barely afloat. Her hull was rotting, her decks were collapsing, and her guns and metalwork were thick with rust. Her rats had not yet left her, though, and were in evidence everywhere. The *Vandalia*'s crew was, if anything, in even sorrier shape. It seemed to be composed of the ragtag and bobtail of the Navy—drunkards, thieves, and misfits of every variety. The incorrigibles of every command seemed to have filtered, at last, down to the *Vandalia*. When Uriah came aboard, only one junior officer bothered to salute him. A number of the crew were missing and, after a tour of Pensacola taverns had rounded up most of them—protesting that they saw no reason why they should not be permitted to drink during duty hours—many were in such an alcoholic state that they had to be lashed into hammocks on the deck. But Uriah was unfazed. With his customary self-assurance, he wrote to his mother that: "I am certainly one of the most capable of putting the corvette in sea-worthy condition." On September 7, 1838, he set about refurbishing his ship. By February the following year she was ready to sail.

As the *Vandalia* moved out of the harbor into the Gulf of Mexico, there was a certain amount of comment on shore as a decorative detail of Uriah was noticed. He had whimsically ordered the *Vandalia*'s guns painted a bright blue. It was his way of giving the ship his personal stamp. It was also very un-Navy. It was, again, his insistence on being his own man, stating his own terms.

The *Vandalia*'s mission was to call on various Mexican ports along the Gulf Coast and to offer support—moral or, if needed, physical—to American consuls who were the butts of waves of anti-American feeling during a period of revolutionary upheaval. In one port after another, the appearance of the now snappy *Vandalia* with her sparkling bright blue guns was enough to quell Mexican tempers and reassure United States consulates. And Uriah, in full-dress uniform, clearly relished being rowed ashore to be escorted to consular dinner parties, where he inevitably was first to raise a toast "To the flag!"

On board his ship, too, he was held in a curious kind of awe. The first day out he announced that he was making a few innovations in regard to disciplinary measures. There would, for example, be no floggings carried out on his ship while he was in command of it. To his junior officers, this was an astounding announcement. How could discipline possibly be carried out, they wanted to know, without the threat of the cat, particularly with a crew that contained the dregs of the naval service? One officer, Lieutenant Hooe, asked Uriah whether he had lost his reason. Flogging was a Navy tradition. To promise that there would be no flogging was an open invitation to mutiny. But Uriah was firm.

On the third night out, one of the most regular offenders in the crew, who had smuggled whiskey aboard, fell over the railing in a drunken stupor and was lost, which left the *Vandalia* in slightly better shape. But the men who remained were better behaved only in a matter of degree. Drunkenness and petty thievery were diseases endemic to the Navy, and Uriah devised unique punishments for these offenses. A man found guilty of stealing would have hung from his neck a wooden sign painted with the word THIEF. A sailor found drunk on duty would wear a sign, cut in the shape of a bottle, marked A DRUNKARD'S PUNISHMENT. Lieutenant Hooe pronounced these measures not only futile but ridiculous. But after a few weeks at sea, an odd fact had to be admitted: they seemed to be working.

Uriah's theory was that to make a man look absurd in the eyes of his companions had a much more lasting effect on his behavior than to torture him physically. And he was an early endorser of the notion that a punishment ought to fit the crime. Sometimes this required him to exercise an unusual amount of imagination. One day, for example, a young sailor named John Thompson was brought to Uriah and accused of mocking—by imitating his voice—an officer. Uriah considered the charge, and then, to a mystified crew member, ordered that a few handfuls of seagulls' feathers be collected. When the feathers arrived, Uriah ordered Thompson to drop his trousers. A small dab of tar was applied to each buttock, and the feathers were then affixed to the tar. The young man was told to stand on deck in this condition for five minutes, to the great amusement of the crew. "If you are going to act like a parrot, you should look like one," Uriah said.

When he returned to Pensacola, Uriah fully expected to be sent out on another assignment with the *Vandalia*. But, without warning, he was ordered relieved of his command and to "await orders." Another long period in professional limbo began. He wrote to Washington asking for assignments, but the Navy remained mute. At last, discouraged, he returned to Monticello and the real estate business.

The Panic of 1837 had left the real estate market severely depressed, and Uriah, whose fortune had not been affected by the Panic, took this opportunity to invest heavily in more Manhattan properties. Soon he owned at least twenty buildings. Three of his rooming houses earned him an income of nearly $3,500 a month, at a time when the average American working man earned $600 a year. Still, he continued half hopefully to think of the sea, and another command. And so it can be imagined with what kind of shock he received, nearly two years after leaving the *Vandalia,* a tersely worded notice from Washington ordering him to appear before a court-martial for "forgery, cowardice, and cruel and scandalous conduct." His sixth.

His accuser, it seemed, was his former fellow officer Lieutenant Hooe, who, in the months since Uriah had left the *Vandalia,* had been conducting a private vendetta to bring Uriah to his knees. The specific details of the charges were almost quaint. "Forgery" referred to the fact that a report submitted by Uriah had omitted two words, through a clerical error. "Cowardice," the charges stated, meant that Uriah Levy had once allowed a man "to wring his nose severely without making any resistance." The "cruel and scandalous conduct" referred to the punishment of John Thompson, and, for good measure, Uriah was also accused of having "failed to set an example of decency and propriety in his own personal conduct," which was a long way of saying that he had had the temerity to paint his ship's guns blue. On the surface, the charges appeared to be by far the most serious Uriah had ever faced. Examined closely, on the other hand, they seemed ridiculous —and Uriah may have made a tactical error at the outset of his trial by telling the court that he considered them so.

Seldom in American history have a sailor's buttocks received so much and such intensive scrutiny from men in the highest ranks of government, including the man with the highest rank of all, the President. The prosecution accused the *Vandalia's* master of having ordered a full-scale tarring and feathering. The defense insisted that a dab of tar "no larger than a silver dollar" had been applied to each member in question. The youth, the prosecution claimed, had been permanently traumatized from the humiliating treatment he had received before the eyes of his mates. Nonsense, replied the defense; the incident had been treated as a good joke and the morale of his ship had improved considerably as a result of it. Page after page of testimony went into the court transcript over the condition of the posterior of a young man who—because he was off on the high seas somewhere—could not be called to testify. As the case dragged on, Uriah became increasingly confident that he would be exonerated. It was a blow of stunning proportions when he heard the court pronounce him guilty, and then heard the sentence—that he was to be dismissed from the United States Navy. It was his second dismissal. He returned to New York in a state of shock.

President John Tyler had been a lawyer before assuming the Presidency, and he looked over courts-martial, when they were sent to him for the customary review, with particular care. It must have seemed to him quite clear that something other than his mode of punishment was "wrong" with Captain Levy where the Navy higher-ups were concerned. Though he did not touch on this in his opinion—anti-Semitism was still such an elusive, vague, ill-defined quantity in the United States—Tyler did say that he considered the punishment excessive, and asked the court to reconsider its sentence.

In its reconsideration, the court became very excited and wrote a shrilly worded reply to Tyler, saying: "We cannot imagine any punishment more degrading and more calculated to produce such feelings than that which was inflicted [on Seaman Thompson]. It involved not only the indecent exposure of the person of the boy at the gangway of the ship, but the ignominy which are attached to only the most disgraceful of offenses. In this view the punishment was not only unusual but unlawful and exceedingly cruel." Even flogging would have been more merciful. Please, the court begged the President, let Uriah's sentence stand, for the sake of "Navy tradition" if for nothing else.

The President's reply was firm. "A small quantity of tar," he wrote, "was placed on the back"—"back" was a suitably Presidential euphemism—"of the boy and a half dozen parrot's feathers put on it was substituted in place of twelve stripes of the cat. And for this Capt. Levy is sentenced to be dismissed from the Service. . . . He meant to affix temporarily to the boy a badge of disgrace, in order to correct a bad habit, and to teach him and others that the habit of mimicry is that of the parrot whose feathers he wore. The badge was worn only for a few minutes. No harm was done to the person, no blood made to flow, as from the application of the cat. And no cruelty was exercised, unless the reasoning of the court be that this badge of disgrace was more cruel than corporal punishment. . . . I therefore mitigate the sentence of Capt. Levy from dismissal from the Service to suspension without pay for the period of 12 months." Once again, Uriah had been saved by having the right man in the White House.

And President Tyler, a just and kindly man, further mitigated Uriah's twelve-month suspension a few months later by promoting him from commander to captain.

But the twelve months passed, and Uriah's official status continued to be "unassigned." Apparently the Navy did not want his services, despite his new rank. Uriah, growing still richer, busied himself in real estate, bustling back and forth between his house in New York and Monticello, and whenever he had a moment, he dashed off a polite note to the Navy Department, asking for an assignment. His requests were always "noted." The Navy would let him know if anything came up. Uriah also, in this period, took up another form of writing—letters to editors of newspapers in New York, Philadelphia, and Washington, on the United States Navy's "antiquated," "barbarous," and "medieval" use of flogging as punishment. Uriah Levy loved to indulge in bombast, and these letters show him at his grandiloquent best. "America shall not be scourged!" he cried. Soon he was taking to the lecture platform with his crusade, and his vivid descriptions of men being lashed held audiences in shocked fascination.

He was, of course, alternately beseeching the Navy for assignments and attacking one of the Navy's most sacred institutions in the press and on the dais. His editorial letters, which were presently being published in pamphlet form, were drawing reactions from the Congress. Speeches, quoting Uriah, were being delivered on the floor of the House, and both pro- and anti-flogging factions were developing. Senator John P. Hale of New Hampshire took up Uriah's cause with particular enthusiasm, and soon he had become Congress' chief opponent of the lash. The Navy, becoming even more deeply entrenched in its position, announced that "it would be utterly impracticable to have an efficient Navy without this form of punishment."

Meanwhile, Uriah's replies from the Navy brass grew chillier and chillier in tone. The months stretched into years, the years to a decade. In September, 1850, Senator Hale succeeded in attaching an anti-flogging rider to the Naval Appropriations Bill. Two years later, further laws were passed, and Uriah was being called "the father of the abolition of flogging," though he shares this honor with Senator Hale. It was now twelve years since he had left the *Vandalia*. Now, when he wrote to the Navy, his letters were sometimes not even acknowledged. He was growing old, but he had not in any way tired of the fight.

In the autumn of 1853, Uriah Levy did a thing that startled his friends and neighbors. He married a young woman named Virginia Lopez. Uriah was sixty-one. She was eighteen. She wasn't just young. She was his niece, the daughter of his sister Fanny, who had married a West Indian banker named Abraham Lopez—a cousin, in turn, of the Lopezes of Newport, the Gomezes, and a number of other Levys. Uriah and his new wife were related, it was once figured out by the family, at least fourteen different ways. Later in the nineteenth century laws were passed —and have since been abolished—banning such consanguineous marriages, but in 1853 it was all quite legal. And Uriah pointed out that he was really marrying Virginia to "protect" her. Her father, who had at one point been quite rich in Jamaica, had made some unwise loans and investments, and had died leaving his wife and daughter almost penniless. It is part of Jewish tradition for the closest unmarried male relative to marry and care for a widowed or orphaned female member of the family. Nonetheless, eyebrows were raised.

In 1855, Congress approved an "Act to Promote the Efficiency of the Navy." Among other provisions, the act set up a board of officers to examine Navy personnel "who, in the judgment of the board, shall be incapable of performing promptly and efficiently all their duty both ashore and afloat." Uriah had no reason to suppose that the act was aimed specifically at him and a few other jostlers of the official Navy applecart—but it was. Within a few months of the passage of the act, Uriah was notified that he was among those adjudged incapable of further service, and that he was therefore "stricken from the rolls" of the United States Navy. The implications of this terse note were even more insulting. The act specified that officers who had achieved their incapacity because of ill health or old age should merely be placed on the reserve list. Those "stricken from the rolls" were those who were "themselves to blame for their incompetency." The final, most cutting touch of all was that the letter was addressed "Mr. Uriah P. Levy, Late Captain, U.S. Navy."

Uriah was outraged. Sixteen years had passed since he had left the *Vandalia,* and he was now sixty-three, with a young and beautiful wife, a fortune, and two splendid houses—at Saint Mark's Place in New York, and Monticello. His chances of reversing the board's decision looked almost hopeless, and would involve virtually another act of Congress. But Uriah, ever the warrior, girded himself for the grandest and mightiest battle of his career.

He rode to New York and hired Benjamin Butler as his attorney. Butler was one of the most distinguished lawyers in the country. He had been Martin Van Buren's law partner and, when Van Buren became President, had been named secretary of war. He had also served as attorney general under Andrew Jackson. Together, the two men sat down to prepare a petition to Congress which declared that the Navy's action was "outrageous, unauthorized, illegal, and without precedent," and that Uriah had been "unjustly dealt with, and was entitled to reinstatement in the Navy and compensated for the illegal and cruel treatment he had received."

In many ways the naval review board that had dismissed Uriah was reminiscent of the Inquisitional courts of Spain centuries earlier, which had sent Uriah's ancestors from the country. The board had conducted its proceedings in total secrecy. No witnesses had been heard, no evidence had been presented. The accused had not been permitted to say anything in his own defense, nor had he had anyone to represent him. Butler reminded the Congress of this in his petition.

He pointed out that the board had vastly overstepped the authority given it. It had been authorized to conduct "a careful examination into the efficiency" of officers, and to submit "the names and rank of all officers who, in their judgment, shall be incapable of performing promptly and efficiently all their duty . . . and when they believe that such inefficiency has arisen from any cause implying sufficient blame on the part of any officer to justify it, they are to recommend that he be stricken from the rolls."

This meant, Butler argued, that unless an officer could be proved "incapable of performing" duties, the Navy board had no business reaching a judgment about him. And how had Uriah's capabilities been tested? Not at all. Despite repeated attempts to return to service, where he might have been tested, he had been repeatedly turned down. The petition was also boldly critical of President Pierce for approving the board's action, and said: "In so far as the President may have been led to a general acceptance of the report . . . by the unsound and fallacious arguments of his cabinet adviser, he has been misguided." The objections to Uriah Levy on the Navy's part, Butler's petition stated flatly, were three: he had not risen through the ranks in the traditional way; he was outspokenly opposed to the tradition of corporal punishment; and he was a Jew. It was the first time in American history that anti-Semitism had been publicly identified as a force in American life and government. The Butler-drafted petition for Levy ran to more than nine thousand words.

Congress was no less slow-footed in 1855 than it is today, and not until a year after the petition was formally submitted did Congress pass a bill which provided that officers, such as Uriah, who had been cashiered could have their cases presented before a board of inquiry. It was an initial victory for Uriah, and now began the long and tedious process of scheduling the hearing—for the following fall—and of gathering evidence and witnesses to a career which, after all, had been cut off seventeen years before. Uriah was sixty-four now, and must have wondered at moments whether it was worth it. But the fire was still in him, and he was determined to end his life proudly, as a Jew and as a United States naval officer. He was driven by a kind of stubborn patriotism, and unwavering faith in the guarantees and freedoms stated in the Constitution, and he seems to have felt that his fight was not for his vindication but that America and all Americans somehow needed to be exonerated, acquitted, declared guiltless of what had happened within its armed services.

He, and his attorney, Mr. Butler, also had a high sense of showmanship, and were determined, in the process of seeking justice and redress, to give Washington, the press, and the public a performance they would not soon forget. When the Levy party arrived in Washington for the hearing in November, 1857, it installed itself in a series of

suites in Gadsby's Hotel, and when ready to depart for the
Navy building, the party chose a route that took them
down Pennsylvania Avenue, past the White House, where
Uriah could dramatically point out his monumental statue
of Thomas Jefferson as it stood, snow-covered, on the
White House lawn. The party—including Uriah, Butler,
his aides, and Mrs. Levy—entered the hearing room pro-
cessionally, and took their seats.

As Butler had warned Uriah, the prosecution opened
with an attempt to introduce Uriah's six courts-martial
into the record. Butler quickly objected, saying that these
courts-martial had been held concerning certain specific
actions in the past which were not relevant to the hearing,
since those acts were not being questioned. He was overruled. Butler then moved that, if the courts-martial were
entered as evidence, the fairness and merit of each decision
should be taken up, and evidence heard—a process that
would have taken months. Once more he was overruled.

When the findings of all the courts-martial had been
read into the record—which took several days—the Navy
then unleashed its major attack against Uriah. One after
another the prosecution brought forth a long string of officers to testify as to Uriah Levy's incompetence, his un-
reliability, and his general undesirability. One officer said
that Uriah was "generally disliked." Another testified that
"His reputation is low." Commodore Matthew Perry commented that there was "nothing particularly remarkable
about him except that he was rather impulsive and eccentric in his manners, fond of speaking of himself and his
professional requirements." Commodore Silas Stringham
said: "He is very vain, and his manner of interfering when
two or three persons were talking together was disagree-
able." The charges were vague and ill-defined, and since
so much time had passed since Uriah's last command the
witnesses had a good deal of trouble with dates, one officer insisting he had worked with Uriah for four years,
though the two had known each other only during his
service on the *Vandalia*, a period of two years. One officer, who admitted he did not know Uriah at all, said that
he felt instinctively that Uriah was a poor sort. "I feel he
is unfit for the proper performance of the duties of a Captain," he said.

Now it was the defense's turn. Benjamin Butler had
lined up no less than thirteen officers on active duty in the

Navy to testify in Uriah's behalf, plus six ex-Navy officers. Three others sent in written depositions. These witnesses were led by Uriah's old friend Senior Commodore Charles Stewart, chief of the Philadelphia Navy Yard, who testified that "When Captain Levy served under me, he performed his professional duties to my perfect satisfaction. I thought he was competent in 1818 and I think he is competent now. I'd be glad to have him on my ship under my command." The others were similarly laudatory, and witness after witness made the point that at the heart of all Uriah's troubles lay anti-Semitism.

When the nineteen witnesses had testified, and the depositions had been read, the court clearly expected the defense to rest its case. But Mr. Butler had saved a special surprise for the end. What happened next was a spectacle on an epic scale such as those devised, a century later, by Cecil B. De Mille. The courtroom doors opened, and in filed a stream of character witnesses composed of some of the most distinguished men in America, from every field and profession, all prepared to testify to the probity and uprightness and courage of Uriah Levy. They included bank presidents, merchants, doctors, commissioners, the editor of the *New York Globe* and the governor of New Jersey. Uriah's distant cousin, Henry Hendricks, was there, and Senator Dix and Congressman Aaron Vanderpoel and Nathan Ely, president of the Peter Cooper Fire Insurance Company, and James H. Blake, the former mayor of Washington. Jews and Christians, heads of companies and famous lawyers, one after another they mounted the witness stand to speak out for Uriah Levy. In all, fifty-three more witnesses gave testimony, bringing the grand total of defense witnesses to seventy-five. It was an overwhelming performance that might have begun to seem comic if it had not been for the distinction and the obvious sincerity of the men involved. And it was of course a grandstand play, for as each new day in court began, with new witnesses called, the American press and public attention became increasingly riveted on what was going on in a tiny Washington courtroom before a relatively unnewsworthy Navy court of inquiry. Americans who had never heard of Uriah Levy, or of such a thing as anti-Semitism, now were aroused, and sides were taken. For weeks, as the trial marched on, it seemed as though the newspapers could write, and Americans could talk, of nothing else.

Seventy-five witnesses were a difficult act to follow, but of course one voice remained to be heard to close the show: Uriah's. He had reached his finest hour. On December 19, 1857, at ten in the morning—the trial had now gone on for more than a month—Uriah rose to his feet and began: "My parents were Israelites, and I was nurtured in the faith of my ancestors. . . ." Three days later, on December 22, he concluded with the words: "What is my case today, if you yield to this injustice, may tomorrow be that of the Roman Catholic or the Unitarian, the Episcopalian or the Methodist, the Presbyterian or the Baptist. There is but one safeguard, and this is to be found in an honest, wholehearted, inflexible support of the wise, the just, the impartial guarantee of the Constitution. I have the fullest confidence that you will faithfully adhere to this guarantee, and, therefore, with like confidence, I leave my destiny in your hands." The members of the board looked stunned and glassy-eyed. Uriah sat down to what a reporter called "a spontaneous outburst of heartfelt applause."

"It was," commented a Washington newspaper, "one of the most glorious, if not brilliant, pleas ever made in the history of the United States Navy: a plea that 'right should be done!' This became the crowning triumph in Uriah Levy's career: it was a half-century of experience speaking, experience as a seaman, but most important of all, experience as an American Jew."

The court's verdict was unanimous: "Levy is morally, mentally, physically and professionally fit for the Naval Service and . . . ought to be restored to the active list of the Navy."

Now that the secret was out, that anti-Semitism afflicted America, too, as it had done for centuries in reactionary Europe, and lay there for all to see—live, quivering, and unpleasant, a fact that had to be dealt with in the armed services as in civilian life—the immediate reaction was one of extreme embarrassment. Now the Navy set about, very late in the game, to atone for the way it had treated Uriah. After years of ignoring his requests to be assigned sea duty, he was, barely four months after the court of inquiry had reached its verdict, respectfully asked by the Secretary of the Navy if he would care to take command of the sloop *Macedonian*, being outfitted in Boston, and sail it to join the Mediterranean Fleet. Uriah replied gracefully that he would be honored, and then—perhaps in a spirit of wicked humor—added an outrageous request. He would like to take his wife along. She was, he explained, "an orphan, and not a native of this country, without any protection during my absence."

It was an unheard-of request. Never before in American naval history—nor since, for that matter—had a captain been permitted to carry his wife aboard. But the Secretary of the Navy, in his new mood of trying to placate Uriah Levy, replied promptly that this would certainly be possible.

Virginia Lopez Levy often seemed in need of some sort of "protection." A curious woman, with an enormous interest in herself, she wrote extensive memoirs in later years, in which she speculated at length about the secret of her immense charm and attractiveness to men. She once asked one of her many men friends, a poet named Nathaniel Parker Willis, whether he could put his finger on what made her so desirable. "I said," she wrote, " 'I think you know me well enough to realize that I am not a vain woman—but it would be idle and ungrateful for me to pretend that I was unaware of the kindness and attention showered on me. Will you tell me the truth, to what do you attribute this popularity I am fortunate to enjoy?' "

The poet replied—according to Virginia—as follows:

> You have indeed set me a hard task. You ask a mere man, an admirer and a poet, to be absolutely truthful to a young and interesting woman, but as your wish is my command, I will do my best. The beauty of a vain woman may command the adoration of men, but it rarely inspires their love. Your power is potent because you use it so little. The infinite variety of your charm is as elusive as yourself and therefore difficult to define, but the brilliant bubbling effervescence of your youth is like a sparkling glass of champagne that you give us enough of to exhilarate without intoxicating. Do you wonder that we quaff it to the last drop?

A sculptor in Florence once asked her to pose for him and—again, according to Virginia—"He wanted me to sit for his *Allegro*. I asked how she was depicted. He said 'buxom, blithe and debonair.' I positively refused to pose for anyone described in this manner, as I was short and plump and possessed of *la beauté de diable*."

She appears to have been an inveterate flirt, and there was a curious episode at Monticello, one day when Uriah was out of town, in which Virginia became involved with a number of spirited college boys who, for some reason, happened to be passing through. She girlishly ordered them off the property, but they refused to go. And after a romping chase over stone walls, through gardens, and in and out of arbors and bowers and gazebos, Virginia wrote that "We all parted friends."

Virginia accepted full credit for the fact that her husband's request to bring her along was granted. "Thé popularity I was fortunate enough to enjoy with the men in power," she wrote, "won for me the unusual distinction of being allowed to accompany my husband. This privilege, which has never been granted since, was passed by both houses and granted without protest."

Her "infinite variety" made her quite a handful for her aging husband. He tried to keep pace with her youthful energy, and dyed his graying hair and moustache jet black. But he also found her an expensive commodity, and whenever they quarreled it was over the extravagant amounts she spent on clothes and trimmings. And she was very nearly too much for the *Macedonian,* where the presence of a solitary female among an all-male crew was, not surprisingly, disruptive. In his diary, a junior officer wrote: "She seemed determined to show off her dresses for every time she came on deck she had a different one." On another occasion, this same officer was disturbed to enter the captain's cabin on an errand and to find "the tables and chairs covered with ladies' apparel, hoops and skirts, bonnets and shoes, etc. etc."

Virginia, on the other hand, found life on shipboard most agreeable, and seemed, at times, to be going out of her way to be kind to the younger officers—particularly at times when the captain was on duty on the bridge and she was alone with time to kill in her cabin. And she enjoyed the stops at Mediterranean ports, where she mingled, as she put it, among "the exalted circles of European society." Everywhere, she wrote, she was admired. From her memoirs: "My sojourn in Italy was as enjoyable as my stay in Egypt. Particularly so in Naples, where I occupied an apartment for some time. Captain Levy was compelled to leave, but everyone was very kind to me, including our Ambassador & his wife, Mrs. Chandler. . . . Spent Yom Kippur with Baron and Baroness Rothschild, who had a synagogue in their home. I have always admired the Rothschild family, and in whatever country I met them was impressed with their nobility of character. They understood perfectly *noblesse oblige."* She dashed off to Paris, where "I went to a fashionable modiste . . . and told her I wanted a white tulle gown, as simple as she could make it, and told her I must have it in time for the ball. She was horrified. Madame must have brocade and point lace, but I insisted on the tulle, and she reluctantly agreed to make it. The night of the ball when these old duchesses adjusted their lorgnettes to look me over and pronounce me *charmante,* I thought I had made a wise selection. But neither the gown nor I had anything to recommend us but our freshness. I have never seen such a collection of jewels and ugly women in my life!"

Her favorite ball that season was the "wonderful costume ball given by the Emperor Napoleon III and where the Empress Eugenie was masked . . . the splendor of its costumes, the scintillation of its lights, the rhythm and intoxication of its music, I think, went a little to my head and I felt that in order to enter into the spirit of the evening I must indulge in a violent flirtation. . . . I learned later that my partner was Prince Metternich. . . ."

Virginia must have been a trial to Uriah, but there were other compensations. In February, 1860, Uriah Levy learned that he had been placed in command of the entire Mediterranean Fleet, and had been elevated to the rank of commodore, which was then the Navy's highest rank. The fleet celebrated this event by presenting him with a thirteen-gun salute. And so Uriah Levy, scorned and beleaguered most of his life in the service, had all the luck at last.

It was all he wanted. The board of inquiry trial had taken its toll on him. He had begun to complain of "stomach distress," and there were other signs that he was getting old. In 1861, he and Virginia came home to the big house in Saint Mark's Place in New York. In April of that year Fort Sumter surrendered, and suddenly the Navy officer corps was split along North-South lines. War seemed inevitable, and many officers returned to the South to count themselves with the Confederacy. Uriah, though he owned property south of the Mason-Dixon Line, announced his allegiance to the Union, and even talked excitedly of Navy service in the Civil War. But early in the spring of 1862, he came down with a severe cold. It developed into pneumonia. On March 22 of that year he died in his sleep, with Virginia at his side.

Uriah's last will and testament managed to say a good deal about his zeal as a patriot, as well as the size of his ego. One of his bequests was for the erection of a statue of himself, "of the size of life at least" and "to cost at least six thousand dollars," above his grave, on which he wished inscribed: "Uriah P. Levy, Captain of the United States Navy, Father of the law for the abolition of the barbarous practise of corporal punishment in the Navy of the United States." He then directed that Monticello—the house and acreage—be left "to the people of the United States," but he attached an odd proviso. He asked that the estate be turned into "an Agricultural School for the purpose of educating as practical farmers children of the warrant office of the United States Navy whose Fathers are dead." Was this Uriah's idea of a joke, or a serious gesture aimed at turning swords into plowshares? Why should the children of dead warrant officers be taught farming? Perhaps Uriah, who considered himself a gentleman farmer as well as a Navy officer, felt that the two occupations complemented each other. In any case, his will left the condition unexplained. There were a number of charitable bequests, and gifts to relatives. Virginia was directed to receive the minimum that the law allowed.

Needless to say, Virginia was not happy with this state of affairs, nor were members of Uriah's family, who had looked forward to splitting up the vast and valuable acreage at Monticello, and who might have been willing to spend less on a monument to the deceased. After Uriah died, his will was contested and his estate went into litigation for several years. Finally the will was broken, and Monticello went to one of Uriah's nephews—appropriately named Jefferson Levy—who, with his family, maintained the big place until 1923, when a Jefferson Memorial Foundation purchased it from him for half a million dollars, a respectable gain on the $2,700 Uriah Levy had paid for it. Virginia Levy remarried rather soon after her husband's death, thus disqualifying herself from much more than the share of the estate she already had received. She survived Uriah by an astonishing sixty-three years, and died in 1925. So it was that the widow of an officer of the War of 1812 lived well into the flapper era. She did not, however, live to see the launching of the destroyer U.S.S. *Levy* during World War II. At the height of the war, the *Levy* was described by the *New York Herald Tribune* as one of "the swift and deadly sub-killers." It was an appropriate monument to Uriah—*more* appropriate than the life-size statue, which never came to be.

16

THE JEWISH EPISCOPALIANS

URIAH Levy's death had been as well publicized as his life, and to the Jewish Old Guard it was all a little embarrassing. He had become the best-known Jew in America, with the word "Jew" emblazoned all over him, and his disputatious image—combined with his wife's flamboyant one—was not exactly the one the Jews wished to cultivate. Families such as the Nathans went to pains to explain that Commodore Levy was "not typical," and should therefore *not* be treated—as he himself had obviously wanted to be treated—as some sort of spokesman for the race.

The Sephardim neither needed nor wanted a spokesman. They had integrated quietly into urban American life, and had become gentlefolk. For these people, their Jewishness was something to be kept privately in the background, not to be noisily defended, or boasted or complained about, in the manner of a Uriah Levy. If they wished to be known publicly for anything, it was for their cultivation, breeding, good manners, and good works. It is perhaps ironic that, as the Jewish elite turned from mere money-making, almost with a disdainful dusting of their hands, to more elevated pursuits of the mind and spirit, they assured themselves of a less forceful role in America than the one they might have played.

There were, in fact, a number of Sephardic men who took pride in the fact that they did nothing at all. Mr. Alfred Tobias was one of these elegantly situated men. The Tobiases were a Sephardic family, originally from Liverpool, who had made a considerable fortune manufacturing chronometers. The first Tobias to emigrate to

America, whose name was Tobias I. Tobias, secured himself rather thoroughly to the New York Sephardic elite when four of his children, Henry, Fanny, Harriet, and Alfred married four of Harmon Hendricks' children, Roselane, Uriah II, Henry, and Hermoine. Alfred Tobias' sole occupation was "handling his investments"—a task he obviously performed quite well, for he increased his own considerable inheritance as well as those of his already wealthy Hendricks wife, and his wife's two orphaned nieces.

Cousin Florian Tobias was also proud to confess that he had never worked a day in his life at anything that could be called a job, and that he never intended to. Oh, he did a few things. He was an amateur billiard champion, and he practiced every day on his full-size Collender table in the billiard room. He had a small carpenter's shop in the house, where he turned out beautiful picture frames, taborets, screens, and delicate objets d'art. He was an admitted dilettante, and his only practical chore in life occurred when coal was being delivered for the furnaces of his father's house in Forty-eighth Street. Cousin Florian always posted himself outside the house, just beside the coal chute—in his best clothes, of course, and in his top hat—where he counted the number of truckloads that went into the cellar, to make sure that the proper tonnages were being delivered. It was not too taxing a job, or life, and Cousin Florian lived to the comfortable age of seventy-four.

The Hendrickses, meanwhile, were doing nicely. With their copper-rolling mills in New Jersey, their big country estate at Belleville, and their town house at 414 Fifth Avenue, they were among the richest of the Sephardic families. They also owned quite a bit of Manhattan real estate, including the blocks between Sixth and Seventh avenues from Twentieth to Twenty-second streets, and thirty acres along Broadway. (Had the family held on to this, the Hendrickses would be among the city's biggest landowners today.) Of course, there were some people who considered the Hendrickses to be a little on the dull side, a little stuffy.

There were also some odd Hendricks family characteristics, and an individual who was accused, in the group, of being a bit "Hendricksy" was someone who was fussy about dirt to the point of neurosis, was obsessive about cleanliness, or repeatedly washed his hands. Several Hendrickses were compulsive hand-washers, and would never touch a stranger for fear of contamination. Once, so a story went, someone said to one of the Hendrickses at the opera, "Aren't the acoustics in this opera house terrible?" Sniffing, Mr. Hendricks replied, "Really? I don't smell anything." But when the United States government needed money to pay for the War of 1812, the Hendrickses point out, President Madison sought loans from individuals. Henry C. de Rham, of the old New York de Rhams, offered $32,300. Harmon Hendricks topped him with $42,000.

By the latter part of the nineteenth century, the Sephardim of New York and other cities were leading lives of comfort and reassurance. If you lived on Fifth Avenue, and most "nice" families lived on or just off it—it ran, after all, along the spine of Manhattan, and one had the nicest views from there—your house probably had a small black box affixed to an inside wall, near the front door. You pulled the handle on the box, a pleasant whirring sound emerged, and presently a messenger boy in knickers and blue cap appeared at your doorstep to carry a letter uptown, or to fetch an order from the druggist's. You rang a servant's bell, it tinkled distantly from the panel in the downstairs kitchen, and within moments a servant appeared to do your bidding. Such were the amenities of those long-ago days. And yet the servants' rooms in the old brownstones were never supplied with baths. Maids, when they bathed at all, were required to use the basement laundry tubs. Wells, where fresh water was drawn, were right on Fifth Avenue.

At the same time, doorknobs were of plated silver, and satin draperies with heavy tassels hung over window curtains of thick lace. Furniture was of gilt rosewood, covered with tufted satin, and tables were of ebony, inlaid with marquetry. A card receiver stood near every entrance. It was the fashion to have, in every formal room, a center table holding ornaments—the Boyer statuettes or the Manet bronzes, or perhaps a Monte Verdi depiction of Benjamin Franklin chaining the lightning. Thanks to the magic of electricity, the house of important downtown businessmen could be supplied with private tickers from the New York Stock Exchange. Mr. Jefferson Levy, Uriah's banker nephew, who later became a congressman, rather topped everyone in the Sephardic community. He also had a ticker from the London Stock Exchange.

In the dining rooms were red Turkish carpets and family portraits. After dinner, the families repaired to parlors, or to music rooms, where they stood about the rosewood piano for a little singing—"Under the Daisies," "Listen to the Mockingbird," "Hidden in the Valley," or "The Last Rose of Summer." An aunt might round out the evening playing the "Anvil Chorus." Music was considered a boon to the digestive juices. It was a cozy and sentimental era, the 1880's and 1890's, and it was hard to believe that it would ever be otherwise, or that the city was changing faster than anyone knew.

Etiquette was stressed more than what went on or appeared in the newspapers. "Always eat your ice cream with a *fork*," the little Nathan children were advised by the governess. "It's those Germans who use their spoons. Remember, while they were still peddling with packs on their backs, your family was having dinner with kings and queens." Of course, there were mésalliances. When Rosa Content (of a pre-Revolutionary Sephardic family) married James Seligman (German, of the then international banking house), she always referred to her in-laws as "the peddlers." As for the Jews of eastern Europe, they were elaborately ignored. Mrs. L. Napoleon Levy (wife of another of Uriah's nephews, and a Hendricks in her own right), embroidering her family tree on a sampler, put the words "from Europe" next to the name of one of her grandfathers because she could not bring herself to admit —even in such a limited public way as stitchwork—that he had come from Poland. Mrs. Levy liked to remind her children that, at her wedding in 1892, the list of guests had included not only Levys, Hendrickses, Lazaruses, Seixases, and Wolffs, but also Roosevelts, Shackelfords, Rittenhouses, Van Rensselaers, and Kings. The Alfred Tobiases (cousins of Levys) were proud to list among their neighbor and friends the Livingstons, the Barclays, and the Auchinclosses.

There were other proofs of social acceptance by Christians. The Hendrickses belonged to and sailed at the Larchmont Yacht Club in Westchester (which Jews have difficulty joining today), and when the Sephardic families summered, they not only went to the Jersey shore—which would later become known as a Jewish resort area—but also to Newport, Saratoga, and Bar Harbor (which were not only non-Jewish but a bit anti-Jewish and becoming more so). A Hendricks granddaughter attended Miss Gayler's School in New York. Invited to a party on a Friday night, she replied that she was sorry, she couldn't attend, "Because that is our Sabbath." There was nothing further said, but from that point on it was noticed that parties for girls at Miss Gayler's School were no longer scheduled for Friday evenings, but were given on Saturday nights instead, out of courtesy to the elegant Sephardim.

Of course, there were scandals, and cases of people who refused to fit into the mold. There was the shocking case of Aunt Agnes Hendricks Wolff, who, in the 1890's, had a notorious affair with a non-Jewish gentleman named Townsend. They went off to Paris together and traveled flagrantly through Europe as man and wife, a state of affairs the family found intolerable. The two were written up in *Town Topics*, the leading scandal sheet of the day, and it all came to a tragic end (as anyone who had read the Maria Edgeworth stories could have predicted) when, one day riding with Mr. Townsend on Long Island, Aunt Agnes was thrown from her mount and killed.

Then there was cousin Annie Lazarus, sister of the poetess Emma, one of wealthy Moses Lazarus' six daughters, who was some sort of revolutionary. She was forever crusading for immigrants' rights, and she married a non-Jewish artist named Johnny Johnston. She favored America's intervention in World War I, and when the country remained isolationist she threw up her hands, declared herself disillusioned with the United States, and she and her husband sailed off to Italy, where they lived in a Venetian palazzo with a beautiful garden. She refused to communicate with or receive any of her American friends or relatives but, it was pointed out at the time, she seemed perfectly willing to go on receiving her considerable American income. Her picture was turned against the wall, and her name was permanently dropped from family conversations. How she and her husband fared during the Second World War, no one knows.

And of course there were quarrels. A schism involving a set of Sèvres china of museum quality has long divided the Hendricks family. Years ago, when an estate was being divided, the Sèvres was split between two cousins—a cup here, a saucer there—and its proper ownership has been in dispute ever since. Visiting Mrs. Henry Hendricks, a cousin once remarked, "Ah, I see you have the rest of the Sèvres." "No," said Mrs. Hendricks frostily, *"you* have."

But in general the Sephardim of the late nineteenth century did as they were supposed to do. The men decorated the boards of directors of the proper corporations, and the correct hospitals, museums, and charities. Women engaged in daintier pastimes—painting, reading, letter writing, going to concerts, operas, and ballets. Women were not given much in the way of formal education (the educated woman, little girls were told, had a hard time finding a husband). But they were cultivated, trained in the arts of charm and wit and small talk on a wide variety of subjects. A surprising number of women—cousin Emma Lazarus is the most famous example—wrote poetry, for their own enjoyment if not for publication.

One of this delicate breed of nineteenth-century woman was Great-Aunt Amelia Barnard Tobias Lazarus, who might have stepped out of the pages of an Edith Wharton novel. Indeed, the young Mrs. Wharton was among Aunt Amelia's circle of friends. Aunt Amelia was not only a Tobias, and therefore connected to the Hendrickses; she was also collaterally descended from Mordecai Gomez, Daniel's brother, and she was therefore connected as well to the Lopezes, Seixases, de Lucenas, and Levys, to say nothing of the Nathans and Cardozos. She was an encapsulation of the great Sephardic strains. In her house in East Ninth Street, just a few doors away from University Place, Aunt Amelia lived a life that had settled elegantly and comfortably into a pattern: congealed, precise, predictable. Her late husband, Jacob Hart Lazarus, who had died in 1891, had been one of the most popular and respected society portraitists of his day—"a nineteenth-century Copley," he had been called. Among other great subjects, he had painted four generations of the Astor family. He left Aunt Amelia amply fixed. The Ninth Street house was a large, three-story affair of red brick where Aunt Amelia was cared for by three maids and her maiden sister, Great-Aunt Sophia Tobias, who "kept house" for Aunt Amelia. On most afternoons, Aunt Amelia could be found reclining —she suffered from angina, and did not move around much—on her long red velvet and mahogany couch in the drawing room, where she conducted what amounted to a perpetual salon.

All the noted personages of the day were her callers: old Mrs. Drexel from Philadelphia, who dropped in on Aunt Amelia whenever she was in New York; Mrs. Delafield; Mrs. Potter; Mrs. Astor, of course. There were also those haughty and rather terrifyingly aristocratic Lazarus cousins known as "the Eleventh Street Lazaruses," who included the formidable and splendid Sarah, and Emma, the poetess, and Frank Lazarus, famous because for years he was to be seen, every day, seated in the same chair in one of the Fifth Avenue windows of the Union Club. For years after his death, the chair was known as "Mr. Lazarus' chair." Another of these Lazaruses was Annie, about whom there had been scandal, and whose name was never mentioned. These Lazaruses kept a summer "cottage" in Newport. Called "The Beeches," it was a huge, gabled affair on Bellevue Avenue, hard by "Belcourt," the Oliver H. P. Belmont mansion, and across the street from "Miramar," built for Mrs. George Widener.

Aunt Amelia was far from beautiful. In fact, though she was thin and always carried herself erectly—a stern and autocratic bearing—she was actually quite homely, with large, imperiously blazing green eyes. (Her sister, by contrast, was a small, plump, gentle lady with wavy gray hair that was always a bit disarrayed.) Aunt Amelia, however, had learned a secret that has made many a non-beautiful woman adored by both sexes: she had charm, she had wit, and she had style. Once, when she was shopping for some handkerchiefs, a salesgirl had said to her, "Mrs. Lazarus, those handkerchiefs you're looking at are very fine—but these other ones might do for mornings around the house." Aunt Amelia shot her a lofty, amused look and replied, "My dear young woman, I would have you understand that my nose is just as delicate in the mornings as it is in the afternoons."

Her dinner parties, served in a dining room that had walls covered with gold brocade, were celebrated for the high quality of the conversation as well as for the high station of the guests. To encourage good talk, there were never more than six at table. Dinner began with sherry and ended with champagne and fresh fruit out of season— which no one ate—purchased at considerable expense from Hicks, the great Fifth Avenue fruiterer. Though em-

inently correct, Aunt Amelia was never totally unapprecia-
tive of the risqué. Frank Lazarus often tried to shock her
with some bit of *mauvaise plaisanterie* he had picked up in
the smoking room at the Union, and, after listening to one
of his tales she would cry out, "Frank! You dirty beast!"
Then she would lean closer to him and, in a husky stage
whisper, ask, "Now what was it you said again?"

The neighborhood around her was deteriorating. She
knew it, but she refused to move or to change her mode
of life in any way. The house on one side of her had become a laundry, and the one on the other side had become
some sort of nightclub—the less said of what probably
went on there, the better. Raucous noises emerged from it
night and day. Aunt Amelia let neither presence disturb
her in the slightest. Inside, her house ran on noiseless machinery. Each morning, her lawyer, "Little Sam" Riker
(his father, "Big Sam" Riker, had been the family lawyer
before him), arrived punctually at eight and opened Aunt
Amelia's mail, attending to whatever needed attention. It
was then Little Sam's duty to go downstairs to the kitchen
to see to it that the servants were at their posts, and to un-
snarl the quarrels that were forever erupting between the
Irish maid and the waitress so that Aunt Amelia's ears
might be spared the unpleasant details. The family had repeatedly urged Aunt Amelia to have, in view of her illness,
a servant sleep in the room next to hers, but Aunt Amelia
would have none of it. That would be lowering the class
barrier too far. Servants belonged on a floor of their own.
Her servants, nevertheless, were devoted to her. Her personal maid, Josephine, had for years been engaged to
marry the coachman for the Alexandre family but, year
after year, the wedding date was postponed. It was because
Josephine could not bear the thought of leaving Aunt
Amelia. Aunt Amelia's only concession to the shabbiness
of her neighborhood was made for her maids' benefit. She
kept a man's derby hat hung on a hat stand in the entrance
vestibule, which was intended to suggest to intruders that
there was a man on the premises, whereas in fact hers was
a household of women. A man from Tiffany's came to
Ninth Street once a week to wind all the clocks.

Great-Aunt Amelia was a stickler for etiquette and the
Right Thing, not because she was afraid of making a mistake in public but because she believed the Right Thing
was one of the obligations and heavy duties of the aristo-

crat. When writing a social note, she enjoined her nieces and grandnieces, a lady should never moisten the entire flap of the envelope, but only the tip. Young ladies were told to sit quietly, with hands folded in laps, legs crossed at the ankles. They were not to fidget or play with their beads. Young men were instructed to sit with one leg crossed above the other, knee upon knee, never sprawled with knees apart, or with ankle on knee. Aunt Amelia was one of New York's great authorities on the intricacies of the calling-card ritual—one that has been compared with the Japanese tea ceremony in terms of the years it took a lady of old New York to master it—and even Mrs. Astor sometimes called upon Aunt Amelia, in those days before there was an Emily Post, for social advice and guidance. Though Aunt Amelia's illness caused her to be in great pain much of the time, she never complained. She believed that complaining indicated ill breeding. Once, before a dinner party, she said quietly to a niece, "If I have to leave the table during dinner, I expect you to carry on as hostess in my place. And of course you must make no point of my absence." Aunt Amelia also believed that it was one of the moral obligations of the privileged and well-placed to care for the fine things that privilege and high estate provided, that it was as wrong to mistreat a good china plate or piece of furniture as it was to abuse a human being. As a result, every item in her house, from the paintings and the rare books to the heavy linen sheets on the beds, was lovingly attended to.

Morality, propriety, and responsibility were instilled in children by the Maria Edgeworth stories. In these, two sisters, the wise Laura and the impulsive Rosalind, were contrasted, and the moral clearly drawn. In one tale, for example, Rosalind foolishly uses money given her to have a shoe repaired to buy, instead, a pretty purple vase that she has seen in a shop window. Alas, a hole appears in her shoe, a sharp stone enters the hole, and, after an agonizing limp home, when Rosalind puts water in her vase the pretty color washes off. Laura is helpfully there to say, "I told you so." For boys, there were stories about a bad youth named Frank who was always made to pay dearly for his naughtinesses. Children were also given copies of the *Illustrated London News* to read for edification and enlightenment. Anything British was considered uplifting.

Great-Aunt Amelia Lazarus exuded such an air of social

security that one would have thought her incapable of being surprised or impressed by anything. But she was secretly delighted to have been invited to one of the great society "Weddings of the Age," that of Harry Lehr, the colorful playboy who once, dressed in full fig, waded into a Fifth Avenue fountain, and who had succeeded Ward McAllister as New York Society's arbiter and Mrs. Astor's pet. Aunt Amelia also believed that social occasions ought to be combined with a certain amount of self-improvement and, when a niece mentioned that she was going to a reception at the de Forests', Aunt Amelia reminded her to be sure to note the fine Indian carving that adorned the wall by the de Forests' staircase. "One must learn first to recognize, then appreciate, beautiful things," she used to say.

Perhaps such an extraordinary degree of refinement and high breeding among the Sephardim is an explanation for the fact that they took a far less active part in the Civil War than they had taken in the Revolution and the War of 1812. Nor did they join the band of aggressive, hungry fortune hunters that emerged after the War—the Rockefellers, Vanderbilts, Guggenheims, Morgans, Mellons, Schiffs, et al. The Sephardim stood politely on the sidelines. The only Sephardic name of any importance to Civil War buffs is that of Judah P. Benjamin, and he had the misfortune to be on the wrong side. One of the great rows in the history of New York's Union Club was over Mr. Benjamin's proposed ouster. Those in the club who wanted him out did so not because Benjamin was Jewish but because he was pro-South. The club refused to expel him, and a group of irate members immediately departed and formed a club of their own, the Union *League* Club.

Judah Benjamin was a member of a West Indian Sephardic family, distantly connected to the branch of the Lopez family that had settled there, as well as to the Mendes family, and in 1818 his parents moved from the island of Saint Thomas, where he was born, to Charleston, South Carolina. Though he attended Yale (without receiving a degree), his youthful orientation was thoroughly southern. After Yale, he went to New Orleans, where he "read" law in a law office, and he was admitted to the Louisiana bar in 1832. In 1852, he was elected a senator from Louisiana, and here demonstrated that he had a Latin temper every bit as fiery as Uriah Levy's. In reply to a slur from another senator, Judah Benjamin rose and declaimed: "The gentleman will please remember that when his half-civilized ancestors were hunting wild boar in the forests of Silesia, mine were the princes of the earth!" (Actually, he was paraphrasing Disraeli, who once, in answer to a similar taunt, said: "Yes, I am a Jew, and when the ancestors of the right honourable gentleman were brutal savages in an unknown island, mine were priests in the temple of Solomon.")

Benjamin resigned from the Senate in order to assist his friend Jefferson Davis in forming his provisional government. He worked in Davis' cabinet, first as attorney general and later as Davis' chief secretary of state, a post he held from 1862 to 1865.

After the Confederacy's surrender at Appomattox, there was a price on Judah Benjamin's head. He managed to make an escape by boat from the coast of Florida and, many months later, after much hardship and bouncing about on troubled Atlantic waters, Benjamin was able to make his way to England, where he lived in exile. He died in Paris in 1884, a lonely and disenchanted man, a long way from the crackling fires and comfortable chairs of the Union Club.

17.

"NATHANS DON'T CHEAT"—
BUT DO THEY KILL?

THE Nathans were such a *proper* family, and could nearly always be counted on to do the correct thing, to rise to the occasion in the right manner, to make the suitable gesture. Young Frederick Nathan was barely more than a boy when he was traveling in the South with Griffith, the family's Negro chauffeur. The two were about to board a steamer when Frederick was told, "He can't ride with you." "Very well," Frederick Nathan said, "I'll ride with him"— and he did, he rode with Griffith in the ship's Jim Crow quarters rather than accept the segregation the South imposed. Nathans were always doing things like that. It was no wonder that, for generations, a Nathan had been president of New York's Shearith Israel congregation.

The great Nathan family patriarch was Isaac Mendes Seixas Nathan. His uncle had been Gershom Mendes Seixas, called "the patriot rabbi" for refusing to let his congregation pray for George III. Isaac M. S. Nathan's grandmother had been one of the old New York Levys, and he himself had married another Seixas and, by her, sired a dynastic brood of fifteen children. He ruled his household with a series of bells—a different bell summoned each child into his father's presence. He also had bells to indicate the various punishments that were to be meted out for whatever misdeed was at hand; one bell meant a birching, another bed without supper, and so on. The combination of children bells and punishment bells made the Nathan house chime like a carillon most of the day. He was a tyrant and a terror, and his children adored him. They all made properly dynastic marriages—one to a

Solis, one to a Cardozo, two to Hendrickses, one to a Gomez, a great-grandniece of Daniel's—and were otherwise a
tribute to their father.

When the little Nathan children were strolled by their
nannies in Central Park during those pleasant decades after the Civil War, they used to hear passersby whisper,
"Look—the Nathans," and "Here come the Nathans!" The
children assumed, naturally enough, that this attention was
due to their celebrated birthright and social superiority.
But the real reason had nothing to do with this. Scandal
in the family, after all, was so rare as to be unknown, and
naturally the dreadful details of it had to be kept from the
Nathan children. It was a scandal that was rocking the entire Sephardic community.

New York in 1870 was entering its most elegant phase,
soon to be christened by Edith Wharton as "the Age of Innocence." West Twenty-third Street at Madison Square
was considered "uptown," and the *New York Herald* referred to this neighborhood as one of the city's "aristocratic purlieus." Here, on broad, tree-lined streets, facing a
leafy park, in tall private brownstone houses, lived the
city's rich, including Mr. Benjamin Seixas Nathan, the
banker, grandson of the founding American patriarch, and
one of New York's wealthiest and most prominent men.
The Nathans—Benjamin Nathan was married to the former Emily Hendricks—and their nine children lived at
number 12 West Twenty-third. On an opposite corner, the
old Fifth Avenue Hotel had gone up a few years earlier
—up to the astonishing height of six stories, and equipped
with something called an elevator, which was said actually
to lift persons with courage to try it to the topmost level.
The Nathans, good parents that they were, had severely
cautioned their children never to enter this unlikely con-
traption.

New Yorkers that summer, when not discussing the elevator, were talking about the weather. It was hot. New
York summers were no less stifling and humid a hundred
years ago than they are today. New Yorkers also talked
about a new war in Europe, which the Prussians had ma-
neuvered France into declaring against them. American
sentiment favored the Germans, due to the unhelpful behavior of Napoleon III during the Civil War. There was
talk, too, of Jefferson Davis, now a private citizen from
Mississippi, who passed through New York—surely feeling

very much amid alien corn—on his way to board a Cunarder to England. It had been a slow season for the theater. *Fritz, Our Cousin German,* was playing at Wallack's, and the Booth was preparing to open with its first offering, *Rip Van Winkle,* with Joseph Jefferson in the title role. At the Grand Opera House, three blocks west of Madison Square, something called the "Viennoise Ballet and Pantomime Troupe" was being offered. It was an age of flounces and ruffles on women's dresses, when men wore bowled hats and braid-trimmed overcoats, and every gentleman of fashion had whiskers. People complained of an infestation of "measuring worms" in the city; they dropped from trees on to women's hats and parasols, and there was a plan afoot to import the English sparrow to consume the worms. By late July, all the "best" people had left the city for lake shores or sea breezes, including the Nathans, who had removed to their summer place in Morristown, New Jersey—or so everyone thought. Then, all at once, at the end of July, all of New York's attention—and much of the country's—was riveted on Benjamin Nathan and his family.

Benjamin Nathan was a quiet, kindly-faced man with mutton chop sideburns and thick spectacles without which he could barely see. Despite this handicap, Ben Nathan had had a distinguished career and, in 1870, he was a vice-president of the New York Stock Exchange, president of Mount Sinai Hospital, a member of the Union Club, the Union League Club, and the Saint Nicholas Society, and a colonel on the governor's honorary staff. He was, in short, the model of a proper nineteenth-century New York gentleman, and there were even some in the family who had the temerity to call Ben a "Jewish Episcopalian."

On Thursday, July 28, Mr. Nathan and two of his sons —Frederick, twenty-six, and Washington, twenty-one— had come unexpectedly to New York from Morristown on business, and had arrived at 12 West Twenty-third Street to spend the night. The men's arrival was quite a surprise to the housekeeper, a Mrs. Kelly, and her son William, who worked for the Nathans as a general chore boy. The house was being redecorated, and most of the furniture had gone out to the upholsterer's. But Mr. Nathan explained that he wanted to stay in New York because he planned, the next day, to go to the synagogue to say prayers in memory of his mother, the former Sarah Seixas,

the anniversary of whose death it was. Mrs. Kelly im-
provised a bed for her employer by placing several mattresses on top of each other on the floor in a second-floor
room, and she did the same for the two boys in rooms
above. Mr. Nathan spent the early part of the evening
with his sons. Then both young men dressed and left, in
separate directions, for gayer surroundings than the half-
empty brownstone. Both returned—again separately, young
Wash Nathan much the later—well after midnight. Each
son looked in on his father, saw him sleeping peacefully in
his makeshift bed, then mounted the stairs to his own
room.

A word should be injected here about Washington Nathan. He was considered one of New York's most dashing
young men. Tall, thin, always exquisitely groomed, he
possessed good looks that were described by one lady as
"agonizing beauty," and it was said that the touch of his
slender, perfectly manicured hand caused the strongest-
hearted woman to swoon. Women fussed over him wherever he went, exclaiming over his "large candid blue eyes,"
and by the time he had reached his twenties he was thoroughly spoiled. It was widely said in the family—and out
of it, for that matter—that the reason why Wash's cousin
Emma Lazarus, the poetess, never married was that all
her life she harbored a "violent passion" for him while he
paid not the slightest attention to her. Poor Emma. She
doubtless possessed intellectual charms and vociferous
opinions (on Zionism, for instance) which attracted to her
male friends like Emerson and Browning, but she was at
best a plain-looking woman, with features that always
seemed too large for her face, and unfortunate skin. It
was also said that Washington Nathan spent thirty thousand dollars a year—a huge sum in 1870—pursuing the
pleasures of his rakish life. And it was known that his father disapproved of his "habits," and that the two had
quarreled often about the young man's spending.

After his sons left the house, Benjamin Nathan had rung
for his housekeeper and asked for a glass of ice water.
This was at around ten o'clock. Mrs. Kelly then locked
and bolted both front and back doors of the house, closed
and locked all the windows, as was her nightly custom,
said good night to her employer, and proceeded to her own
room. Around eleven she was awakened by a brief thun-
derstorm, which subsided well before midnight. This is all

that is known for sure of events that night at 12 West
Twenty-third Street. Early the following morning, a guest
at the Fifth Avenue Hotel looked out his window and saw
two young men come running down the steps of the house
shouting for help—the Nathan boys, one half dressed, the
other dripping with blood.

Upstairs, Benjamin Nathan lay dead, murdered in the
most deliberate and brutal fashion. This kindly and gentle
man, who no one could believe had a single enemy, had
been repeatedly beaten by a heavy weapon and clearly by
someone intent upon his total destruction. Ghastly wounds
covered the body, bones had been broken, and there was
a particularly savage wound in the center of the forehead.
He had apparently been dragged from the room where he
had been sleeping, and his body lay in a doorway between
that and an adjacent room, used as a study, in a pool of
blood. There were clear signs of a terrible struggle. Furniture was overturned, and blood was spattered on the floor,
walls, and frame of the door. In the study, a small safe
had been forced open and on top of the pile of mattresses
was an open cashbox. A large and heavy object, covered
with blood, was found in another room—a "carpenter's
dog," a J-shaped instrument used for gripping and hook-
ing—clearly the murder weapon. Since the family had
been away, and the house was being redecorated, nothing
of value had been in the safe. A quick inventory of the
items stolen was pitifully small: three diamond shirt studs,
two watches, and a gold medal. Of course no one could
say what might have been removed from the cashbox, but
Mr. Nathan surely would not have kept much cash in his
empty house. Immediately a telegram was dispatched to
Morristown: FATHER IN AN ACCIDENT. COME AT ONCE.

There ensued one of the most bizarre murder cases in
the history of New York crime, and before it was over it
had received worldwide attention, even in Russia, where
the Jewish press commented on "the murder of a wealthy
and influential New York Jew." It was a traumatic experience for a family that had always studiously avoided publicity of any sort whatever.

Immediately—awful though it sounded—the prime suspect became Washington Nathan, with his dissolute nature,
who was suspected of having murdered, in Lizzie Borden
fashion (though that case was still more than twenty years
away), his own father. Frederick, the "good son," known

to have worshiped his father, was never for a moment under suspicion. What must have happened, it was argued, was this: Wash Nathan had come home from his evening on the town, had stepped into his father's room to ask for money, and had been refused. The two had argued. Finally, in a rage, Wash had grabbed the odd instrument—carpenters working in the house might have left it lying about—and attacked his father. He had then rifled the safe and cashbox. New York newspapers were soon hinting that "someone from inside" must be the guilty party. How could a murderer have entered a locked and bolted house? Wash Nathan's guilt seemed terribly likely.

At the inquest that followed, a long series of contradictory and confusing facts began to emerge. The doctor who first examined the body testified that he did so at 6:05 A.M., and that in his opinion Mr. Nathan had been dead for three to four hours, no longer. This would place the time of death at between 2 and 3 A.M. The policeman on the block, John Mangam, testified that he checked the front door of the Nathan house at 1:30 and 4:30 A.M., as a matter of routine, and on both occasions found the door securely locked, and saw no signs of any disturbances within the house. Other residents of the neighborhood, however, stepped forth to say that Officer Mangam was not as diligent as he claimed to be, and that they had never known him to check the door of any house.

Then there was the testimony of the guest at the Fifth Avenue Hotel, and the matter of which Nathan brother had been partly dressed and which had been covered with blood. This was important because the brothers had told the police that Washington had been the first to come downstairs that morning, dressed and ready for the early visit to the synagogue. He had seen his father and immediately cried out to Frederick, who then came running down the stairs, partly dressed. Frederick told the police that he knelt briefly beside his father, and touched him, thus becoming covered with blood, and then both brothers had run shouting down another flight of stairs to the street—through a front door that, both claimed, was standing wide open. At first, the hotel guest—a Major General Blair—identified Frederick as the bloodied and undressed one, and Washington as the clothed one, thus corroborating both brothers' story. But then he changed his mind, and insisted that it was the other way around, making liars out of both

Mr. Nathan's sons. Frederick Nathan had a heavy beard. Washington Nathan had a small moustache. There was little family resemblance, and it would be difficult to mix them up. On the other hand, General Blair had viewed the scene from diagonally across the street, through trees and from an upper story, in the early morning light and through sleepy eyes. His testimony could not be weighted too heavily.

Then there was the altogether baffling fact that although four other people were sleeping in the house at the time, no one had heard a sound of what must have been a terrible and screaming ordeal—furniture overturned, a body bludgeoned again and again, dragged across a room. The two sons, just one floor above, claimed to have heard nothing. Mrs. Kelly had heard the storm earlier, but nothing after that. Her son William had heard nothing. The Walton Peckhams, who owned the house nearest to the Nathans'—separated from it by eighty feet—said yes, they thought they had heard noises, thumping, a bang or two, a door slammed. At first, they thought it was the storm, then perhaps a burglar in their own house, and finally conjectured that it might be coming from next door. Mr. Peckham said he was positive the hour of the noises was 2:30 A.M., though he had not consulted his watch. He knew because he had had "a good sound sleep" before being awakened, and that meant it had to be two-thirty. His bumps and slams had to be discounted.

Though it was a stifling city night, all windows in the Nathans' neighborhood appeared to have been firmly shut against the slightest breeze. This seemed strange to some people, but of course there had been that storm and there was also, in 1870, a belief some householders shared that night air was injurious to health, even deadly. From across the street, meanwhile, General Blair's hotel window had been open all night long, but he had heard nothing until the brothers came running into the street.

Then there was the problem of the murder weapon. Where had it come from? One of the workmen at the Nathan house said yes, he thought he had seen something of the sort lying about in the days previous to the murder. But another said no, there had definitely never been a "dog" of that sort in the house. Though it was described as a carpenter's dog, the Nathan carpenters said it was not theirs; it was not, in fact, a tool used in their sort of work but was used primarily in logging operations. Logging operations! The killer had carried his weapon a long way to a fashionable address in Manhattan. It was also not a tool customarily employed by safecrackers, although it was quite possible that it could be used that way. Another expert on "dogs" came forth to say that this was not a logging implement at all, but was used "to lay the flooring of yachts and other small vessels." The inquiry appeared to be leading nowhere.

All sorts of unlikely people came forth now to contribute evidence leading to an explanation of what might, or might not, have happened that night at 12 West Twenty-third. A young newsboy, James Nies, said he had been delivering his papers on that street at around 5 A.M. and, when passing the Nathan mansion, saw a man "dressed like a mason" walk up the steps of the house, stoop, and pick up a strange piece of yellow paper which "looked like a check." The alleged mason studied the piece of paper, pocketed it, and departed. Who was the mason? The murderer returned to the scene of his crime when he discovered he had dropped some incriminating document? A mere passerby curious to see what scrap of paper might be lying outside the front door of a rich man's house? And what had the piece of paper been—something dropped from the burglar's haul? Neither the piece of paper nor the mason ever turned up, and the investigation struck another blind alley.

Next came a report of mysterious midnight goings-on outside the mansion of Samuel F. B. Morse, the inventor of the telegraph. The Morse house, on West Twenty-second Street, backed up to the Nathan house and, according to the Morses' caretaker, a Mr. Devoy, he had returned home about twelve-thirty on the night in question and had seen a strange coach and pair standing in front of the Morse stables. A man was lying inside the coach, and Mr. Devoy asked him to move on. Mr. Devoy said he believed a second man was inside the coach, and that he had heard at least two men "whispering" within—but he could not be sure. Later, his wife told him that the coach had been there since at least ten-thirty, and that it remained there for at least another hour after Devoy told the occupant to go, and that around two o'clock a heavily cloaked driver mounted the box and drove rapidly away.

Perhaps the oddest testimony of all came from a Miss

Annie Keenan, a music teacher from New Jersey. Miss Keenan had been walking along Twenty-third Street on the evening of the twenty-eighth, at around 8:30 P.M., and had seen a man with "a crazy look" in his eye poking furtively about the front stoop of the Nathan house. He appeared to have "some rigid object" stuffed up the sleeve of his coat—the "dog," of course. While Miss Keenan watched, the man entered the Nathan house through a basement window and, as he did so, there was a loud "clank" as his arm struck the window frame—proving that it was the dog. A letter, signed "A.K.H.," arrived at police headquarters under a Washington postmark and, in return for eight hundred dollars, "to be left inside the railing of Grace Church," the writer offered to return "the papers" that would solve the case. An attempt was made to draw some connection between "A.K.H." and Annie Keenan's initials, but this proved fruitless, as did an effort to connect these "papers" with the newsboy's yellow slip.

At around the same time, a lawyer named Thomas Dunphy got himself sorrily entangled with an already hopelessly entangled case. Mr. Dunphy, who had a theory of how the murder had been committed, was acting out his theory for the benefit of some women friends in Brooklyn. Unfortunately, he chose to demonstrate the murder method using the first person pronoun—"I lunged toward him," etc.—and must have given a convincing performance, because an eavesdropping neighbor overheard the scene, was certain she was listening to a firsthand account of the Nathan murder, and called the police. Mr. Dunphy spent an uncomfortable night in jail before it was demonstrated that he could have had nothing to do with it.

Naturally, the person the press and public were most eager to hear testify was Washington Nathan. He arrived on the witness stand looking cool, composed, and well-tailored, carrying a gold-handled stick, gray gloves, and a tall silk hat. He described himself as "commission merchant," with offices at 25 Water Street downtown, but his account of the evening of July 28 was nowhere near so simple. After leaving his father, he said, he spent "an hour or two" simply strolling around New York. First he walked up Fifth Avenue to the Saint James Hotel, then over to Twenty-fourth and Broadway, then into Madison Square Park—very near his home—where he listened for a while to a band concert. Meeting a friend there, he walked back to the Saint James, where each had a glass of sherry. Next he walked down Broadway to the point at which it met Fifth Avenue, where he met "these two girls"—and he waved his hand, indicating that the young ladies were in the courtroom. The three then walked to Delmonico's, and he said good-bye to them there, going into the coffee room to read the papers. For a celebrated *bon vivant,* he was having a singularly dull evening.

He then went back to the Saint James *again*—but no sherry this time—and then toward home, popping into the Fifth Avenue Hotel on the way. He met a friend there and stayed for a chat. At about nine, he left the hotel and headed for a crosstown bus. He rode down to East Fourteenth Street, near the Academy of Music, and entered a house at number 104. He stayed until around midnight— delayed slightly by the storm—and then went back uptown to Broadway and Twenty-first Street, entering Brown & Kingsley's restaurant, where he had supper: Welsh rarebit. From there he went straight home, let himself in with a key, locked the door behind him, and went upstairs. He looked in on his father, saw him sleeping peacefully, and continued upstairs to his own room. He heard nothing during the night, saw nothing more of his father until the following morning, when he found him lying on the floor in a pool of blood—with the front door standing wide open.

He testified that it was not true that he and his father had ever had any serious quarrels. He insisted there was no foundation for reports that he spent thirty thousand dollars annually on pleasurable pursuits, and doubted that he spent more than three thousand dollars. His father, he said, had given him a five-thousand-dollar stake to start him in business, and any arguments about Wash's spending had been minor. He painted a picture of a warm relationship between father and son, and on the whole gave a confident, poised performance.

For some reason it was deemed necessary to verify Wash's account of his whereabouts between nine and twelve. The reason may have been the sheer delectation of the courtroom audience, because it was soon entertainingly clear just what sort of house it was that the young man had visited at 104 East Fourteenth Street during those three hours. A lady called Clara Dale was summoned to the stand, and a great deal of space in the press was devoted to her costume and appearance. The *Herald* reported:

> Miss Dale was very gaily attired in a costly dress of green striped silk, embellished with all the usual paraphernalia of panier, flounces and trimmings. She wore light colored lavender kid gloves and over a jaunty round hat of the latest pattern was spread a green veil which hung down over her face almost completely hiding it from view. Beneath this she wore a black lace "masked battery" which totally covered the upper portion of her face.

The reporter from the *World,* meanwhile, despite the veils and masks, found that "her face was full and fair, with large blue eyes, and her physique and carriage were stately." It also noted her hair, in "waterfall and puffs," and her shoes, "with preposterous high brass heels and white pearl buttons and tassels." Miss Dale testified that Mr. Washington Nathan had been with her during the hours of nine and twelve on the fatal night—which, of course, did nothing to establish his whereabouts at the time of the murder, two hours later.

But who killed good Benjamin Nathan? As the months dragged on, the answer seemed to grow increasingly elusive. For all the suspicion that surrounded young Wash, there was not a shred of evidence. Where was he at the time? Home in bed, he said, and there was no one to prove otherwise. The New York Stock Exchange—which had lowered its flag to half staff to mourn the passing of a member—had offered a ten-thousand-dollar reward for the apprehension of the killer. The Nathan family had added to this, and presently the Nathan murder reward had mounted to over thirty thousand dollars. This led to the usual number of crank letters with offers to provide information, which proved unfounded, and to a series of false "confessions." Several suspects were arrested, then released for lack of evidence. The months turned into years.

At one point a convict at Sing Sing named George Ellis —who could have obtained a pardon for bringing a murderer to justice, and therefore had much to gain—came forward and announced that if he could see the murder weapon he could identify the murderer. In great secrecy, Ellis was brought down to New York from prison and

taken into a room where Police Chief Jourdan had as-
sembled some twenty-five carpenters' dogs, of assorted
shapes and sizes, collected from hardware stores across the
city. Without hesitation, Ellis walked to the murder weapon and pointed: "This is the one." It belonged, he said, to
a burglar he knew named Billy Forrester, who had once
told him of a plan he had to rob the Nathan house. Forrester was traced to Texas, brought to New York, and subjected to intensive interrogation. One of the "witnesses"
brought to confront him was Annie Keenan, the New Jersey music teacher, who immediately identified him as the
man with the "crazy look" she had seen that night—despite the fact that over two years had passed, and the woman was demonstrated to be extremely nearsighted. In the
end it was decided that despite Ellis' astonishing identification of the weapon—which could, of course, have been a
coincidence—and Miss Keenan's testimony, these two facts
did not add up to a case against Billy Forrester, and he
was released. Because there never was a solid suspect, there
never was a trial. Today, a hundred years later, the case
remains unsolved.

A number of people have taken up the Benjamin Nathan murder, and reexamined all the confusing, contradictory evidence. One of the stranger accounts is in a book
called *Recollections of a New York Chief of Police,* written seventeen years after the event by ex-Chief George
Walling. Walling builds up a damaging case against Washington Nathan, and speaks of the young man "clinking
glasses with the *demi-monde*" on the night of the killing.
He also claims that, in the weeks following his father's
death, Wash Nathan wore "a handkerchief like a bandage" around his neck, despite the fact that this was not
mentioned in any of the contemporary newspaper reports,
nor at the inquest. Walling implies, of course, that Wash
Nathan wore the bandage to cover wounds earned in a
mortal struggle with his father. But then, after all but accusing Wash—who was still living at the time, and presum-
ably could have sued—Walling reverses himself and points
to William Kelly, the housekeeper's son, who, Walling
claims, admitted burglars to the house that night. Walling's
final claim is equally illogical. He says that Police Chief
Jourdan, the chief at the time of the crime, failed to solve
the murder because "the full horror of it was too much
for him to bear."

Most theorists on the case end up with burglary as the motive, and a number believe that Kelly—who, at the time of the inquest, was shown to have a number of unsavory friends—may have been an accomplice. They speculate that a burglar, or burglars, entered the house that night, and were in the process of opening the safe, using the carpenter's dog as a prying tool, when they were overheard by Mr. Nathan, who rose from his bed and went into the study, surprising them at their work. But it was a clumsy tool for a burglary, and a foolish time to do it, with five people in a house that was empty of furniture and rugs, where the safe had been emptied of all important valuables. Was the open safe just the killer's way to make burglary *seem* to be the motive?

One tiny fact may be significant. Benjamin Nathan, we know, suffered from extreme myopia, and was virtually blind without his thick, steel-rimmed spectacles. The first thing he did on rising each morning was to clamp his glasses across his nose. He did this before he put his feet on the floor. Would he, if he had heard strange sounds in the night from the room next door, have risen to investigate a possible burglary without putting on his glasses? The glasses were found, carefully folded, on the table beside his makeshift bed of mattresses a long way from that bloodied scene, as though their owner had been dragged out of bed with intent to kill.

In the Nathan family, there has never been a moment's suspicion that Washington Nathan could have murdered his father. To a Nathan, it would be something "not done." And newspaper reports at the time of the tragedy, despite the grisly sensationalism attached to such a possibility, always pointed out that "Parricide is extremely rare among Jews."

Several private facts about the case have long been available within the family. For one thing, Wash Nathan was, at the time, having a love affair with a New York society woman somewhat older than he, who happened to be married. His honor as a gentleman, and as a Nathan, would not permit him to tell his exact whereabouts that night, for that would have disgraced the lady's name. Hence his incongruous account of wandering up and down New York streets and in and out of restaurants. "Clara Dale," in her green and purple flounces and spiky shoes, had merely been a bit of window dressing suggested—and hired—by family lawyers. The Nathans also feel that the murderer would have been found if the case had not been mishandled from the start—and by a relative, at that. Judge Albert Cardozo, Benjamin Nathan's brother-in-law (and the father of the future Supreme Court justice), had been running for political office at the time. He had immediately taken charge of things, paying great attention to what was "seemly," and thus good for his political career. Whenever an unseemly fact turned up, the judge took pains to bury it.

The Nathans never moved back to 12 West Twenty-third. Its associations were too painful. The family used to recall, a little sadly, how proud Ben had been of his new house when he built it; he was particularly proud of the massive thickness of its walls. He wanted his house to be soundproof. If he had not been so successful, someone might have heard his cries for help.

Like so many beautiful young men of golden promise, Washington Nathan came to a sad end. He received $75,000 under his father's will, another $25,000 from a grandmother, and $10,000 from an aunt. But his life continued to be dissolute and wasteful, and in a few years he had gone through it all. He was seldom seen as a "commission merchant" down on Water Street, but more often at Delmonico's, or the Fifth Avenue Hotel, or at Brown & Kingsley's. These lounges were his favorite haunts, and he could usually be found there, with this or that young lady "of fashion" or of the Clara Dale variety, and people commented that he was not aging well. By thirty, he looked haggard and old.

In 1879 his mother died, leaving an estate—huge for its day—of over a million Hendricks dollars, $100,000 in a trust fund for Wash. This money was tightly controlled by family lawyers and the bank, and was designed to give Wash a fixed income of a hundred dollars a week. On this skinflint sum he apparently did poorly, and the year of his mother's death his name appeared again—and unpleasantly—in the newspapers. While calling on an actress named Alice Harrison in a hotel suite, he was shot and wounded in the neck by a woman named Fanny Barrett. The bullet lodged in his jaw, and was never removed. At the time, though, one New York physician offered a unique plan. He would operate on Wash's jaw and, when he got his patient drowsy and talkative under morphine, he would dredge the truth out of him about the Nathan murder. No one took him up on his offer.

In 1884 Wash married a non-Jewish widow named Nina Mapleson Arnott, and left the United States. For a while the couple lived in London, then they went to Paris. As he moved into the Mauve Decade, Wash Nathan was often seen in the bar at the Hotel Chatham, alone and looking bewildered, and it was noted that he had grown quite fat.

In 1891, he was sued by French creditors for $1,590 and an attempt was made to break the trust in order to collect the debt. But at home in New York the courts ruled that his mother's trust could not be violated for this purpose, and the French debt went uncollected.

By the late 1880's Washington Nathan had been reported to be in poor health. In the summer of 1892, he went to Boulogne for some sea air. On July 25—the anniversary, very nearly, of the death of his father, who, on the night of his *own* death, had remained in New York to commemorate the anniversary of yet another Nathan's death—he collapsed and died after a walk alone on the beach. He was forty-four years old. His hair, they said, had turned completely white.

18.

"CARDOZOS DON'T CRY"

UNCLE Albert Cardozo, the judge, continued to exert a baleful influence on the House of Nathan. He had been elected justice of the Supreme Court of the State of New York—a post his father, Michael Hart Cardozo, had been nominated for, though the senior Cardozo died before the election—and the Cardozos took themselves very seriously and lived every bit as grandly as their Nathan cousins (Albert was married to Benjamin Nathan's sister Rebecca). The Cardozo house stood at 12 West Forty-seventh Street, diagonally opposite the Jay Gould mansion, which was always bustling with the arrival and departure of carriages, footmen, and liveried servants; from their earliest days the Cardozo children were made to feel part of a world of wealth and consequence. Cardozos were said to come by their lofty position naturally. During the Inquisition, a Cardozo had actually claimed that he was the Messiah. Refusing to convert, he was marched to the stake boldly proclaiming: "Hear, O Israel, the Lord is our God, the Lord is One!"

Albert Cardozo's children—there were seven—were all carefully taught to be able to recite, upon command from any of their elders, the words from the prophet Micah: "To do justice, to love kindness, and to walk humbly with thy God." They were taught to "treat the rich and the poor alike, be kind and civil to those in thy employ." They were instructed to "avoid not the society of your brethren but be firm in faith. Be good citizens and seek the welfare of the community in which you dwell." Unfortunately, Judge Albert Cardozo, from his high position on the New

York State bench, had difficulty adhering to the letter of these worthy mottoes, particularly the latter.

"Boss" William Tweed and his infamous Ring ruled New York in those days, and Tweed was finding the friendship of prominent judges most useful in his operations. Tweed seemed to find Albert Cardozo—with his distinguished façade, his gift of oratory, his air of complete incorruptibility—a particularly helpful man to have on his side. Tweed was interested in naturalization: not the slower legal kind, but the instant and illegal kind, whereby thousands of new immigrants were daily made into American citizens, who naturally were eager to vote for Boss Tweed. Justice Albert Cardozo was one of a trio of judges—the others were George G. Barnard and John H. McCann—who countenanced this activity.

Another ally of Boss Tweed's was Albert Cardozo's neighbor Jay Gould, the railroad manipulator, for whose machinations—he bought and ruined railroads to the right and left of him—it is said that American railroading has been paying to this day. Jay Gould—for financial support —could be very useful to Boss Tweed, and Boss Tweed— for political support—could be useful to Jay Gould. Soon it appeared that at another point of the triangle, within the state judiciary, Justice Albert Cardozo was also being helpful. When a railroad went bankrupt, it was up to the courts to appoint a supposedly impartial referee to help it put its affairs in order and settle its debts. Certainly Cardozo was uncommonly partial in his appointments of refereeships whenever Gould-wrecked railroad companies were in need of financial reorganization. Out of almost six hundred refereeships that Cardozo was authorized to bestow, over three hundred were given to one of Boss Tweed's nephews, and more than a hundred went to Boss Tweed's son. Jay Gould's most notorious adventure, of course, was the one by which he enormously inflated, then utterly destroyed, the stock of the Erie Railroad, a feat that made millions for Gould and rocked the American economy for months thereafter. In the financial carnage that followed, it was necessary to appoint a receiver for the railroad. At the suggestion of Boss Tweed, Albert Cardozo appointed another Tweed henchman. This was too much for the New York State Bar Association, which ordered an investigation into Mr. Justice Cardozo and his activities.

In the Sephardic community as well as within the fam-

ily, it was assumed that Uncle Albert would do the manly
thing: stand up to the investigation, lay his cards on the
table, and demonstrate that he had been guilty of no
wrongdoing. But Uncle Albert failed them utterly. Instead
of submitting to the inquiry, he resigned his post on the
bench, leaving a distinct impression of guilt behind him,
and an odor of malfeasance surrounding the Cardozo
name. Had Tweed and Gould paid off their good friend?
Uncle Albert always insisted that they had not, but no one
quite believed him, since, by resigning, he had sidestepped
the inquiry. Also, it had appeared to many people that the
Cardozos lived awfully well—far better than would seem
possible on a state justice's salary. After stepping down
from the bench, Uncle Albert resumed a quiet practice of
law, and the Cardozos lived less well.

All this was in 1873, when Albert's youngest son, Benjamin Nathan Cardozo, was just three years old. (Benjamin had been just a few months old when the uncle after whom he was named had been so brutally murdered.)
Six years later, when he was only nine, his mother died,
and an even darker atmosphere fell upon the Cardozos'
house. Mr. Gould and Boss Tweed were no longer friends
of the family. More and more the ostentatious style of life
across Fifth Avenue at the Gould mansion was in painful
contrast with that at 12 West Forty-seventh. Albert Cardozo used to complain in his twilight years that he was
"the victim of politics." "I was a victim of politics, a victim of politics," he would insist again and again, and his
family, out of loyalty and love, took this sympathetic line.
But everywhere the bitter truth was well known: Albert
was a weakling.

Within the tight little world of the Sephardim, Albert's
plight was the cause of deep embarrassment. After all, if
such disgrace could befall a member of one of the oldest,
one of the leading families, what did it say about all the
others who considered themselves the "few" elite, but-
tressed against the ruffian horde that stood outside the gate?
This, on top of all the leering publicity the Nathan murder trial had generated, seemed almost too much to bear.
What was the point of being able to say (as some of the
Gomez descendents liked to say, rather slyly, apropos of
the new-rich Germans), "We made *our* money in wam-
pum," when a member of the family of Albert Cardozo's
stature could prove himself to be so easily corruptible? If

anything, Albert Cardozo's misfortunes had the effect upon the Sephardim of making them draw together into an even tighter knot of privacy and privilege. Now the Sephardim seemed to want to pull a shell around themselves, a chrysalis that would be impervious to prying from outside.

Within these contours of Sephardic life, Benjamin Nathan Cardozo grew up. His was a notably unhappy childhood. And yet, if it had not been for the family misfortunes, in particular his father's disgrace, it is quite unlikely that Benjamin Cardozo would have become the man he came to be. Because, from his earliest boyhood, he set out upon a life plan designed to exonerate, or at least vindicate, his father, and bring back honor to the Cardozo name.

His growing up was not particularly helped by his father's choice of tutor for him. Albert Cardozo was a snob —which may have been at the root of many of his troubles—and keeping up with the Joneses was one of his preoccupations. In the 1880's the family to keep up with was, of all people, that of Joseph Seligman, the German Jew who had arrived in New York in the 1830's with one hundred dollars sewn in the seat of his pants, had started off as a foot peddler in Pennsylvania, and had succeeded to the extent that he now headed an international banking house that did business with the Rothschilds. To the older Sephardic group, it seemed that the Seligmans and their ilk had taken on preposterous airs, and they were actually getting into select clubs such as the Union. A few years earlier, Joseph Seligman had startled New York's Jewish community, and the rest of the city as well, by hiring Horatio Alger to tutor his children. Not to be outdone by an upstart immigrant German, Albert Cardozo decided to do the same for his son Ben, and Mr. Alger joined the Cardozo household.

Small and roly-poly, with a round bald head and squinting, nearsighted eyes, Mr. Alger was described by one of the family as "a dear, absurd little man." He was certainly a far cry from his rags-to-riches newsboy heroes in such then-popular romances as *Ragged Dick* and *Tattered Tom*. He was flutily effeminate, with mincing ways and a fondness for practicing ballet positions in his spare time, crying out such exclamations as "Oh, lawsy me!" or bursting into wild tears when things went wrong. Yet he once seriously announced his candidacy for President of the United States after a friend, as a joke, told him he could defeat Garfield.

The immense popularity of his books had made Alger a rich man, but he always considered his true forte to be poetry, which he wrote very badly. He once wrote a poem—of which the kindest critical word was "interminable"—explaining American life. And because he had created boy folk heroes, he saw himself as a kind of missionary to youth. This was why he accepted tutoring posts, and why he gave so generously to causes for the betterment of orphaned boys, shoeshine boys, hoboes, and derelicts on the Bowery. As a teacher he was hopelessly ineffective in both the Seligman and the Cardozo households, where healthy growing boys kept him perpetually cowed. They locked him in closets and tied him to chairs, and played all manner of cruel tricks on their tiny tutor. Benjamin Cardozo once said, in a remarkable example of understatement, "He did not do as successful a job for me as he did with the careers of his newsboy heroes." And yet one thing may have rubbed off on young Ben Cardozo: Alger's love of poetry. All his life, Benjamin Cardozo was an avid reader of poems—he occasionally tried his hand at poetry himself—and had a fascination, and tremendous respect, for the English language.

At the same time, there was no doubt that, despite any deficiencies in his education, young Ben possessed a brilliant mind—a mind that would carry him into Columbia as a freshman at the age of fifteen (he graduated at nineteen) and, with what he described as "an almost ecstatic consecration to the law," into a career that has hardly been equaled in the history of American jurisprudence. With only two years of law school, instead of the usual three, and without even an LLB degree, he became a member of the bar, moved on to become chief judge of the court of appeals of New York State, and at last achieved the highest judicial post in the country, justice of the Supreme Court of the United States. But was it his brilliant mind alone that pushed him to these accomplishments? A great deal is known and has been written about Benjamin N. Cardozo, the great jurist, humanitarian, and towering public figure. Somewhat less is understood of the man, who was lonely, tortured, obsessed.

Despite moments of inadvertent hilarity provided by Horatio Alger, the Cardozo household grew increasingly gloomy during the years of Ben Cardozo's youth, and a pervading air of melancholy and dissent settled upon the place. Though the Cardozo children were bound together by natural ties of love and family, the strongest bond between them seemed to be sadness. There were endless quarrels with relatives, sometimes over money or business matters, but more often over real or imagined social slights. As Ben Cardozo's cousin Annie Nathan wrote:

> As a child, I was always trying to tread a path warily through the maze of family feuds. "Was it Aunt Becky or Aunt Rachel," I would ask myself, "who didn't speak to Uncle John?" "Which aunt was it with whom Mama had quarreled?" These perplexing feuds always had their start in the failure of some relative to "ask after" one of the family. There were fourteen aunts and uncles—almost all with numerous progeny —so some slight, quite unintentional lapse might easily have been pardoned. But not in our family. It was the crime of crimes. It was with us as the laws of the Medes and the Persians that on meeting a relative (particularly an "in-law") however fortuitously, however pressed for time, one must inquire meticulously into the state of health of each and every member of that particular family. Any deviation, any temporary forgetfulness, was set down as a deliberate slight, to be resented as such.

At times, it must have seemed to young Benjamin Cardozo that a terrible curse hung over his branch of the Nathan family, rather like that which afflicted the Greek House of Atreus: somehow, before he was finished, each member of the Cardozo family must be made to pay for the father's sins. Not long after his mother's death, an older sister, Grace, died at the age of twenty-five. That same year, Ben's father died. That was the autumn Ben started at Columbia. Next year, Ben's twin sister, Emily— described as "the one high-spirited member of the family" —was married, but in the family this was treated as another tragedy. The man she married, Frank Bent, was a Christian and, though Emily was the only one of the seven Cardozo children to marry, she was thereafter treated as dead. The family actually "cut *kriah*" for her— that is, they held a service for the dead for her. (To cut kriah is to cut a tiny snippet of one's clothing—always in an inconspicuous place, or one easily mended—symbolic of the Biblical practice of mourners rending their garments over the deceased.) This particular family service, Benjamin Cardozo once recalled, "disgusted" him. Emily Cardozo's name was dropped from family conversation, and her portrait, literally, was turned against the wall.

A few years later, Ben's only brother (another had died in childhood), Allie, whom he idolized, died, also at an early age. That left Ben and two older spinster sisters, Ellen and Elizabeth—plain, shy Nell and beautiful, excitable Lizzie. Lizzie wanted to be a painter, and she studied art under Kenneth Hayes Miller, who described her as "the end of a long line of aristocrats. She looked like a feminine edition of Dante. Eyes so dark and intense, the aquiline, aristocratic nose." For all her beauty and the intensity of her personality, Lizzie Cardozo had very little artistic talent, which few people—including Mr. Miller—could bring themselves to tell her. She painted incessantly nonetheless, and also wrote fervid, morbid poetry full of death and loss and desolation. She suffered from a recurring back ailment which, by the time she reached maturity, kept her in almost perpetual pain. But it was clear to many that more than this was wrong with Lizzie. She had visions, hallucinatory fantasies which may have been heightened by drugs prescribed for pain, but which certainly sprang from some deeper psychosis, and when Lizzie's "bad periods" became impossible for Nell and Ben to manage, a trained nurse, Kate Tracy, had to be hired to handle her. Miss Tracy remained Lizzie's companion for life, and the two women retired to a little cottage in Connecticut. Was Lizzie Cardozo perhaps too highly bred? She was descended on both sides from people who had married their close relatives. Both sets of grandparents had been marriages of cousins, as had at least two sets of her great-grandparents. Was some weak and fatal strain coming to the surface, threatening to fling apart permanently the closely knit fabric of Spanish Jewish families? Was Lizzie indeed "the end of the line"? Such thoughts must have darkened the mind of Ben Cardozo as he set out with "ecstatic consecration" to be a great lawyer and jurist.

And so, at 803 Madison Avenue, where the family had moved after Albert Cardozo's downfall, it was now just Miss Nell, eleven years older than her brother, and Ben.

Their father had left a depleted estate of less than $100,000, and much of this was required to care for the afflicted Lizzie. Young Ben, working furiously in law offices downtown, became the breadwinner. Nell kept house for him. Darkly handsome, but small and frail of physique—he was described by one of his Columbia professors as "desperately serious"—Ben buried himself in study and work from early in the morning until late at night. At Columbia he had been too young for the social life—he was a sophomore before his voice began to change—and by the time he began to practice law he had lost all taste for it. He usually brought work home with him from the office and, after a quiet dinner with Nell, he would be back at his desk until after midnight. His girl cousins used to try to persuade him to accompany them to dances or to concerts or the theater. He always refused, using the press of work to do as an excuse. Sometimes he would break his routine with a bit of four-handed piano with Nellie of an evening, but that was all. He had, he once admitted, hesitated before deciding to go into law. He had considered studying art. But he hadn't hesitated for long, because forces from the past stronger than he were driving him to expiate his father's guilt.

Benjamin Cardozo brought a particular and individualistic "style" with him to American justice. Though he was often called a "lawyer's lawyer," with a photographic memory that could cite cases, chapter and verse, without looking them up in the lawbooks, he was also an early champion of the little man against what often seemed the giant and uncaring mechanism of urban or corporate society. For instance, in an early—1916—automobile-safety case that came before the New York State court of appeals, a man named McPherson was suing an automobile company for injuries incurred when a new car he had bought turned out to have a defective wheel. The manufacturer had argued that it was not responsible, since it had not sold the car directly to McPherson, but to a dealer. There was no proof, the company argued, that it had known of the defect—though the car had collapsed when being driven at eight miles an hour. This defense had been upheld by the lower court.

Not so, replied Judge Cardozo in his reversing opinion. He wrote: "Beyond all question, the nature of an automobile gives warning of probable danger if its construction is defective. This automobile was designed to go fifty miles an hour. Unless its wheels were sound and strong, injury was almost certain. It was as much a thing of danger as a defective engine for a railroad. The defendant knew the danger." Cardozo also pointed out that the company obviously knew, when it supplied its dealers with cars, that they were for the ultimate sale to motorists, and that any claim to the contrary was silly and "inconsequential." He added: "Precedents drawn from the days of travel by stagecoach do not fit the conditions of travel today. The principle that the danger must be imminent does not change, but the things subject to the principle do change. They are whatever the needs of life in a developing civilization require them to be."

Cardozo was also one of the first American jurists to spell out clearly that what is a legal wrong is not necessarily a moral wrong, and that this fact must be considered in, for example, judging the crimes of the criminally insane. Cardozo was the kind of jurist who always looked for ways in which the laws, as written, were either too vague or too universal. There was the case of a cigar packer named Grieb who, under the instructions of his employer, was delivering a crate of cigars to a customer and stumbled on a staircase and fell. The accident proved fatal but, since the man had been delivering the crate after regular working hours, his employer had argued that his widow and children were not entitled to the customary death benefits under the Workmen's Compensation Act. The man was not, his employer insisted, legally employed at nighttime. This position had been upheld in the lower court.

But, said Judge Cardozo in his reversal:

> Grieb's service, if it had been rendered during working hours, would have been incidental to his employment. To overturn this award, it is necessary to hold that the service ceased to be incidental because rendered after hours. That will never do. The law does not insist that an employee shall work with his eye upon the clock. Services rendered in a spirit of helpful loyalty, after closing time has come, have the same protection as the services of the drone or the laggard. . . . What Grieb then undertook to do with his employer's approval was just as much a part of

the business as if it had been done in the noonday sun. . . . If such a service is not incidental to the employment within the meaning of this statute, loyalty and helpfulness have earned a poor reward.

For all the clarity of his thinking and the lucidity of his judgment, he remained an exceedingly modest man and often expressed a low opinion of himself. Once, accepting an honorary Doctor of Laws degree from a university, he described himself as "a mere plodding mediocrity." When asked what he meant by this, he said: "I say plodding mediocrity, for a mere mediocrity cannot go far, but a plodding one can go quite a distance." This was about as generous with himself as he permitted himself to be, though he once went so far as to describe himself as a "judicial evolutionist." And he remained a solitary, moody man who entertained—with sister Nell acting as his hostess —only when it seemed to him an absolutely inescapable necessity, and who spent his leisure time reading poetry, studying law, or—for a rare diversion—studying Italian and playing a bit of gentlemanly golf.

He spent a great deal of time answering letters. Each letter he received—even as a Supreme Court justice—was personally answered by him, and in longhand. He wrote a beautifully flowing script. One of his lifelong friends was Mrs. Lafayette Goldstone and, throughout his long correspondence with her over a period of more than twenty years, the wistful, self-deprecatory spirit of melancholy pervades. When he was appointed to the New York State court of appeals, in 1914, a certain amount of time spent in Albany was required, and he always treated these "exiles," as he called them, as though Albany were Devil's Island. Years later, after his appointment to the United States Supreme Court, he took an apartment in Washington, and his view of life in the capital was equally dismal. From his apartment at 2101 Connecticut Avenue he wrote in a characteristic vein to Mrs. Goldstone: "The letterhead tells the story. Alas! I am homesick for the old scenes and the old faces. The apartment is beautiful, but my heart is far away." The following year, he wrote: "I feel more than ever an exile. . . . [New York], the great city— election is on, and I am condemned to take no part in it. 'Hang yourself, brave Crillon,' said Henry IV after a great victory had been gained. 'Hang yourself, brave Crillon, we fought at Argeres, and you were not there.' "

Of life in Washington, he wrote: "I call myself Gandhi, an ugly old saint—or at least a putative saint—to whom the faithful pay obeisance. They come here in great numbers, young and old, stupid and clever, some to stare and some to talk. Among the clever was Irwin Edman. . . . What a delightful youth he is!"

His great idol was Oliver Wendell Holmes, whom he replaced on the Supreme Court bench, and after a visit with Holmes at Beverly, Massachusetts, Cardozo wrote: "Holmes is a genius and a saint, enough of the mischievous devil in him not to make the sainthood burdensome, but still, I think, a saint, and surely a genius." Yet Cardozo's own reticence and shyness hampered him during the visit and, writing again to Mrs. Goldstone, he said: "I wish I could talk freely like you. I'm fairly paralyzed when I visit strangers whom I admire and revere. But the old man sent word to me that he entreated me to visit him, so what could I do? My friend, Felix Frankfurter, who knows him well, drove me there from Boston, and back to my hotel. What an egocentric letter! I'm ashamed of it. . . ."

When Holmes died, Cardozo wrote: "Holmes was great. His life work had been finished, but he remained a magnificent symbol. The world is poorer without him. I was the last person to visit him before he took to his bed."

Cardozo was capable of a certain gentle humor. Once, after a visit to New York's Metropolitan Museum, he wrote: "Almost as one enters, one is greeted by two gigantic effigies of the Pharaoh of the Exodus, a gift of the Egyptian government, brought from the Temple at Luxor and wrought by some Egyptian sculptor about 1250 B.C. If the effigies could see, they would probably surmise that New York was the place to which the Jews, driven forth from the land of Egypt, had been guided by the wise old Moses."

But the note of sadness was forever creeping in. "May all happiness be yours in your bright and sunlit dwelling," he wrote to Mrs. Goldstone. "I cling to you, says an Italian (I am airing my new learning) 'come l'edera il muro,' as the ivy to the wall. That is the way I feel about my friends as I watch the devastating years." And, a little later, from his summer home in Rye: "I am glad you like me for myself and not for my supposed greatness which, alas, is non-existent. . . . Whatever greatness I have is the greatness of a drudge."

As he grew older, and more celebrated, people—particularly his female relatives—kept trying to make matches for him, but to no avail. He remained steadfastly a bachelor, and increasingly devoted to and dependent upon his sister Nell. They were like mother and son, she reminding him to take his umbrella if it looked like rain, telling him to bundle up warm in case of snow. It is likely that if he had ever wanted to marry, strong-willed Nell would not have let him. Her entire life revolved around him, and she was jealous every moment they were apart. His biographer George Hellman wrote: "He knew all that he meant to her—the jealousy as well as the depth of her affection. He made allowances for the jealousy; he was grateful for the affection." To a cousin who once asked him why he denied himself the pleasures of a wife and children, Cardozo replied quickly, "I can never put Nell in second place!" And once, at a New York dinner party, a young woman seated next to the great jurist had the temerity to say to him, "Won't you tell me, Judge Cardozo, whether you were ever in love?"

He looked briefly startled, and said, "Once." Then, adroitly, he changed the subject. He never revealed any more than that.

It is possible that Cardozo saw himself as a kind of missionary, not only to redeem the Cardozo name but also to restore prestige and authority to Sephardic Jewry in general—to help this tiny band ("We few," he used to say) retain its place in history. Because certainly the spunk and individuality that characterized the earlier generations in America seemed to be disappearing as the world moved into the twentieth century. After two hundred fifty years, the fabric of Sephardic life seemed to be shredding, flying apart, no longer a knit thing and all of a piece. Cardozo had always been fiercely proud of his forebears, the ancestors who had fought as officers in the Revolution, who had founded banks and captained vessels, who had sat at the right hand of Presidents from Washington on down. And yet the tragic fact was that the importance—economic, political, and social—of the oldest Jewish families was diminishing. They were being eclipsed by Jews from other lands and, at the same time, the old standards were disappearing. Suddenly, in the finest and oldest families, there were suicides, divorces (his cousin, the writer Robert Nathan, had already been divorced three times), alcoholics, wastrels, and people who had to be locked away with custodians. Did Cardozo see his father's troubles as symptomatic of a larger trouble—a trouble reflected also in his sister Emily's marriage to a Christian, and his sister Lizzie's unhappy state? Was the end of the line at hand for "we few"? He may have sensed this, and spent much of his life attempting to reverse the trend.

The year 1868 was a shattering one for all the Sephardim. It was the year that the splendid new Reform Temple Emanu-El opened its doors, with a cluster of the wealthiest German Jews in New York on its committees and board of directors. Not only was the new edifice splendid, and obviously expensive, and not only was it right on Fifth Avenue at Forty-third Street, far north of Nineteenth Street, where Shearith Israel then more modestly reposed (inherent in Emanu-El's choice of site was the statement that the forties were now more fashionable than the area around Thirty-third Street), but it represented —on a national scale—a triumph for the Reform movement, which the Sephardim had so long opposed. When the temple was dedicated, the *New York Times* editorialized that Emanu-El's congregation was "the first to stand forward before the world and proclaim the dominion of reason over blind and bigoted faith." The Judaism of Emanu-El was praised as "the Judaism of the heart, the Judaism which proclaims the spirit of religion as being of more importance than the letter." The farsighted Germans behind Emanu-El were extolled for having "become one with progress."

Immediately there was a great deal of grumbling within the Shearith Israel congregation, and it wasn't long before a faction had formed that talked of the need for a new building and of "modernization" and "improvements" in the service. One group wanted to introduce family pews— eliminating segregated seating—and to install an organ. Another urged that the fixed prayers should be fewer in number, with less repetition, so that "in these modern, busy times," the service would be shorter. Still another group thought that the ancient Spanish music had outlived its usefulness and meaning. By 1895, the debate had reached such a point of ill feeling and crossed purposes that a meeting of the elders of the synagogue was held.

The meeting started off stormily. Then Ben Cardozo, still a young lawyer, got to his feet. Nothing, he said, must be allowed to change the Sephardic ritual of the synagogue, the oldest in America. Its very name, meaning "Remnant of Israel," indicated that there were values here worth clinging to at all costs. Perhaps the weight of his Nathan-Seixas-Levy-Hart ancestors added strength to his words, for he was certainly effective. After his speech, a vote was taken, and the proposed changes and updatings were defeated by a count of seventy-three to seven. Thus Sephardic tradition stepped into another century of imperturbability.

He may not consciously have meant to, but as Mr. Justice Cardozo he became Sephardic Jewry's proudest figure, restoring the old families' oldest pride, a pride of history, of heritage, of race—which was the way *he* felt it.

Cardozo watched with dismay as his beloved Nell grew old and frail. They continued their old routine: winters in Albany, then home to New York, then to the house at Allenhurst, on the Jersey shore, for summers, and the quiet evenings of cards and four-handed piano. Then Nell became paralyzed and could no longer play. He wrote: "Our rides along Ocean Avenue have lost the point and tang that they had in former years. Sea Bright has lost its brightness." As the summer drew to a close: "I have been worried again about Nell. She hasn't been so well for the last week—a slight temperature in the afternoon, a quicker pulse at times, and speech more incoherent. Dr. Woolley has visited her daily. . . . So the summer creeps its weary length along."

Then an improvement: "There has been no recurrence of the alarming seizure of a fortnight ago, but I cannot tell when one may come." And, a few weeks later: "I am sending you some snapshots of Nell that were taken a few weeks ago while she was sitting on the porch. I think she looks sweet, and remarkably well, all things considered." But by the following summer he was despondent again. "She seems to have lost strength," he wrote in August, 1928, "and her power of speech has not at all improved. The effect of these long silences, when once she was so full of animation, is something that I do not need to describe. . . ." A few months later, Nell died. This woman who had been so possessive of him and ambitious for him did not live to see the capstone of his career, his elevation to the United States Supreme Court three years later. And without her the achievement seemed empty to him.

He was even reluctant to accept the appointment. To a cousin he wrote: "Indeed I don't want to go to Washington. Please telegraph the President not to name me." Two days later, he wrote: "I'm trying to stave off the appointment. . . . Most of all, I don't want to live in utter loneliness . . . away from all my relatives and friends here whom I love." At last, he accepted the post, but with a deep sigh. And he hated Washington.

A few days after Nell's funeral, Judge Cardozo paid a call on a cousin, Sarah Lyons, who lived in a large and somewhat disheveled apartment not far from his own now-empty house on West Seventy-fifth Street. Miss Lyons, a peppery spinster in her eighties, never at a loss for a quick opinion, admonition, or piece of her mind, and whose bombazine was always stiff with family pride (her mother was a Nathan), poured tea for them both. As they talked, some mention was inevitably made of Nell, and Judge Cardozo's eyes misted over. "Now, Ben Cardozo," said Miss Sarah sternly, "you're not to cry!"

The judge answered quickly, like the dutiful little boy he had always been, "I'm not crying, Aunt Sally."

A few years later, at his funeral, someone said, "If only his father had been strong enough, had had the grit enough, to resist Boss Tweed, Ben would have had a happy life."

True, but then we might not have had the Supreme Court justice.

19.

THE EMBATTLED SISTERS

If the Sephardim of New York needed more Nathans to gossip about, there were suddenly the two fighting Nathan sisters, Annie and Maud. Everyone knew that the two girls did not "get on," and that there had been "troubles" within that branch of the Nathan family—the girls were daughters of Robert Weeks Nathan, Benjamin Nathan's brother—but nothing had ever erupted in any sort of public way. Then, in 1933, Maud Nathan wrote and had published an autobiography called *Once Upon a Time and Today*, which, among other careful glossings-over, painted an idyllic picture of a happy girlhood in New York and, later, in Green Bay, Wisconsin. When, several years later, her sister Annie countered with her own book, called *It's Been Fun*, her version of the Nathan story sounded like no fun at all.

Robert Weeks Nathan was a handsome and cheerful man with a fondness, in the phrase of his day, for a well-turned ankle. In her book, Annie told of how, as a little girl, she was out walking in New York one afternoon with her nurse when who should she see coming from the opposite direction but her father, with an elegantly turned out young lady on his arm. Annie rushed up and hugged her father, who did not seem particularly pleased to see her. In fact, he actually pushed her off, and back into the nurse's clutches. As she and the nurse proceeded, the nurse explained that the man they had met was not Annie's father, though there was "some slight resemblance." Annie Nathan was bewildered. Certainly she knew her own father. But the nurse was very firm, and for years Annie believed that the man she had encountered on the street that afternoon was not her parent but his exact double.

Then she told of the beautiful and mysterious Lazarus cousin whom no one in the family was supposed to "receive." Annie's mother, though, did secretly receive the lady, and the two whispered together over teacups. What was the scandal? Annie could never get to the bottom of it because no one would ever tell her. But it all had to do, she gathered, from "the way of life" the beautiful cousin had chosen to live.

Annie's mother had been a Florance, an old Sephardic family from the South. Florances had first come to Charleston, South Carolina, in the eighteenth century, and from there had migrated to New Orleans and Philadelphia. The Florance men, Annie Nathan revealed in her memoir, were said to have a weakness for hard liquor. That was said to be Uncle Ted's problem. Nonetheless, some Florances were very grand. One of Philadelphia's noted hostesses in the nineteenth century was "Mrs. William Florance of Rittenhouse Square"—she was always so identified except at such times when she was simply "Mrs. Florance," as though there could not be two of her elevated rank. Mrs. Florance was a formidable woman. Looking down her Rittenhouse Square dinner table one evening, she noticed a guest whose gown revealed somewhat more décolletage than Mrs. Florance thought proper. Without a word, she rose from the table, left the room, and returned a moment later with a shawl, which she draped carefully around her guest's shoulders. "You look chilly, my dear," she murmured, and the dinner party proceeded.

Uncle Ted was something else again, and his reputation in Philadelphia left something to be desired. He, too, had married a Nathan—Benjamin Nathan's daughter Rosalie —but he had left her to live openly with another woman. By this woman he had gone so far as to have a daughter —or so "everybody" said. He insisted that his lady friend had been a widow, with a daughter, and that the daughter was not his. Naturally, nobody believed Ted Florance's trumped-up explanation. When the lady friend died, the daughter—quite naturally, it seemed—went to live with her father. It can be imagined what consternation greeted the news that Ted Florance was going to marry this young woman. He was going to marry *his own daughter*. Tea tables in New York rocked with the news for weeks.

Whether or not she really was his daughter will, of course, never be known, but the feathers flew so high in the Nathan and Florance families that the marriage was called off.

His wife, meanwhile, Aunt Rosalie, was not to be outdone by her husband's flamboyant ways. In the 1880's, a "mature" woman with grown children, she suddenly took off for an extended tour of Europe *with another man*. She was accused of "flying in the face of decency," but despite the criticism she continued on her travels, explaining that a man made a more useful and entertaining travel companion than another woman. It saved her no end of trouble and being "put upon," she said. The man was an oculist—he and Aunt Rosalie had first met "on a professional basis"—and, she explained, he also tended to her eye needs while they traveled. (Like Ben Nathan, she was extremely nearsighted.) It seemed, at best, a little incongruous; they were both well past middle age—"Old enough to know better," the Nathans muttered—but the arrangement continued pleasurably for both. Aunt Rosalie's oculist was with her when she died in Switzerland. She was cremated, which was a scandal in itself.

Annie Nathan's father had been a prosperous stockbroker, but he had got caught in the stock market crash of 1875 and had lost everything. It was the beginning of another tragic episode in the Nathan family. A friend, David Kelly—"a devoted admirer of my mother," Annie wrote obliquely in her book—offered Mr. Nathan the unlikely job of general passenger agent for the Green Bay and Minnesota Railroad in Green Bay, Wisconsin. It was a moment of great upheaval for the family, and its impact was not helped by the fact that when the Nathans had established themselves in a house in Green Bay, Mr. Kelly moved in with them. It was an odd ménage—Mr. Nathan seldom spoke to Mr. Kelly, and made no secret of his dislike for him, though both he and an older son worked for Kelly's railroad—and it grew even odder when Mr. Nathan began entertaining his own group of lady friends in the house. Before long, however, Mr. Nathan grew tired of the Middle West and returned to his old Wall Street haunts, leaving his wife, children, and Mr. Kelly in Green Bay.

Annette Florance Nathan was, as they said, "delicate." Feminine and woundable, she had been born in the South and raised by attentive nurses and servants, and she knew nothing of housekeeping before her marriage. (After she was married, her first maid asked her how she wished her potatoes cooked for dinner and she knew so little of cooking that she couldn't answer.) She would have inherited a share of a large fortune, but her father, an unreconstructed Southerner, cut her off without a penny for marrying a Yankee. Though she had no business experience whatever, she hit on the idea, in Green Bay, of trying singlehandedly to recoup the family fortunes. "She had been told wonderful tales of profitable returns from running rooming houses in Chicago," her daughter wrote, and so she set off for Chicago to acquire such an establishment. Several days later, she returned to Green Bay, ecstatic. She had met "a kindly and lovely blue-eyed woman" who had helped her find a house—a place somewhat larger than she had originally thought of buying—and her new friend had helped her spend a great deal of money on furniture and redecoration.

The Chicago venture was a disaster from the beginning. The charming blue-eyed friend had helped Mrs. Nathan buy far too large a house for far too much money, in a neighborhood unsuited for rooming houses, and the friend had also required a sizable cut of the cost of the proceedings. It wasn't long before the house and Mrs. Nathan's investment in it were lost, and the family staggered under another heavy blow.

It was one from which the poor lady never recovered. Her "nervousness" had already become pronounced, and now there were terrible temper tantrums followed by tears and long periods of depression. She had trouble sleeping, and doctors had prescribed both morphine and chloral for her—which she took alternately, or together, and in increasing doses—and by the time the family realized her addiction it was too late. There followed awful scenes, with the children struggling to keep the "medicine" out of their mother's hands, with the arrival of relatives who tried to help, with—ultimately—the tortured woman's confinement in a hospital, her children shipped back East to grandparents, and Mrs. Nathan's death. Robert Weeks Nathan returned to his wife's side for that. Mr. Kelly had, in the meantime, vanished.

All this—her father's philanderings, his financial ineptitude, her mother's relationship to Mr. Kelly—was in

Annie's book. She even pointed out the "Florance family drinking habit." What was not explained in the book was how, out of these shambles of unhappy lives, two women as effective and successful as Annie Nathan and her sister Maud could have emerged. Strong-minded and opinionated, they were too much alike, and too competitive, to get along. But between them they managed to lift the Nathan name out of its Victorian doldrums into twentieth-century prominence.

Maud Nathan, the older of the two, became a double Nathan when, at the age of sixteen, she married a first cousin, Frederick Nathan. She was a great crusader for women's rights. She became a leading suffragist, and marched alongside such doughty women as Harriet May Mills, Mary Garrett Hay, Mrs. Clarence Mackay, and Carrie Chapman Catt. Her name is engraved on a plaque in the New York State Capitol at Albany as one of those responsible for women receiving the vote. She was also a founder of the New York Consumers' League, a welfare group devoted to improving working conditions for women in shops and factories. Though small and soft-spoken, with large dark eyes, she loved nothing better than a fight. Once she became so incensed about what she considered rude treatment by a Manhattan taxicab driver, and the subsequent handling of the matter by the police, that she wrote a stinging letter about it to Police Commissioner Theodore Roosevelt. Her letter so impressed Mr. Roosevelt that he sent for her, and she converted him to the cause of the Consumers' League by taking him on a tour of sweatshops. The future President remained an admirer for life. Once, when foot traffic was being diverted from a street where a luncheon was being given for Prince Henry of Prussia, Mrs. Nathan—on her way to a social welfare meeting—refused to be diverted, and challenged police officers to arrest her. They didn't dare, and she passed through. At one point, the list of organizations on whose boards she sat, international conferences she had attended, and delegations before which she had spoken gave her the longest biographical sketch of any woman listed in *Who's Who in America*.

Longer, even, than her sister Annie's, which was a painful thorn in Annie's side. The sisters' first important falling out was over the issue of women's suffrage. Annie Nathan, who had been the first woman in New York to ride a bicycle—in a day when that sort of thing shocked society and made the newspapers—and who seemed to stand for everything connected with progress and enlightenment for her sex, took the astonishing step of joining the antisuffragists. "She did it mostly to spite Maud," one of her cousins wrote, but whatever the reason, it was the end of peace in the family. On the occasion of one of their rare confrontations, Annie said to Maud, "How would you like your *cook* to vote?" Maud replied coolly, "He does!" Needless to say, the girls' two brothers took Annie's side, as did most men (Judge Cardozo was an important exception; he favored women's voting). And Annie Nathan, meanwhile, had undertaken a separate battle: education for women.

"As far back as I can remember, I was filled with a passionate desire to go to college," she wrote in her memoir. Her father took her on his knee and told her, sadly, that if she pursued this ambition she would never marry, because "Men hate intelligent wives." Nevertheless, she enrolled in what Columbia College then called its "Collegiate Course for Women," and, before she was twenty, was happily married to a successful doctor, Alfred Meyer. She found the "Collegiate Course" dismayingly restricted, however, devoted as it was largely to teaching women to roll hems and balance teacups, and she dropped out in 1886 without a degree, only to discover that the only other institution of higher learning for women within a reasonable distance was the Harvard Annex (a forerunner of Radcliffe), but even that did not offer a degree. There was literally no college for women in New York City, nor anywhere nearby.

So Annie Nathan Meyer set out to start her own college. She set out, on her bicycle, to solicit funds and support from people all over the city who were either indifferent or unalterably opposed to women's colleges. She pedaled hundreds of miles up and down New York City streets, storming the fortresses of the rich and influential, demanding to be seen and listened to. Her friends and family—except her husband—immediately gave up on her, and decided that Annie and her crazy crusade were both hopeless. One of the women on whom she called was a Mrs. Wendell, the mother of a Harvard professor, who "actually wept"—so she said—"thinking of that sweet young girl wasting her *life* in the *impossible* attempt to found a woman's college connected with Columbia."

And yet, little by little, she began to get support for her project. One of the earliest to back her was Ella Weed, headmistress of the then fashionable Miss Annie Brown's School on Fifth Avenue, where proper young ladies of New York society attended classes. Another enthusiastic supporter was Chauncey Depew, the wealthy clubman, and he was joined by such luminaries of the day as Richard Watson Gilder, the former editor of *Century* magazine, and Josephine Shaw Lowell. Suddenly it began to seem as though Annie Nathan Meyer on her bicycle really *was* going to start a college. Barnard College, named after a former president of Columbia (a tactic by which Annie Nathan got the support of Dr. Barnard's widow), received its charter in 1889, and its founder had wasted astonishingly little of her life in the effort. She was just twenty-two years old.

Though Barnard flourished and grew, it remained for years New York's only women's college, and it took New York an uncommonly long time to realize what Barnard was and what New York had. In the 1890's, Mrs. William Astor—*the* Mrs. Astor of the famous ballroom—met her friend Mrs. Duer at a party and asked after Mrs. Duer's daughter, Alice, who later would become the poet Alice Duer Miller. "I haven't seen Alice at any of the dances all winter," said Mrs. Astor. On being told that Alice was attending Barnard College, Mrs. Astor cried out, "What! That sweet young thing?" Several years later, a Barnard fund-raising group was speaking before a wealthy chapter of the Daughters of the American Revolution. Because of the prominence of the women in the group, and the size of their pocketbooks, the Barnard ladies were certain that large contributions would be forthcoming. But, after several weeks had passed, and no gifts arrived, a call was paid on one of the Daughters. Had she been interested in Barnard's financial needs? she was asked. "Ah, yes," the lady replied, "it was so interesting. I wish I could do something, but you see there is so much to do right here in New York. I can't give to anything so far away."

Fund raising for Barnard continued to occupy much of Annie Nathan Meyer's life, and she lived to be nearly ninety. Obviously she was successful, for Barnard has grown from a handful of girls educated on a first-year budget of just over ten thousand dollars to an enrollment today of nearly two thousand women and an endowment in the tens of millions. Annie Meyer wrote:

> A successful beggar must possess many conflicting qualities. She must possess a shrewd knowledge of human nature. And yet not too shrewd. It must be a shrewdness tempered and warmed by a magnificent confidence, a glorious awareness of the heights to which human nature may rise, as well as the depths to which it may fall. Obviously, the slightest tinge of cynicism plays havoc with the faith which is to move mountains. Never did I press the bell of a millionaire's home with a finger that did not tremble. Never did I stand upon the top step before a millionaire's mansion without a fervent prayer that the one I had come to see would prove to be "not at home."

Annie Nathan Meyer's only persistent failing was that she grew hysterical at funerals. When this happened, the wig she wore in later years would come flying off. Her husband would cry out, "Give her a thump! Give her a thump!" It all made Nathan family funerals something of an ordeal.

For all their separate successes, relations between the two Nathan sisters remained stormy. There were moments of good feeling between them, but those were few and of brief duration.

It seemed incongruous that these two small, compact, effective women—who happened to be sisters but who also had done so much for the common cause of women—should remain enemies, and yet they did. Toward the end of their lives, at a large reception for a welfare cause in which they both happened to be interested, the Nathan sisters showed up—separately, as usual. The two remained at the party for more than an hour before they left, separately. During the whole time, the founder of Barnard College and the great crusader for women's rights remained on opposite sides of the room, elaborately ignoring one another.

20.

"FOUL DEEDS"

IN 1928, one of the last attempts was made—publicly, at least—to have ancient Sephardic lineage stand for something: probity, dignity, authority. It involved, appropriately enough, the ancient family of de Fonseca-Brandon, and the American public was reminded—fleetingly—of the grandeur that this family could look back upon.

James de Fonseca-Brandon (1764–1843) of London was a shipping magnate of considerable proportions who owned several fleets of India merchantmen. His mansion in town contained so many "taxable lights" (a man's house was taxed according to how many windows it had) that it became something of an eighteenth-century landmark, and an advertisement of its owner's great wealth. On the de Fonseca side of his hyphenated family, James de Fonseca-Brandon traced his descent directly back to the illustrious de Fonsecas of Madrid, one of whom, Cardinal de Fonseca (a *Converso,* obviously) was Grand Almoner to Ferdinand and Isabella at the time of Columbus' voyage.

The Brandon side of his genealogy was equally, if not more, illustrious. The Brandons were English, and included Charles Brandon, Duke of Suffolk, who had been consort to Mary, Queen of France, and related to various English monarchs, including Henry VIII, "Bloody" Mary, Elizabeth I, Edward VI, and Mary, Queen of Scots. James de Fonseca-Brandon married Sarah Mendes-da Costa, an heiress whose family fortune came from West Indian plantations; she traced herself back to the first Jewish settlers in the New World, who established a colony on the island of Curaçao. When Sarah Mendes-da Costa de Fonseca-Brandon died, the family pointed out proudly, if somewhat sorrowfully, she left her huge fortune—all of it —to "the poor of London of all denominations."

One of *her* ancestors had, at one point, been considered the richest woman in England: Caterina Mendes-da Costa Villa-Real Mellish, called "the Belle of Bath" and celebrated in court circles as "Kitty" Mellish. Kitty Mellish was the mother of Elizabeth, Lady Galway, and a sister of Lady Suasso d'Auvergne Le Grand, and her father had been Antonio Mendes-da Costa, seventeenth-century governor of the Bank of England. Her mother, a cousin of her father's, Dona Caterina Mendes, had been the godchild of Queen Caterina of England, the childless consort of Charles the Second. This lady, Dona Caterina, had actually been born in Britain's royal palace, where her family lived with the prince and his consort; Dona Caterina's father, Don Fernando Mendes, a fellow of the Royal College of Physicians and Surgeons, had been the most famous surgeon of the seventeenth century, physician to three monarchs—King John IV of Portugal, Queen Caterina of England, and King Charles II of England. His portrait in court robes hangs—somewhat inappropriately, since he was a Marrano—in Westminster Abbey.

But by 1928 the de Fonseca-Brandon family—a number of whom had dropped the cumbersome Spanish part of the double name—despite the fact that it had become connected, in various ways, to the Hendricks family (a Brandon brother and sister married Hendricks counterparts), as well as to a number of Da Costa and de Fonseca cousins, had diminished to the point where the family consisted largely of a handful of spinster aunts and a young man named Lyman Brandon, who married and then divorced his wife, a New York lady lawyer who practiced under the name Frances Marion Brandon. It was she who put the Brandon name back under public scrutiny of a certain sort. In a lawsuit, Mrs. Brandon was claiming that she had been made the victim of a huge and nefarious swindle, one that involved not only herself but a number of her legal clients. This was what she claimed happened:

Mrs. Brandon, like some of her Nathan and Hendricks connections, had been an ardent feminist and, early in the twenties, she had been introduced to a Miss Annie Mathews, a Harlem dressmaker, who was running on a feminist platform for the office of New York county registrar.

Mrs. Brandon gave liberal amounts of time and money to the Mathews campaign, which was successful, and in the process she became acquainted with one George J. Gillespie, a religious zealot who claimed to be a saint. Mrs. Brandon soon fell under Gillespie's charismatic spell, and before long Gillespie was a regular visitor at her house. The poor woman had just lost her mother, to whom she had been devoted. Thus she claimed that "While stricken in mourning, and completely under the influence of his astounding 'saintliness,' something I had never expected to find on earth, this rare bird-of-paradise by enslaving my mind, through his religious grip on me, and by his evil council, gradually got into entire control of my every thought and act, of my gilt-edged law practice, and, what is more to the point, of my amplitudious fees!"

For months on end, Mr. Gillespie and Mrs. Brandon had met at her house, where they chanted quotations from the Bible, sang hymns—he sang "Nearer My God to Thee" in a high soprano—and prayed. He brought along others of his flock, called "angels," and she invited her friends—"Society folk," as she described them—and mass conversions to the Gillespie sect took place. In the process, Mrs. Brandon and her friends were frequently called upon to contribute cash and gifts to Gillespie and his angels, as well as to Gillespie's wife, a "wretched paralytic," who never presented herself. The Gillespians were so devoted to holiness and purity that they would not drink, smoke, swear, or even eat an egg "unless assured the hen that laid it was married." Mr. Gillespie also claimed himself to be "one of Cardinal Hayes's personal attorneys," representing himself to be "a religious man of deep piety, an exemplary Catholic living the life of a holy man of high principle, virtually a saint, withdrawn from the world and worldly interests and affairs." Mrs. Brandon began to believe that Gillespie was her "second but superior self."

Gillespie was particularly interested in one of Mrs. Brandon's clients, Miss Alice A. De Lamar, a maiden lady who had inherited a multimillion-dollar fortune from her father, Captain Raphael De Lamar, a mining magnate, whose estate Mrs. Brandon's law office managed. Presently, in his role as Frances Brandon's alter ego, Gillespie had a new "life plan" to offer her. He asked her, "What is your object in life?" And she answered, "To devote myself ultimately to the poor and helpless." Solemnly he intoned,

"God sent me to you." What she needed, he said, was a
seat on the children's court bench, where "Your great
heart, great mind, irreproachable character, all are needed
right there. There you must work as I do for the honor
and glory of God. But first you must serve a brief ap-
prenticeship doing court work for the city, to learn the
ropes." When Frances Brandon demurred, saying that she
had a law practice to tend to, Gillespie said that was simply taken care of; he would take over her law practice and
run it for her. Delighted, Frances Brandon agreed, and applied for the office of assistant corporation counsel for
New York City, a post she was promptly given.

Not surprisingly, it wasn't too long before certain "irregularities" began to turn up in the accounts of some of
the Brandon clients, particularly that of the biggest Brandon client, Alice De Lamar. Presently the irregularities
seemed to amount to more than half a million dollars.
When the new assistant corporation counsel attempted to
get information from Gillespie, he put her off soothingly,
assuring her that all was well. He, meanwhile, seemed to
have made off with all her clients' files, records, and accounts, but Mrs. Brandon, still under his spell, could not
believe that her "angel from Heaven" could be guilty of
any wrongdoing. When her clients expressed anxiety, Mrs.
Brandon attempted to put more pressure on her friend. She
found him suddenly strangely hostile. In fact, when she
suggested that she might have to go to higher authorities
about the situation, the holy man threatened her life, saying—as she remembered it—"You're a squealer, are you?
Well, one squeal and I'll have you bumped. I'll have you
jobbed!"

The situation continued to worsen. After more than one
meeting, over tea and sandwiches, at Gillespie's office,
Frances Brandon got the distinct impression that Gillespie
was trying to poison her. Some discreet research revealed
that George Gillespie had been known elsewhere, and at
other times, by such names as Ginger-Ale George, Brother
Gillespie, and Slippery George. He nonetheless continued
to exercise "complete control and mastery" over her. And
so, when he offered her a final and grotesque "deal," she
immediately accepted it. He said he would return her law
practice to her if she would marry him. His "paralytic"
wife, he explained, had conveniently died in the meantime.

On March 15, 1925, Frances Marion Brandon formally

announced her impending marriage to George Gillespie. She was, to be sure, somewhat apprehensive about the future of the union. She approached it in "fear and trembling, amid nameless premonitions." Mrs. Brandon did not lack for a sense of the dramatic, and she actually went so far as to purchase a black wedding gown. It was, as she saw it, "A marriage I had agreed to as *the only* way of recovering quiet possession of my records from this Gillespie, and unravelling those financial irregularities, without painful notoriety."

But her public announcement had the inadvertent effect not only of creating notoriety but also of catching Gillespie off his guard and trapping him. Obviously he had had no intention of marrying Frances Brandon, and was simply offering marriage as a way of putting her off and keeping her out of his account books. When the announcement appeared, it created a certain stir. For one thing, he was more than twenty years her senior; he was a self-proclaimed celibate, for another. When Gillespie was approached by a newspaper reporter for a statement about the upcoming nuptials, he protested, "I am a holy man!" And then, "I do not even know the woman. What is she? Some sort of city employee? Then how would I know her? The thought of marrying her never entered my mind! If a million other women had made that announcement, I could not have been more surprised."

Needless to say, to Frances Brandon this statement "came like a thunderclap, or rather, a roar of thunder that tore at the very core of my life." There followed a period where she "remained as one dead for two years or more." Then she instigated the swindle suit against Gillespie, asking $575,000 in damages.

It was, of course, a classic and pathetic case of a susceptible and perhaps foolish woman who had been successfully duped by a confidence man. And Frances Brandon might easily have won wide popular sympathy for her predicament, if she had not chosen to inject the issue of social "class"—and alleged Sephardic superiority—into the case. While it was still pending trial, she wrote and published a pamphlet intended to place her name above reproach, and thus disassociate herself from the shady doings of the nefarious Gillespie. Titled "The Truth at Last!!" it consisted of sixteen tightly packed pages filled with shrill vituperations and fulminations, besprinkled with quota-

tions from the Old and New Testaments, Shakespeare, and
Saint Thomas a Kempis, hectic with italics and spiky with
picket fences of exclamation points. But at the heart of her
exercise, alas, was the assertion that, in terms of background and breeding, George Gillespie was Frances Brandon's social inferior.

"Gillespie is Scotch," she wrote, "judging by his name,
and of sordid, squalid origin, a street gamin, a ruffian;
salesman of children's dresses, etc.; then a dockhand at
the New York Customs House; married a creature, her
father a stablehand, her aunt a cook; menials; illiterates.
In line therewith, his daughter married the son of a Bronx
veterinary." For all that, she wrote, "He palmed himself
off as a 'Society man and philanthropist,' and then was always concealing his family connections and their record as
habitual petty jobholders, this ingrate . . . identified *me*
. . . as a despicable 'some sort of city employee.' . . . Why
should I, a recognized executive, with a phenomenal record
of achievement, and a priceless law practice, exchange
cake for crumbs, *retrogress* into the political rank and file,
into a nominal public office, regardless of remuneration?
For bread and butter? Hardly. My financial circumstances
preclude that possibility. Then how? Through *Gillespie!*"

As for herself, she pointed out in her manifesto:

> My sister, years ago, married the cousin of a beloved
> First Lady of the Land, our *American* equivalent for
> the bluest blood of Royalty. No fuss; no feathers;
> just unpretentiously. We are like that . . . though my
> own blood and kin traces back through America's
> proudest aristocracy, those PIONEERS, who tamed the
> wilderness with their bare and bleeding hands; sturdy
> stock; backbone of America. . . . First Settlers back
> beyond the Revolution, tracing ancestry not to the
> landing of the Pilgrim Fathers, but even back of that,
> to AMERICA'S FIRST SETTLER, The Founder, Sir Wal-
> ter Raleigh.

As if that were not enough, she crowed: *"I wear the
crimson of nobility by right of that proud name* [Bran-
don], *and wear that peerless name as a diadem of stars
upon my brow: When we were very young, I married
Lyman da Fonseca Brandon!"* She then proceeded to recite all her ex-husband's genealogical credentials—the

Duke of Suffolk, Mary, Queen of Scots, Kitty Mellish, and all the rest.

Her pamphlet went on to quote a lengthy testimonial in her behalf from Lyman Brandon. "I know Frances Marion Brandon," her former husband wrote somewhat elliptically. "She is an Ace . . . A phenomenon, a paragon among women; one in a thousand thousand, to know her is to love, respect, honor, and cherish all womanhood as epitomized in her. Cast in heroic mold, modest, self-sacrificing . . . of invincible courage . . . gladly go to the scaffold for principle, for THE TRUTH . . . inspiration to women . . . her great soul . . . glorious womanhood. . . ." Lyman Brandon's prose sounded suspiciously like his former wife's, and he was every bit as prolix.

Finally, after a detailed recitation of Mr. Gillespie's "foul deeds," Mrs. Brandon's paper terminated with these words:

> Duped? Humbugged? Hoaxed? I was. *We all were!* But CREDIT ME ALWAYS WITH THIS, THE HIGHEST FEATHER OF MY CAP: *It was I, who called Gillespie's bluff; smoked him out; treed him!* I who rendered that *supreme service* to my fellow citizens. The Artful Dodger caught at last! Another prize captured by me; or rather, a *prize capture.* But those of you who do not yet know me may ask, have I any proofs? Have I? *Have I? My turn to thunder now!*
>
> What was it Crockett said? *"Come on down, Gillespie; you're a gone coon!"*

And as the date for the trial approached, these words turned out to be prophetic. Mr. Gillespie was indeed gone. He had vanished without a trace.

And as for Frances Brandon, poor woman, her pompous and windy pamphlet had made her a laughingstock. While she attitudinized, New York giggled. While she fumed and ranted and exhumed fifteenth-century ancestors, readers of New York newspapers hugged their sides. She had made being related to the Grand Almoner of Ferdinand and Isabella seem—simply—funny.

To the Sephardic community of New York, Mrs. Brandon's behavior was a deep affront. She was, after all, using a Sephardic connection by marriage in order to establish her integrity; a pedigree she had merely married was being tossed around and advertised for all to see. Furthermore, Brandon was now no longer her husband but only her ex-husband. It was all just another reminder of how thin the fabric of Sephardic life had grown to be. As one of the Nathans wrote to a Philadelphia cousin: "In case it isn't obvious by her behavior, this Brandon woman is *not* one of us."

But of course the feeling that there is some sort of mystical advantage in being a Sephardic Jew, or even in bearing the traces of Sephardic "blood," has persisted, persists. In the opening paragraphs of his autobiography, the late Bernard Baruch, whose father had been a German immigrant, wrote: "My grandfather, Bernhard Baruch, whose name I bear, had an old family relic, a skull, on which was recorded the family genealogy. It appeared that the Baruchs were of a rabbinical family and of Portuguese-Spanish origin. . . . Grandfather also claimed descent from Baruch the Scribe, who edited the prophecies of Jeremiah and whose name is given to one of the books of the Apocrypha."

At the same time, the great financier admitted in a sheepish tone that was quite unlike him: "Somewhere along the line there must have been an admixture of Polish or Russian stock."

And John L. Loeb, the present head of the banking firm Loeb, Rhoades & Company, is more ancestrally proud of his mother, the former Adeline Moses, than of his father, who founded the giant banking house. The Moseses were an old Sephardic family from the South who, though somewhat depleted from the days when they had maintained a vast plantation with slaves and cotton fields, were nonetheless disapproving when their daughter married Mr. Loeb, "an ordinary German immigrant."

Both Messrs. Baruch and Loeb are dutifully listed in Dr. Stern's registry of the Old Guard.

21.

"AN ALTOGETHER
DIFFERENT SORT"

SEPHARDIM in the New World might dream of titled ancestors in plumes and crests and jeweled swords, who had been the poets, philosophers, physicians, judges, astronomers, and courtiers during Spain's most glorious moments. But there were hundreds of thousands of other Jews, also Sephardic but with less elaborate claims, who descended from Spain's Jewish tailors, cobblers, blacksmiths, and knife grinders. At the time of the Epulsion Edict, these families had not been able to afford the enormous bribes demanded by Inquisitional officers that would get them sent, along with their property, to lucrative northern ports in Holland, Belgium, and England. Being poor, they could not afford to become Marranos, who had to live by paying bribes. Being poor, they also lacked the sophistication and poise it took to lead the Marrano's double life. Finally, being poor and unsophisticated, they lacked the adaptability that would have allowed them to accept conversion.

There was nothing for these Jews but to surrender their money and their houses and escape. Some had fled to northern Africa. Others went eastward, across the Mediterranean, to Turkey, where they accepted the sultan's invitation, or to the islands of Rhodes and Marmara, or to Salonica and the Gallipoli Peninsula, areas where the Jews knew they would be well treated because these lands were still ruled by the Moslems.

There, in backwaters of history, it was as though a giant door had swung closed on these Sephardim, leaving them frozen in time. They were poor, uneducated, living in tight little communities of their coreligionists, proud, mystical, working by day as farmers or fishermen or small trades-people, returning at night to their fires and their prayer books, and their evenings of singing *cantos* and *romanzas*, in the pure medieval tongue. As "guests" of the Moslems, they were considered a separate and autonomous people, permitted to preserve their religious and cultural habits, as well as their strange language. For they did not, as the upper-class Spanish Jews did, speak Castilian. They spoke Ladino, a Judeo-Spanish mixture which sounded like Span-ish but contained many Hebrew words and expressions, and was written in Hebrew characters. In Spain, Ladino had helped them preserve the privacy of some of their bus-iness dealings. Now it simply served to isolate and insulate them further as the world passed them by.

While Reform Judaism was remaking the pattern of Jew-ish life, threatening to topple the traditional orthodoxy, these Jews knew nothing of it. Word of the European po-groms never reached them, nor did any kind of anti-Semi-tism. At the same time, they remained fiercely and proudly Spanish, and were convinced that one day they would be asked to return to Spain again. When they left Spain, the heads of families had taken the keys to their houses with them. Now the key to *la casa vieja*—the old house—was passed on from father to son, while decades turned into generations, and generations into centuries. These Jews had developed a rationale to explain why they had been ex-pelled from Spain. It was, they decided, the Lord's punish-ment. Like the Jews in the Old Testament, they were being made to suffer because they had failed to cleave sufficient-ly to Judaic precepts. They had been insufficiently pious, and had failed to obey every letter of every Talmudic law. And so, while Jews elsewhere were modernizing and liber-alizing their attitudes, practices, and rituals, these Sephar-dim were moving in the opposite direction, not only toward a greater piety and a more intense mysticism, but also be-coming hyper-ritualistic, more orthodox than the Orthodox, their ways all but incomprehensible to others.

In the synagogues, the women were not only seated sep-arately from the men, but behind heavy curtains, so that they would not distract the men from their prayers. Se-phardic home life in such outposts as Rhodes and Salonica became heavily centered around the dinner table, where the preparation and serving of food was a formalized adjunct of religion; indeed, the Meal, the Bath, and the Prayer were a kind of trinity of Old World Sephardic life. Much of a mother's day was spent in her *cochina,* working at her stove preparing such traditional Spanish dishes as *paella, pastelitos con carne,* and *spinata con arroz* for her family. If callers dropped in, the woman of the house, no matter how poor she was, was required to urge food on them— wine and nut cookies, perhaps, or sesame seed pretzels, or eggs baked in their shells for days and days until the whites had turned honey-colored. And to refuse food when it was offered was regarded as the highest form of insult.

In these Sephardic households, it was very much a man's world. The man of the house was known as *el rey,* the king, and his sons were *los hijos del rey,* and were treated accordingly. In skullcaps and shawls, the men of the house were served their meals first, with the women waiting upon them, bringing them saucers of warm water and towels between courses so that the men and boys could wash and wipe their hands at the table. The woman might stuff the grape leaves—plucked from the inevitable grape arbor planted outside each door—but it was the man's job to go into the market to shop for meat, to find the best eggplants, tomatoes, spinach, and rice. It was also considered proper for a husband to supervise his wife's cooking procedure, to stand at her shoulder with suggestions and criticism, and periodically to sample and taste, perhaps even picking up the spoon himself to stir in a bit of grated clove or oregano if he felt it was needed. A wife would never resent this sort of treatment from a husband because every good Sephardic woman knew that the worst punishment a man could inflict upon a woman was to reject—by pushing aside his plate—food that she had prepared.

Sabbath meals particularly were surrounded by rules and rituals. All generations of a family gathered about a patriarchal table on which was spread a stiff white cloth reserved specifically for Sabbath use, and the meal proceeded with strictest formality. Everything used at the Sabbath was kept in special storage. Even Sabbath clothing was stored separately from the clothes of every day. Each item of food must be cooked in its traditional pot, served on its appointed platter, and eaten from its assigned plate. Onion could not mix with garlic, nor could meat dishes be served with fish, milk, or eggs. Even threads of different origins—linen, cotton, and silk—could not be used in the same fabrics if these were to be brought forth, or worn, on the Sabbath. To carry anything on one's person—so much as a handkerchief—was a violation of Sabbath rules.

The Sephardic women were the custodians of the secrets of *endurcos,* the ancient folk magic the Jews had carried with them out of Spain. *Endurcos* was supposed to be white magic—used exclusively to cure the sick—and so it worked hand in hand, rather than at odds, with both orthodox medicine and orthodox religion. The ingredients of *endurcos* were, for the most part, herbs and spices—salt, garlic, clove, oregano, marjoram, honey, almonds, halvah—and its forms (chants, prayers, songs in Ladino, spells, and gestures) were traditionally in the hands of women past the age of menopause, called *tias* or "aunties."

In an old world Sephardic community, a *tia* is a woman of considerable importance. Sometimes she is summoned to help a doctor and to coordinate her work with his. Or she may be called in when the doctor has done all he can for his patient and ordinary medicine will no longer suffice. When this happens, the *tia* must be given complete authority, and often the first thing she will do is to shoo everyone else out of the house so that she can work single-mindedly with her patient. She may begin her treatment by brewing a stiff tea of mint or marjoram, according to recipes known only to her, and there will follow a strict regimen based on diet, regular bathings of the patient, and recitals of the *tia*'s ancient incantations. A cure may take days or even months before the assorted demons, devils, and evil spirits (or *buena gente,* "good people," as they are guardedly called) are cast out of the patient's body and the *tia*'s work is done. There is never a charge for the services of a *tia,* for hers is both an art and a gift, and she must therefore give it away.

A *tia* also may be consulted on matters less crucial than life or death. For instance, Turkish candy may be prescribed by a *tia* for an infected finger. Sugar from the table of a Rosh Hashanah festival is considered a cure for sterility in childless women. Marjoram or oregano tea will cure, according to the *tia,* both insomnia and fright. Sugar in water is the simple remedy for "crying children." For severe cases of insomnia, tea should be placed outside the window of the victim and left there for three days, during which the victim must not touch fire. After the three days, she should rise early in the morning and drink the tea quickly before breakfast. Old people in these Sephardic communities follow this routine regularly, once a month, and therefore have no trouble sleeping—as long as they are careful to remember that it must never be practiced when a baby who has not yet teethed is in the house. Otherwise, the evil eye will fall upon the baby. If it does, of course, it can often be dispelled by hurling cloves into the fire or tossing salt into the wind while chanting exhortations in the names of Jacob, Isaac, Abraham, and Moses.

To ward off the evil eye, bedrooms of children are strung with garlands of garlic cloves, and young people are instructed to carry garlic with them for luck. Older women carry blue and amber beads from the Holy Land, strung together on silk threads, for the same reason. For a little boy's first visit to a new household, it is important that he carry with him something sweet—an almond cookie, perhaps—along with something silver in his pocket, if the visit is to be a success. And so it has gone, for centuries, in an endlessly complex pattern of ritual, tradition, mystery, and magic. In the 1960's, for example, the State of Israel inaugurated "Operation Magic Carpet," which was designed to fly Sephardic Jews to Israel out of Yemen and North Africa. But the Jews refused to fly. The situation had reached an impasse until someone recalled the words from Isaiah: "I will bear you on the wings of eagles." Thus reassured, the Jews consented to board the aircraft.

At the same time, these Sephardic Jews were fiercely independent, proud to the point of crustiness, disdainful of Christians and the "fairy tales" of Christianity, filled with a sense of heightened religiosity and superior purpose.

In the semifeudal world of the Ottoman Empire, this "lost" Sephardic life could continue uninterrupted, unchanged, its tribalistic injunctions and habits passed on from generation to generation. The home was a kind of shrine, and for a son to leave his parents and venture out into the world beyond was the worst sort of transgression. It was possible to believe that nothing could disrupt these changeless ways. In the early 1900's a handful of adventurous youths from Greece and Turkey came to the United States, and wrote home to friends and relatives with tales that were scarcely to be credited—of Jewish millionaires with automobiles and yachts and mansions, who headed banks and corporations. A trickle of emigration began.

With the outbreak of World War I, the trickle increased to a stream of considerable proportions. Then, at the end of the war, the revolution in Turkey marked the end of an era. Jews swarmed out of the Near East and the Levant by the tens of thousands, and these were presently joined by Jews from northern Africa. In New York, they looked for Sephardic synagogues and found elegant establishments that were the oldest synagogues in America, still controlled by an aristocratic if somewhat diminished Jewish Establishment. Because they felt entitled to, these Jews curled up on blankets and bedrolls in the corners of the synagogues until they could find shelter, and the effect upon the existing community was cataclysmic. It was a confrontation, some 450 years later, of two streams—two social classes, really—of Sephardim, and the two groups encountered each other with the impact of a collision. Here were these Greek- and Turkish-looking people (with skins darkened from generations in the Mediterranean sun, plus a certain amount of intermarriage) claiming to be cousins of the Lazaruses, Cardozos, Nathans, Seixases, and Levys. These were people who were poor, ignorant, superstitious, who practiced an exotic form of Judaism no one comprehended, who spoke a language that sounded "worse than Yiddish," some of whom—the Jews of North Africa, for instance— had actually lived in caves.

To the old American Sephardim—Boston Brahmin-like, entertaining their little circles of friends and relatives at tea parties, over teacups of fragile porcelain, with antique silver spoons, under darkening family portraits of Revolutionary ancestors in powdered wigs and lacy collars—the newcomers were like primitives from another planet. No one knew what to make of them. They were, plainly and simply, an embarrassment to families grown accustomed to thinking of themselves as the grandest people in America.

Vainly the rabbis of the community at large tried to explain these Oriental strangers to their congregations, as well as to explain the existing congregation—its mood and texture—to the strangers. It was no use. One sermon of the period even went so far as to point out that food cooked in oil is no less nourishing than food cooked in butter or vegetable shortening—for the newly arrived Sephardim continued to cook in olive oil, even to spread it on their bread, a practice which to other Jews seemed barbarous. The Sephardic communities were split even further as the old-timers pointed out—with certain accuracy—that they were descended from Spain's Jewish gentry, while the newcomers descended from the riffraff.

The Levantine emigration of the twentieth century also changed the traditional locations of Sephardic communities. Up to then, Sephardic congregations existed primarily in the older eastern cities—Newport, New York, Philadelphia, Charleston, Savannah. Many of the new arrivals settled in New York, giving New York today the largest Sephardic population of any American city. But many others headed westward. Many Greek Jews were fishermen, and they were attracted to the fish markets of cities such as Portland and Seattle. Others headed for southern California. Today, the second-largest Sephardic congregation is in Los Angeles. Seattle, where the Jewish community of Rhodes has transplanted itself almost intact, is third.

In the United States, the Near Eastern Sephardim made a determined effort to keep to their old cloistered ways, to cling to the comforts of ritual and the mysteries of *endurcos,* and the tight family structures they had enjoyed for centuries. But their removal from New York's Lower East Side soon after their arrival, the prevailing laws of compulsory education, and their children's association in schools and on playgrounds not only with other Jews but with people of other ethnic backgrounds had an inevitable effect, and a familiar process of Americanization began rather rapidly. The edges of old distinctions began to fade and blur. The Sephardim have staunchly retained their special ritual, songs, and prayers, but old world embellishments have been steadily disappearing. Only a few old people understand the rites of *endurcos* now, and even the treasured key to *la casa vieja* has become a charming anachronism. These Jews no longer seriously consider returning to a golden age of Spain.

Probably the greatest loss has been the Ladino. It was always an amorphous, uncodified tongue, written—like Hebrew—from right to left, and in characters similar to (but not exactly like) Hebrew, and learning to speak it was always like learning to play a musical instrument by ear. Spoken Ladino ignores all rules of grammar and of spelling, and written Ladino simply overlooks them. A writer in Ladino can employ the grammatical rules, or conventions, of any Western language he chooses—French, Spanish, Italian, or even English. Ladino words even pop up oddly in Hebrew texts, as happened when an American professor of Hebrew at the University of California found the word *empanada,* written in Hebrew characters, when reading the *Shulhan Aruk* of Karo. He could find *empanada* in no Hebrew dictionary. He eventually discovered that an *empanada* is a dish prepared by the Sephardic Jews of Salonica, a casserole of chopped meat and fish baked with a layer of pie crust on the top. In Spanish dictionaries, *empanada* is defined as a meat pie.

The new settlers from the Near East quickly began introducing English words and American expressions into the Ladino, thus making the language even harder to decode. One of the strangest examples of this sort of thing is the Ladino verb *abetchar,* meaning "to bet," which came directly from the Americanism "I betcha." Expressions came into being such as *Quieres abetchar?* meaning "You want to bet?" and *Yo te abetcho,* meaning "I bet you." The verb "to park" became, in new Ladino, *parkear,* and the verb "to drive" was *drivear.* Therefore, *Esta driveandro el caro* translated as "He is driving the car," and "He is parking the car" was *Esta parkeando el caro.*

Thus undermined by grotesque intrusions from the prevailing language, and gradually forgotten by children when they entered English-speaking schools, Ladino, lacking any newspapers or even a dictionary, has become an exotic language as rare as the whooping crane, preserved only in the memories of a few rabbis and teachers. No doubt in a few more generations it will all but have disappeared.

The Levantine Sephardim who came to America in important numbers in the 1920's and 1930's may have been poor and uneducated and believers in the evil eye. But, like other immigrants of other eras, they have largely succeeded in pulling themselves out of poverty and educating themselves out of ignorance and parochialism, and on the whole they can claim as good a record in the United States as any other group. In Los Angeles, several dark-skinned Sephardim became shoeshine men. In a few years, a shoeshine man had a shoe repair shop and, a few years later, he had a chain. In Seattle, a fisherman from Greece became a canner of fish, and by the second generation his cannery became a large factory. By the time these Sephardim had begun sending their sons and daughters to American colleges and universities, whole new sets of American middle-class values had been accepted. Although it was still considered anathema to marry a Christian, it was no longer a disgrace for one's daughter to marry a *tedesco*—a German—particularly if he was rich. When this happened not long ago a Sephardic mother commented tellingly, "Well, at least he's an American, and at least he's not black."

The impact on the old congregations in the older cities—Shearith Israel in New York, Mikveh Israel in Philadelphia—was, in the meantime, lasting. The two Sephardic strains enjoyed a truce that was, at best, uneasy. Annie Nathan Meyer was somewhat ruffled when a New York society woman suddenly said to her, "You speak such beautiful English! How long is it since your parents came to America?" She immediately brought out miniature portraits of the Colonial ancestors on both sides of the family. Of one lace-capped great-grandmother, Mrs. Meyer said impishly, "She looks rather like Martha Washington, doesn't she?" When her visitor, confused, said, "Oh, but I thought you were Jewish," Mrs. Meyer waved her hand and said, "These people are an altogether different sort."

And when Shearith Israel's great rabbi David de Sola Pool approached a lady of his congregation and asked her why, when for years he had seen her at Friday evening services, he now saw her no more than twice a year, at the high holy days, the woman looked wistful and said, "It isn't the same. I look around in the synagogue now, and I see nothing but strangers."

22

SMALL GESTURES . . . AND A
HUSH AT CHATHAM SQUARE

ON December 17, 1968, readers of the *New York Times* may have encountered a small item which could have struck them as ironic, or mystifying. The story was datelined Madrid, and began:

> Four hundred and seventy-six years after King Ferdinand and Queen Isabella ordered the Jews expelled from Spain, the Spanish Government declared tonight that the order was void.

In other words, that fateful edict beginning with the words "It seems that much harm is done to Christians by the community or conversation they have held and hold with Jews . . ." which had had such a shattering effect on Spanish Jewry, and on the history of Spain itself, was at last nullified. Judaism was legal in Spain once more. In practice, the Spanish Constitution of 1869, which had proclaimed religious tolerance in general terms, was considered to have superseded the Catholic monarchs' order. But Spain's Jewish community, numbering about eight thousand people, had long been seeking an explicit revocation of the Expulsion Edict itself. It had taken the government of Generalissimo Francisco Franco to bring this about.

Generalissimo Franco himself has always been friendly in his treatment of Spain's Jews. In the 1930's, he issued an "invitation" to Jews, advertising in the Jewish press, asking the Jews to return to Spain. A few families actually did come back. During World War II, Franco embarked on an emphatic campaign to rescue Jews from Hitler's po-

groms, and he has been personally credited with saving as
many as sixty thousand Jewish lives. One little-known incident of that war is that on January 8, 1944, Franco
made a personal telephone call to Adolf Hitler concerning
the fate of Jewish prisoners at Bergen-Belsen concentration
camp. Franco demanded that the prisoners, many of whom
were Sephardim from Greece, be released. Hitler complied,
and 1,242 Jews were sent to safety in Spain. Franco went
to the Spanish border personally to meet and escort these
refugees into his country. When informed that the Germans had confiscated all the Jews' money and possessions,
Franco placed a second call to Hitler. The result was that
the Jews' property was sent after them.

Why was the Spanish leader—in so many other ways
sympathetic to Nazi policies—so opposed to Hitler in the
matter of anti-Semitism? Historians of the war have never
been sure, and Franco has, typically, never explained. But
it may have had something to do with the strong possibility that Franco himself is of Marrano descent, as so
many other Spaniards are. Franco is a common Sephardic
name, particularly among Sephardim from the island of
Rhodes, and it all may mean that El Caudillo is a distant
connection of the beautiful Tory Franks sisters of Philadelphia. It may also explain Franco's refusal to accede to
Hitler's attempts to come into Spain: perhaps he feared
that he himself could become a victim of the Führer's policies.

During the years of Arab-Israeli warfare, Franco's government has continued to help Jews in Arab countries to
escape persecution. It has taken such steps as to issue them
Spanish passports, thereby making them honorary Sephardic Jews, as it were.

When the announcement that the Expulsion Edict was
at last void was made to the Jewish congregation of Madrid, the *Times* report continued, it caused "a profound
stir," and it came simultaneously with another event of
vast symbolic importance—the opening of the first synagogue to be built in Spain in six hundred years. Ever since
Inquisitional days, Jews had been meeting for worship in
the secrecy of apartments and private houses, behind closed
shutters and drawn curtains. Even under the relatively benevolent Franco regime, Jews had been too unsure of their
position to risk erecting a permanent public building. At
the opening ceremonies, nineteen men in top hats and

prayer shawls filed into the new synagogue bearing velvet-encased sacred scrolls topped by silver bells. Dr. Solomon Gaon, grand rabbi of the Sephardic communities of Great Britain, who is considered the world's leading Sephardic figure, flew to Madrid for the occasion; he stood in the white marble and wood hall and declared: "We witness a historic moment, when past and present meet. The most brilliant history of our people in the Diaspora was written in Spain. May this mean the beginning of a new time of moral and spiritual progress for all the people of this land."

In the United States, where some 100,000 Spanish and Portuguese Jews have now settled like so many birds after a long flight, the news of a new synagogue in Madrid was of less significance. Though the occasion was officially celebrated with prayers of thanksgiving, word that Ferdinand and Isabella's Expulsion Edict had finally been invalidated met privately with a kind of grim amusement. The reaction was: "It's about time."

In New York's Shearith Israel congregation, a strong feeling continues that here is something precious that must, at all costs, be preserved. Though the congregation is splintered and factionalized, split down the middle between the Old Guard and Levantine newcomers, and further cast into disagreement over the choice of an Ashkenazy (of all things), Dr. Louis C. Gerstein, as head rabbi (a tradition-minded faction wanted London's Dr. Gaon, a Spaniard), and what is felt to be a continuing Germanization of American Jewish life,* today's members of the Jewish First Families see themselves as keepers of a flame, pre-servers of something that was once of great importance— to history and to the human spirit—and is still worth re-membering.

Most members of the Old Guard families today are not particularly pious, and make merely token observances of the Sabbath and the other holy days. Hendrickses, Laza-ruses, Cardozos, and Nathans of the 1970's do not, for

---

* Despite all sorts of socially discriminatory measures, snubs and countersnubs. In New York, for instance, the elite German-Jewish men's club, the Harmonie, would not admit Sephardic members. In retaliation, the Sephardic Beach Point Club in suburban Westchester would take no Germans. This condition persisted well into the twentieth century.

the most part, keep kosher households, nor have they for several generations. What they have undergone, over the long centuries, has been a peculiarly American phenomenon. In an aura of religious tolerance and, in the case of the Old Guard, social acceptance, their early need for their religion seems to have diminished considerably. Perhaps religion flourishes strongest, and its forms have more fierce importance, when it is prohibited or proscribed. One effect of the Inquisition was the opposite of its intent: it made Spain's Jews more determined to be Jews. In the new world, with pressures against Jews gradually diminishing, this determination has diminished also.

What has happened is that reverence for the past has replaced religious conviction. The old Sephardic families today often appear to worship history more than a Judaic God. The old portraits and the lacy family trees, the escutcheons and coats of arms, have become their testaments and prayer books. The lists of great-grandparents' birthdays in the frontispiece of the family Bible seem to have more meaning than the text within. Even the insistence of the Sephardim on retaining the orthodox form of worship—against the trend toward modernization and Americanization that has been marked among Jewry all over the country—seems a gesture of nostalgic sentiment, a gesture in deference to the past, more than one of pure religiosity. After all, the past has placed these "few of us"—now all so thoroughly interrelated—in a position in America that is particular, peculiar, unique.

In 1897, when Shearith Israel finally got around to moving its congregation uptown into a handsome new building, there was no possibility that the move would be hailed as an attempt "to become one with progress." Instead, the building was an attempt to become one with the past. Within the walls of the larger synagogue there stands a second, much smaller synagogue—an exact replica of the first synagogue in America as it stood on New York's Mill Street three hundred and more years ago. Step into the "little synagogue," and you step not only into old New York but further back, into medieval Spain. On the wall, an old Spanish calendar marks off the hour, day, and week with the letters *H, D,* and *S*—for *hora, dia, semana.* The heavy brass candlesticks may have come from Spain also. The Sabbath lamp was the gift of the family of Haym Salomon. The tin bells were made by the colonists around 1694, before they had silver. The scrolls within the Ark are tattered and stained from water and blood. During the Revolution, a drunken British soldier fired on the reader in the synagogue; they are his bloodstains. Later, a second drunken soldier threw the scrolls in the mud. (Both offenders, it is recorded, were court-martialed by the British.)

Outside, in the synagogue proper, the seating is of course segregated. The beautiful music of the Sephardic service —another strong emotional bulwark of the congregation— traces back to old Spanish folk songs. Only a few changes have occurred over the centuries. Three hundred years ago, the official language of the synagogue was Portuguese. In 1728, however, the congregation revised its "wholesome Rules and Restrictions," and resolved that "the Parnaz shall be obliged twice a year to cause these articles to be read in the Sinagog both in Portugues [sic] and English."

A prayer for the government, then part of the ritual, also had to undergo revision, for obvious reasons. The original prayer blessed:

> *Sua Real Magestade nosso Senhor Rey Jorge o Segundo, as suas Reales Atezas Jorge Principe de Veles, a Princesa Douger de Veles, o Duque & as Princesas & toda a Real Familha, a sua Excellencia o Honrado Senhor Governor y todos os Senhores de sea Concelbo, o Magistrado desta Cidade de New York e todos os seos Deredores ...*

Blessings are no longer offered to "His Royal Majesty, our Sovereign George the Second, their Royal Highnesses George Prince of Wales, the Dowager Princess of Wales, the Duke and Princesses and all the Royal Family, his Excellency the Governor and all the gentlemen of his Council, the Mayor of the City of New York and all its environs." Otherwise, nothing has changed.

Shearith Israel stands sedately at the corner of Seventieth Street and Central Park West. Rather pointedly, Shearith Israel appears to have chosen an address on the older, homier West Side, rather than on grander, flashier Fifth Avenue. Shearith Israel faces almost directly across the park toward the new Temple Emanu-El in an attitude of reproach.

Once a year, on Memorial Day, members of Shearith Israel meet at the synagogue for breakfast, and then proceed downtown to pay commemorative visits to the graves of early American ancestors in the oldest Jewish cemeteries in America. In all, three cemeteries are visited: the tiny one at Chatham Square, the even tinier triangular cemetery on West Eleventh Street in Greenwich Village, and the somewhat larger one on West Twenty-third Street, not far from the site of Benjamin Nathan's murder. All are Spanish and Portuguese cemeteries, though the Twenty-first Street enclosure contains the grave of one of New York's Presbyterian Cadwaladers, who must have done something very scandalous indeed to have been placed there in alien corn.

The most important of the three is the Chatham Square Cemetery, for it is the oldest. The earliest grave there dates 1683, just one year after the land was purchased. Chatham Square Cemetery is a hushed and peaceful place, just a bit removed from the dither of Chinatown nearby, and the ground is covered with sturdy green ivy, graveled walks between the old stones, shaded by the lacy branches of three ailanthus trees. Not all the inscriptions are legible now. The cemetery was once six times as large, but the city has intruded upon it, pressed in on it, squeezed it and narrowed it to such an extent that the distinct impression is left that here remain only the doughtiest of that early, doughty breed. There are Gomezes, Lopezes, Seixases, de Lucenas, Harts, Peixottos, Lazaruses—a number of them slain Revolutionary soldiers—and a young doctor who had worked during one of New York's periodic yellow fever epidemics, and whose inscription reads:

IN MEMORY OF WALTER J. JUDAH,
STUDENT OF PHYSIC, WHO WORN DOWN
BY HIS EXERTIONS TO ALLEVIATE THE SUFFERINGS
OF HIS FELLOW CITIZENS, IN THAT DREADFUL CONTAGION
THAT VISITED THE CITY OF NEW YORK IN 1798 FELL
A VICTIM IN THE CAUSE OF HUMANITY . . .
THE 15TH OF SEPT. 1798 AT
20 YEARS 5 MONTHS AND 11 DAYS

At the Memorial Day ceremonies, a brief tribute is read over each grave, and then a small American flag is placed on it by one of the deceased's living descendants. For all the simplicity of this service, a distinct understanding is generated of the Jews' belief that a cemetery is a *beth hayyim*, a house of the living, that these Americans are not dead but with us still, that a man's ancestors are arrayed behind him in the past, each generation looking over the shoulders of the generation that follows, in endless continuity.

At a recent service, thirty-four persons were counted.

The Jewish First Families honor the past in other ways, large and small. Several years ago, the family of Harold L. Lewis, who are collateral descendants of Commodore Uriah Phillips Levy, became concerned about the way their ancestor and his relationship with Monticello were being represented in history books. The "official" text, for instance, which is on sale at the gift shop at Monticello, makes this typical reference to Uriah: "Within the year [of Jefferson's death] Monticello was sold to liquidate the debts of the estate. Later the property was purchased by Uriah Levy for $2,500! . . . Almost one hundred years has passed since the death of Thomas Jefferson, and the mansion has suffered from the neglect of the many occupants who had neither the funds nor the interest to preserve the historic building." No mention is made of the extensive restorations that Uriah Levy made during the many years when he was the mansion's only occupant. Another text, "Monticello," by Gene and Clare Gurney, contains the following reference:

> Mr. Levy did not live at Monticello. Instead he leased it to a succession of farmers who brought Jefferson's beautiful house close to ruin. They used the once-lovely drawing room to store grain. Refuse was allowed to collect on the portico steps until a horse and wagon could be driven up to the drawing room door. Unused outbuildings were torn down and no repairs were made anywhere on the estate.
>
> Belatedly realizing that something should be done to save Monticello, Mr. Levy willed it to the government when he died in 1862. His heirs successfully contested the will, and one of them, Jefferson M. Levy, did make an effort to repair some of the damage that had been done to the historic house, but he

lacked the resources to carry out such a tremendous task.

Over the years a number of prominent people recommended that the government buy and restore Monticello as a memorial to the third President. Nothing was done, however, and Monticello continued to deteriorate.

This account does a great disservice to both Uriah and his nephew. Jefferson Levy had no lack of "resources," and was an extremely rich man who spent enormous sums restoring and refurbishing Monticello. He made repeated trips to Europe in search of the mansion's original furniture, wallpapers, and rugs, and when the originals were unobtainable he had costly copies made from whatever sketches could be found. Under Jefferson Levy's stewardship, Monticello became one of the great showplaces of the early twentieth century—it attained, in fact, the sort of elegance and grandeur that Thomas Jefferson had conceived for it, but had never lived to see. The house was the scene of many lavish parties and entertainments. Jeff Levy's sister, Mrs. Amelia Von Mayhoff, acted as his hostess, a role she clearly relished, and a long list of dignitaries from official and diplomatic Washington, as well as titled folk from Europe, were frequent guests at Monticello. Levy nieces alive today remember being ushered into the great drawing room, where a typically opulent reception was going on, the guest list including the President of the United States, Theodore Roosevelt. And yet, for some reason, no history book has yet taken note of any of this.

Today, most of the guides at Monticello look blank when any mention is made of Uriah Phillips Levy, and only a few have the vaguest knowledge of Monticello's associations with the Levy name. None of the guides, on a recent visit, was aware that Uriah's mother, Rachel Levy, is buried on the grounds. Her grave is in a small enclosed plot not far from the gift shop.

Several years ago, Harold Lewis, whose wife was one of Jefferson Levy's nieces, was astonished and outraged on a visit to Monticello to discover a bronze plaque which stated simply that a certain Uriah Levy had at one point bought the estate for $2,500 and later sold it for $500,000. The implications of Jewish greed and sharp practice seemed quite clear. After a great deal of difficulty and much correspondence with Monticello's trustees, Mr. Lewis was successful in having the plaque reworded.

Others have been equally dutiful to the past. In Manhattan in the late 1960's, one of the historic areas threatened by real estate developers was a triangular piece of land between East Ninth and Eleventh streets and Second and Third avenues, through which narrow Stuyvesant Street passes diagonally. Within this area are the old Church of Saint Mark's in-the-Bowery, dating from 1799, and thirty-three neighboring houses from the eighteenth and early nineteenth centuries. This is the site of the bouwerie—or farm—of Governor Peter Stuyvesant, and in the churchyard of Saint Mark's are buried eight generations of Stuyvesants, along with the Dutch governor himself. Early in 1969, New York City's Landmarks Preservation Commission announced that it had succeeded in having the district declared a historic one, meaning that no exterior changes to the church, the churchyard, or any of the buildings can be made without the approval of the commission. (There has since been a controversial decision to let the old graveyard, which was being desecrated by vandals, double as a children's playground.)

The announcement of the designation of the area, which should in any case preserve it for some time to come, was made by Harmon Hendricks Goldstone, a New York architect, and chairman of the Landmarks Commission. The announcement made much of Peter Stuyvesant's grave, but overlooked the fact that Mr. Goldstone is himself a direct descendant of Abraham de Lucena, one of the first Jews to arrive in Manhattan in the year of the Twenty-Three.

It gives Mr. Goldstone a certain amount of quiet pleasure, and a feeling of the right thing done, to know that he has been at least partly responsible for protecting the final resting place of the choleric little governor who gave his ancestors such a shabby welcome all those hundreds of years ago.

Mr. Goldstone's mother, Mrs. Lafayette Goldstone, is, of course, as bewilderingly connected as her son to all the old families—Hendricks, Tobias, Levy, Seixas, Hart, Nathan, and the rest. It is she who was such a faithful correspondent, through the years, of Mr. Justice Cardozo, and she achieved considerable acclaim as a poet, writing under the name May Lewis, a combination of her middle and maiden names. (She is a sister of the above-mentioned Harold Lewis.) She became, at one point, an ardent Zionist, at a time when that was not a popular stance among upper-class Jews.

During the Hitler era, at the point when the Third Reich decreed that Jews must wear the badge of the yellow star, as their Inquisitional predecessors had done, Rabbi David de Sola Pool of Shearith Israel had a yellow star stitched to his vestments to symbolize what his people in Europe were suffering. The sight of the New York rabbi wearing the star stirred Mrs. Goldstone deeply, and moved her to write what she considers her most important poem:

> O earliest morning stars that sang together,
> And choruses of night that answered them,
> The ancient stars, the sacred, the resplendent,
> The shepherds' star
> That rose on Bethlehem;
>
> And even those small emblems that men make,
> The stars of knighthood, bright for honor's sake;
> The little service stars that shall burn through
> Their hours of grief and pride,
> And liberty's white spangled stars that ride
> Valiant forever on their field of blue.
>
> Is this the symbol that the brutal hand,
> The blundering will to harm, the vicious hate,
> Has wrought into a badge, a mark to brand?
> Wear it, O Jew, upon your helpless arm;
> Your race is worthy such insignia;
> Be proud, be grateful it is not your fate
> To bear a swastika.

Mrs. Goldstone has already celebrated her ninety-second birthday. She lives comfortably in a large Park Avenue apartment with a view of Central Park, surrounded by fine old furniture, silver, china, and some splendid family portraits, several by her ancestor Jacob Hart Lazarus, the Astor family portraitist. She doesn't get out as often as she used to but still entertains regularly at little teas, with a merry fire going in the fireplace, and she goes regularly to the synagogue. She has watched many of her relatives drift away from their ancient faith, and takes it philosophically, but was saddened that a relative who had married a non-Jew now considers herself—from a religious standpoint—"nothing." In the family, both Jewish and Christian holidays are celebrated.

She is still an energetic lady. Not long ago, walking in the park, she avoided ruining a new pair of shoes by taking them off and running barefoot to the nearest exit to escape a downpour. A favorite taxi driver, who serves as a kind of chauffeur, taking her on errands and visits around the city, asked her the other day the secret of her good health, spirits, and great age. Stepping out of the cab, she answered, "I believe in God."

SOURCES

ABRAHAMS, ISRAEL. *Jewish Life in the Middle Ages*. Philadelphia: Jewish Publication Society of America, 1896.

BARRETT, WALTER. *Old Merchants of New York City*. New York: Carleton, 1870.

BARUCH, BERNARD M. *Baruch: My Own Story*. New York: Holt, 1957.

BYARS, WILLIAM VINCENT. *B. and M. Gratz, Merchants in Philadelphia, 1754–1798*. Jefferson City, Mo.: Hugh Stephens Printing Co., 1916.

DIMONT, MAX I. *Jews, God, and History*. New York: Simon and Schuster, 1962.

DUBIN, MAXWELL H. *Jews in American History*. Los Angeles: privately printed and circulated, 1930.

ELZAS, BARNETT A. *The Jews of South Carolina*. Philadelphia: Lippincott, 1905.

FEIN, ISAAC M. "Baltimore Jews During the Civil War." *American Jewish Historical Quarterly*. Vol. LI No. 2, December 1961.

FITZPATRICK, DONOVAN, AND SAPHIRE, SAUL. *Navy Maverick: Uriah Phillips Levy*. Garden City, N.Y.: Doubleday, 1963.

FRIEDMAN, LEE M. *Early American Jews*. Cambridge: Harvard, 1934.

———. "Boston in American Jewish History." *Publication of the American Jewish Historical Society*. Vol. XLII No. 4, June 1953.

HANDLIN, OSCAR. *Adventure in Freedom*. New York: McGraw-Hill, 1954.

HELLMAN, GEOFFREY T. "Collection." *The New Yorker,* June 12, 1965.

HELLMAN, GEORGE S. *Benjamin N. Cardozo.* New York: Whittlesey House, 1940.

HERSHKOWITZ, LEO, AND MEYER, ISIDORE S., eds. *The Lee Max Friedman Collection of American Jewish Colonial Correspondence.* Waltham, Mass.: American Jewish Historical Society, 1968.

HÜHNER, LEON. *Jews in America after the American Revolution.* New York: Gertz Brothers, 1959.

————. *The Life of Judah Touro.* Philadelphia: Jewish Publication Society of America, 1946.

KAYSERLING, MEYER. *Christopher Columbus and the Participation of the Jews in the Spanish and Portuguese Discoveries.* New York: Longmans, Green, 1894.

KORN, BERTRAM WALLACE. *The Early Jews of New Orleans.* Waltham, Mass.: American Jewish Historical Society, 1969.

KRAUS, WALTER MAX. "The Arrival of the *Saint Charles." The Saint Charles.* Vol. I No. 1, January 1935.

LANGDON-DAVIES, JOHN. *Carlos: The King Who Would Not Die.* Englewood Cliffs, N.J.: Prentice-Hall, 1963.

LONDON, HANNAH R. *Portraits of Jews.* New York: William Edwin Rudge, 1927.

————. *Shades of My Forefathers.* Springfield, Mass.: Pond-Ekberg, 1941.

MADARIAGA, SALVADOR DE. *Christopher Columbus.* New York: Macmillan, 1940.

MADURO, J. M. L. "A Genealogical Note on the Pimentel, Lopez, Sasportas and Rivera Families." *Publication of the American Jewish Historical Society.* Vol. XLII No. 3, March 1953.

MARCUS, JACOB RADER. *Early American Jewry.* 2 Vol. Philadelphia: Jewish Publication Society of America, 1953.

MARS, DAVID. "Justice Benjamin Nathan Cardozo: His Life and Character." *Publication of the American Jewish Historical Society.* Vol. XLIX No. 1, September 1959.

MEYER, ANNIE NATHAN. *Barnard Beginnings.* Boston: Houghton Mifflin, 1935.

————. *It's Been Fun.* New York: Henry Schuman, 1951.

MICHENER, JAMES A. *Iberia.* New York: Random House, 1968.

NATHAN, MAUD. *Once Upon a Time and Today*. New York: G. P. Putnam's Sons, 1933.

PEARSON, EDMUND L. *Studies in Murder*. New York: Macmillan, 1924.

POOL, DAVID DE SOLA. *An Old Faith in the New World: Portrait of Shearith Israel*. New York: Columbia University Press, 1955.

————. *Portraits Etched in Stone*. New York: Columbia University Press, 1952.

PRITCHETT, V. S. *The Spanish Temper*. New York: Alfred A. Knopf, 1954.

ROTH, CECIL. *A History of the Marranos*. Philadelphia: Jewish Publication Society of America, 1932.

————. "On Sephardic Jewry." *In the Dispersion*. Spring 1966.

SACHAR, ABRAM LEON. *A History of the Jews*. New York: Alfred A. Knopf, 1930.

STERN, MALCOLM H. *Americans of Jewish Descent*. Cincinnati: Hebrew Union College Press, 1960.

VAN DOREN, CARL. *Secret History of the American Revolution*. New York: Viking, 1941.

WIZNITZER, ARNOLD. "The Exodus from Brazil and Arrival in New Amsterdam of the Jewish Pilgrim Fathers, 1654." *Publication of the Jewish Historical Society*. Vol. XLIV No. 2, December 1954.

WOUK, HERMAN. *This Is My God*. Garden City, N.Y.: Doubleday, 1959.

INDEX

HOW MANY OF THESE DELL BESTSELLERS HAVE YOU READ?

Fiction

1. **THE NEW CENTURIONS** by Joseph Wambaugh $1.50
2. **THE TENTH MONTH** by Laura Z. Hobson $1.25
3. **THE SCARLATTI INHERITANCE** by Robert Ludlum $1.50
4. **BLUE DREAMS** by William Hanley $1.25
5. **SUMMER OF '42** by Herman Raucher $1.25
6. **SHE'LL NEVER GET OFF THE GROUND** by Robert J. Serling $1.25
7. **THE PLEASURES OF HELEN** by Lawrence Sanders $1.25
8. **THE MERRY MONTH OF MAY** by James Jones $1.25
9. **THE DEVIL'S LIEUTENANT** by M. Fagyas $1.25
10. **SLAUGHTERHOUSE-FIVE** by Kurt Vonnegut, Jr. 95c

Non-fiction

1. **THE SENSUOUS MAN** by "M" $1.50
2. **THE HAPPY HOOKER** by Xaviera Hollander $1.25
3. **THE GRANDEES** by Stephen Birmingham $1.50
4. **THE SENSUOUS WOMAN** by "J" $1.25
5. **I'M GLAD YOU DIDN'T TAKE IT PERSONALLY** by Jim Bouton $1.25
6. **THE DOCTOR'S QUICK WEIGHT LOSS DIET** by Irwin Maxwell Stillman, M.D. and Samm Sinclair Baker $1.25
7. **NICHOLAS AND ALEXANDRA** by Robert K. Massie $1.25
8. **THE GREAT AMERICAN FOOD HOAX** by Sidney Margolius 1.25
9. **THE DOCTOR'S QUICK INCHES-OFF DIET** by Stillman & Baker $1.25
10. **SURROGATE WIFE** by Valerie X. Scott as told to Herbert d'H. Lee $1.25

If you cannot obtain copies of these titles from your local bookseller, just send the price (plus 15c per copy for handling and postage) to Dell Books, Post Office Box 1000, Pinebrook, N. J. 07058. No postage or handling charge is required on any order of five or more books.